D1032515

The Lost America of Love

SHERMAN PAUL

The Lost

America of Love

REREADING ROBERT CREELEY,

EDWARD DORN, AND ROBERT DUNCAN

Louisiana State University Press

Baton Rouge and London

Manufactured in the United States of America

Design: Patricia Douglas Crowder
Typeface: Trump Medieval
Composition: G&S Typesetters, Inc.
Printing and binding: Thomson-Shore, Inc.

LIBRARY OF CONGRESS CATALOGING IN PUBLICATION DATA
Paul, Sherman.
The lost America of love.
1. American poetry—20th century—History and criticism. I. Title.
PS323.5.P3 811'.54'09 80-27470
ISBN 0-8071-0865-0

Grateful acknowledgment is made to the publishers and the poets for permission to quote longer passages from these works:

For Love: Poems 1950–1960. Copyright © 1962 by Robert Creeley. Reprinted by permission of Charles Scribner's Sons.

Words. Copyright © 1967 by Robert Creeley. Reprinted by permission of Charles Scribner's Sons.

Pieces. Copyright © 1969 by Robert Creeley. Reprinted by permission of Charles Scribner's Sons.

The Charm. Copyright © 1969 by Robert Creeley. Reprinted by permission of Four Seasons Foundation.

Later. Copyright © 1979 by Robert Creeley. Reprinted by permission of New Directions.

The Collected Poems, 1956–1974. Copyright © 1975 by Edward Dorn. Reprinted by permission of Four Seasons Foundation.

Hello, La Jolla. Copyright © 1979 by Edward Dorn. Reprinted by permission of Wingbow Press.

The Opening of the Field. Copyright © 1960 by Robert Duncan. Reprinted by permission of New Directions.

Roots and Branches. Copyright © 1964 by Robert Duncan. Reprinted by permission of New Directions.

Bending the Bow. Copyright © 1968 by Robert Duncan. Reprinted by permission of New Directions.

Photographs by Lynn Swigart

For Jim

Tell me what you see vanishing and I
Will tell you who you are

—W. S. Merwin, "For Now"

Blow again trumpeter! and for thy theme,
Take now the enclosing theme of all . . .
Love, that is pulse of all . . .

—Whitman, "The Mystic Trumpeter"

Contents

Preface

Some Others was the title under which this book first proposed itself to me. It comes from the concluding sentence fragment of Charles Olson's letter in reply to "On Poets and Poetry," a review-article by Grover Smith in the *New Mexico Quarterly* (1953). The date alone is probably enough to call up the situation in poetry that provoked Olson to defend Pound, Williams, Crane—"And some others." This book, a sequel to *Olson's Push*, is about some of the others, younger poets of Olson's generation of poets who were closest to him and shared his adventure and who, he says, were "at the job" of making good the declaration of *Others* (1915–1919) that he may very well have had in mind: "The old expressions are always with us, / And there are always others."

In choosing another title I did not dismiss this working title so much as answer the claim of a phrase that, once heard, has remained for me the summary notation of the experience of a generation of writers. This generation of writers—my generation—came to consciousness during the years of the Great Depression and the Second World War. It was not a lost generation but a generation that, having its youth in the still-recognizable "Old America," knew loss—loss, as so much testifies, of community, household, love.

I might have called this book *A Book Beginning with a Phrase by Ginsberg*, for "the lost America of love" is the most resonant and telling phrase in his poem "A Supermarket in California" and led me on to write a book that, as much as anything, is about Kore in America, about her absence and the work of her recovery. Inevitably, the phrase, associated with Whitman in Ginsberg's poem, sounds for me whenever Whitman is evoked, and I find now, on rereading my work, that at the beginning Whitman immediately suggested himself and that the logic of meditation—a logic of metaphor, as Crane knew—quickly brought this phrase to mind. So, while this book about Kore concerns some of the others in their relation to such modern and postmodern poets as Pound, Williams, H.D., Crane, and Olson, it also concerns, much more than I imagined, their relation to a beloved predecessor, the progenitor, Whitman, our first great poet of love.

The form—the method—I employ also belongs to a sequel. Could I have studied Olson and not have heeded his insistence on enacting thought, on finding a form for the immediate activity of thought itself? The distinction here, as Olson says, "is between language as the act of the instant and language as the act of thought about the instant." The open, serial, meditative form I adopt answers to that. It is, I think, a form for open criticism, an open form for critical thought comparable to open forms of poetic thought.

The practice is meditative and depends upon rereading. *Rereading* names a present activity. One of course has read the poems—is full of the work—but attends the poem again to prompt present thought, not only the kind of responsiveness Cid Corman has in mind when he speaks of taking poets "at their word" but responsiveness to all that the occasion of reading calls forth. Meditation itself is open and wayward, answering (it is all an answering) less to intention than to the desire to write—to enter that wonderful activity—in whatever way and to whatever end the occasion prompts one. To trust language and the particular moment—and the particulars of the moment—and to encounter the poem with one's *present* resources! That is the risk. Now. And no revisions, no second thoughts, just first thoughts, the best thoughts, Ginsberg believes, those, as Emerson found, that agree with third thoughts!

Criticism of this kind is also open because it waives judgment, no longer assumes a sovereign mind speaking for established tradition. It belongs with our recent art which, Meyer Schapiro says, has become "more deeply personal, more intimate, more concerned with experiences of a subtle kind"—yes, and freer in its attitudes toward the medium, seeing in the random or accidental the beginning of an order. As my frequent misspelling of *meditation* tells me, its work is *mediation*. It opens space—is spacious—and it mediates the poem for both writer and reader, gives both their rights of participation. I find it especially rewarding because it permits me to address the poem with all possible closeness and (another aspect of this intimacy) to be deeply addressed by it. Rereading, necessarily, is answering, and the wonder of it is that one's answers are not foreknown, that what might otherwise remain hidden or silent gets acknowledged. I little expected, for example, to concern myself with the difficult, and still unresolved, problems of poetry and politics or to find myself so strenuously engaged in putting the green tradition to the test of the black (but then, as Duncan says, "It is life / that tenders green shoots of / hurt and healing / we name Love").

Nor did I know the extent or limits of my sympathy and the depth at which, at times, I would be moved.

A final word. Every critical book, and especially one of this kind, should be prefaced: to be read in the company of—as an accompaniment to—the poems.

Acknowledgments

Isn't the fact that books have a place for acknowledgments a profound recognition of the nature of book-making? My indebtedness to the thought of others is everywhere evident in my work. What especially needs to be mentioned here, with gratitude, is sustenance of other kinds.

I probably would not have written a book of meditations if William Spanos hadn't invited me to write on Robert Creeley in whatever form I pleased and generously given me the needed space in *Boundary 2*. (Even then, it was necessary to cut the manuscript, which is fully printed here.) Without the confirmation of readers I might not have continued. Their kind, unsolicited responses were heartening, as was the encouragement of Beverly Jarrett of the Louisiana State University Press. Public readings of the meditation on Creeley's "Later" also helped—one at Marycrest College, at the invitation of Sister Benita Moore, the other at the N.E.H. Institute on Writing of the University of Iowa, at the invitation of Professor Carl Klaus.

Writing the meditations was occasional. Readiness was the all-important factor, but there were also occasions, the most notable the Charles Olson Festival at Iowa City in November 1978. The conjunction of the publication of "Later" by the

Toothpaste Press and Creeley's reading of the sequence at the festival prompted my writing about it. Similarly, Ed Dorn's lecture and reading (demonstration) from *Hello, La Jolla* moved me to write about that book when I did. The high excitement(s) of that week—the most overwhelming Duncan's (ever) presence and his reading of the *Dante [Etudes]* and the new Whitman poem—had much to do with this book. So did the subsequent viewings and reviewings, in the company of Bruce Wheaton, of the video-taped proceedings. The photographs by Lynn Swigart gratefully included here were taken at discussions during the festival.

My heaviest scholarly debts are personal: to George Butterick, director of the Charles Olson Archives of the University of Connecticut Library, and Robert Bertholf, director of the Poetry Collection of the Lockwood Memorial Library of the State University of New York at Buffalo. The Beinecke Library of Yale University and the libraries of the University of Iowa were also generous with their holdings. And the Department of English, the Research Council, and Graduate College of the University of Iowa were, as always, unfailing in their support.

ROBERT CREELEY

I

15 June 1977

Begin anywhere. It will unravel. Why not take up his *Whitman*? Or that Sparrow essay on "life tracking itself"?

20 June 1977

The juxtaposition of biographical notes on Whitman and Creeley in the Penguin *Whitman* (1973). "Poet to Poet." Yes, "the response of one poet to the work of another can be doubly illuminating." Fill in the dates (1819–92; 1926–   ).

He wanted to do Wyatt but seized the chance to do Whitman. Admits that Ginsberg, Duncan, and Zukofsky, who prompted his appreciation, were better able (more deserving? more in the tradition?) than he was. But now, should he reissue *A Quick Graph*, he could add this introduction to section two, where he treats his predecessors—put Whitman there where he belongs, before Crane. In any case, it is characteristic "criticism": testamentary, generous in acknowledgement, directed to use. One of his best essays.

More is involved than what he says in the first sentence, with his obsessive *lovely* and *insistences*. (Call these notes "The Lovely Insistences of. . . .") So Whitman instructs us to speak for ourselves. Creeley had learned this from Williams and Olson. But it enables him to open the essay according to instructions: in his own voice, telling only what he knows; unassertively, with only that authority ("seems to me," he says). It makes possible—opens *possibility*, another insistence—a stance in criticism of the kind he takes in poetry. Open criticism.

And the subsequent consideration of *person* and *personal* speaks for what *Pieces* (1969) and *A Day Book* (1972) most fully permitted him ("the biases and distortions and tediums of the personal . . . are . . . invited into the writing"). That kind of openness; what the long open poems of his contemporaries invite; what "Projective Verse" had called for, "a process of . . . endless gathering, moving in the energy of his own attention and impulse," he says here of Whitman's method.

Like the image of nest-making—weaving—in *Maximus*. And his image of *agglomerate*, "a ball, primarily of clay but equally compacted of shells and pebbles which the actions of the waves had caused the clay to pick up. . . ." An appropriate place, the beach, to think about Whitman. At Bolinas, all the continent away. *Away* (1976), *a-way, a wave*; a water book. He says of his image of cosmos, so different from Olson's, so much more dense and compacted, "I like too that sense of the spherical, which does not locate itself upon a point nor have the strict condition of the linear but rather is at all 'points' the possibility of all that is." In time, he says, these clay spheres become stones.

Personal and *common*, another equation. Presumably the greatest lesson he learned from Whitman. This speaks for his preoccupation with self and its close ("domestic") world; with what others experience and he would gladly share with them.

See "People," in *A Day Book*: the marginalia, "from Descartes to Whitman." Doesn't he gainsay Lawrence's harsh judgment of Whitman's democratic sympathy, the scornful quotation, "I am he that aches with amorous love"? Doesn't he now endorse it? In 1954, he felt that Lawrence was "incredibly right"; that the Whitman of amorous love is "a bore of immense proportions." But in that note on *Studies in Classic American Literature*, he accepts Crane's Whitman, the Whitman, Lawrence said, who charged men's blood.

21 June 1977

Creeley and Dickinson, and why not Whitman, so private and troubled, not the bard or prophet but the poet whose presence in the poems moved Mrs. Gilchrist to answer with declarations of love? Mentioning this, Creeley says: "It would be sad indeed if books could not be so felt as entirely human and possible occasion." This is the way he feels Crane had felt Whitman. (And Dickinson, whom Crane also put in his poem.) And doesn't Crane, who speaks for Creeley in *Origin # 1* and opens *For Love*, speak for him now, for the wanderer he was and remains? Recalling the 1940s when neither Whitman nor Crane was critically esteemed, he tells of the paper on Crane he requested permission of Matthiessen to write; cites the lines that then were embarrassing:

> yes, Walt,
> Afoot again, and onward without halt,—
> Not soon, nor suddenly,—no, never to let go
> My hand
> in yours,
> Walt Whitman—
> so—

A poet of love. In responding to Crane, already responding to Whitman. Crane, another deeply troubled poet, brings him to Whitman. Those brilliant recognitions of Crane, the essays of 1953 and 1954: Crane brought him to the tradition that the poets of his generation so fully—and critically—repossess, that here he now repossesses for himself.

Isn't love the outstanding debt we owe Whitman? In Whitman, Creeley notes, Ginsberg found the much needed line that enabled him to "*build up* large organic structures." But Ginsberg also found the poet he addresses in the supermarket—"dear father . . . lonely old courage-teacher. . . ." This is the Whitman, in the words of Lawrence with which Creeley concludes, who enables us to pioneer our wilderness, "the wilderness of unopened life." "Respondez!," included here, reminds us that Whitman is already the poet of "the lost America of love": "If our America now is a petty shambles of disillusion and violence, the dreams of its possibility stay actual in Whitman's words." We owe him that possibility. In acknowledging this, Creeley speaks for the cultural and political endeavor of the postwar generation. By tracing the postmodern movement and treating its poetics in terms of Whitman (it is all here: the "field of activity," of enactment, the "web of coherence," the "flexibility of diction," the invitation to the reader to participate, the unending poem of a man's life)—in doing this, he restores Whitman in respect to all the new work done, the work that he made possible.

Whitman, he tells Williams in 1960, "demonstrates the appetite for a new occasion for the poem, for speaking. . . . [not] that analytic appetite peculiarly European [but] . . . accumulative, 'creative' action."

He might be speaking of Olson when he notes Whitman's "affection for the pragmatic" and the fact that he emphasizes "space and process [as] unremittingly our condition." And why is this important? Because it gives us "the literal possibility of a life," allows us to go on: "the process permits the material ('myself' in the world) to extend until literal death intercedes." Song of myself.

The wilderness of unopened life. Life tracking itself, the autobiographical motive, he says in *Sparrow 14* (1973). ". . . life *is* preoccupation with itself," Olson insists in "Introduction to Robert Creeley," taking the salient phrase from Ortega's essay, "In Search of Goethe from Within." Doesn't Creeley have this in mind? He calls the lecture "Inside Out"; names the two modes of narration Olson considers, acknowledges his own essentially *inside* mode but also (now) bringing it closer to Olson's *out*—at least the Olson of *Maximus I–III*? Olson thought Creeley, whose prose was featured in *Origin #2*, "the push beyond Lawrence," the "total IN":

22 June 1977

> the narrator taking on himself the job of making clear by way of his own person that life *is* preoccupation with itself, taking up the push of his own single intelligence to make it, to be—by his conjectures—so powerful inside the story that he makes the story swing on him . . .

That was a way to restore phenomenology: "you get a man back in, among things, the full motion and play comes back."

Ortega. His "modern theme" ours—Creeley's and Olson's—the restoration of "vital reason," Olson's "single intelligence." How well Olson read the essay on Goethe (in *Partisan Review*, 1949), the essay I read then in preparing to write about Emerson and Thoreau. "Not the within of Goethe," Ortega says, "but the within of his life, of his drama"—not Goethe's subjective vision but the drama of his engagement with life. Certainly Olson owes Ortega a great deal for this radical transformation of the idea of "our life." And also for the long

22 June 1977

footnote in which Ortega, in defending his originality against the assumption of indebtedness to Heidegger, succinctly presents his philosophy and provides the mandate for the new generation of poets. "Human life," he insists, "has to go out into the 'world'"—"the resorption of the environment is the concrete destiny of man."

See Creeley's letter to Corman in *Origin # 2*: "Fragments. Like any man, is himself that collector, that center round which: such fly." (Olson's style) And why? ". . . to say I'm alive." To declare content. Form is the extension of content, the content within a man: "The phenomena outside the given man, around him, OBJECTS . . . are that which the content IN the man uses to declare itself—that this declaration, this COMING OUT by means of the materials, MAKES the form."

"Forms are—there are no 'dead' forms; form is the declaration of life." Creeley in *The Black Mountain Review*, 1954.

Inside out = projective. The project of projective verse. Differs from the Transcendentalists' practice: projection is not symbolic; there are no correspondences. Instead *form* is the result of the activity of writing, the object one makes.

23 June 1977

True of autobiography, *his story*. Not at all a matter of confession, of relieving yourself. You write in order to recover the situation, the occasion in its fullness, prior to abstraction. Also, as he says of Williams, you put the fact of your own life against "abstract commitments."

Such writing locates the self in the fullness of its existence: mind in body, mind-and-body in the world.

yes, yes,
    that's what
I wanted,
        I always wanted,
I always wanted,
        to return
to the body
        where I was born.

Ginsberg's poem; epigraph to *Pieces* (1969). Put the pronoun in quotation marks ("I"). Now it has Creeley's insistence. "Come *back* into the body," he says in the lecture, thinking of Ginsberg's "heroism." Thinking, too, of Jung, of the maternal body, the earth. Makes the return to that body the work of his generation: "We saw what Jung might call the 'individuation process' enter the nightmare of 'divided creation,' torn from centers of physical reality." He writes autobiography in order to "Tell me who I am." Tell *me* who *I* am. Like Lawrence, in the epigraph, "to depart to where *I am.*" *Where.* Such location is *place,* the preferred condition. "I *am* a poet! I/am. I am." Williams, in "The Desert Music." The poem is a place that makes place.

Unopened life is wilderness, space not place. ". . . the thickets / of this wilderness" in Olson's "In Cold Hell, in Thicket." You write to open life, to have possibility, to have place. Writing itself is the *activity.* It keeps you open and vulnerable, in the condition of poetry, ready to answer "the adventurous muse" who, William Spengemann says, inspired our classic literature. And still inspires our literature. And that other muse, Olson's necessary goddess.

> How shall he who is not happy, who has been made so unclear,
> who is no longer privileged to be at ease, who, in this brush, stands

reluctant, imageless, unpleasured, caught in a sort of
hell, how
shall he convert this underbrush, how turn this
unbidden place,
how trace and arch again
the necessary goddess?

He might have called the lecture "Against Generality as Such." So aggressive. Delivered as written (no David Antin), and written for himself. "I know that I, as an artist, have never dared to imagine in working that an actual audience might be literally attentive to what I have to say." Yet he has a *they* in mind. Prods them with abrasive remarks, hoping perhaps to awaken their response and thereby meet them. "There's no pleasure in being by yourself finally, always alone." The lecture itself is witness, as he says, to "what the words have done to *me* as *I* gains locus."

Yes, he presses toward what is existent and real, inalienable in experience, to forfeit which is to forfeit life. Doesn't this refusal to be cheated account for his fundamental seriousness? The exigent condition Olson calls "nakedness." He endorses this.

The Puritan tradition of autobiography he mentions is his own. Thoreau, Lawrence, Dahlberg, Williams. ". . . a specific isolated consciousness in the universe . . . intensifies the attraction of this situation of statement." And the sentence of Marisol's he cites applies as well to him: "When I show myself as I am, I return to reality." Both use themselves in their work, become presences in it; hence *A Day Book* gives an accumulation of selves, and the collaborative volume, *Presences* (1976). In her Steinesque closing statement, she says, "People should think of themselves when they live alone."

Method and project. "You begin at any point, and move that point forward or backward, up or down. . . . In and out the system, as Buckminster Fuller would say. It's a system—of valuation, habit, complex organic data, the weather, and so on." Modus operandi of *Pieces, A Day Book*, and all that follows. And, increasingly, going forward by tracking backward. To what end? To witness. To tell *his story*. To do what Williams, cited here, does in "The Desert Music." Yes, to tell what he sees and hears. And hearing the music, dance the poem, the "agony of self-realization / bound into a whole / by that which surrounds us."

That names the particular work of many postmodern poets.

25 June 1977

That's his poetics:

> What device, means, rhythm, or form the poem can gain for its coherence are a precise issue of its occasion. The mind and ear are, in a sense, stripped to hear and organize what is given to them, and the *dance* or *music* Williams has used as a metaphor for this recognition and its use is that which sustains us, poets or men.
>
> The *dance*, the acts of a life, move to that *music*, the life itself, and it is these which it is the poet's peculiar responsibility to acknowledge and recover by his art.

Life tracking itself. "*I am given to write poems*": the testament of his calling. All the touchstones are there; ever-repeated because he had to find them for himself, on the way.

"The Desert Music": *the* demonstration for him, *the* test poem, "for myself the loveliest form he left us." It steadies him, he tells Williams during the terrible time following his divorce. Trying to hang on: "I thought of your, 'I am a poet. I am. I am. . . .' I don't want any other 'excuse.'"

He speaks the lovely truth when he tells Williams, "You've really made a whole world possible."

He is to Williams as Olson is to Pound. With none of Olson's resistance to fathers. Williams is the man he most reveres, whose poems he knows as well as any man living; the man after whom he names a daughter.

He says it at the start of their remarkable correspondence: "I've put myself to school with your work." In a letter making the usual request for material for a new magazine. The magazine that never appeared, but that in many respects *Origin* became, and, later, the *Black Mountain Review*. Even before he hears from Olson, he wants to begin the push, to create a center, make a *polis*. The correspondence begins in 1950, with talk of a magazine and the literary situation. By the time Williams' death closes the correspondence, the new movement is established. Scribner's publishes *For Love*, a decade's work, in 1962; Williams supplies a blurb.

Never the sense in these letters that he is the incompetent husband depicted in *The Island*, though he readily admits his difficulties. He comes on wonderfully, direct, generous, warm, clearly knowing what he's about. No question that as much as Olson—or Corman, or anyone—he put the movement in motion, the Divers Press for one thing doing some of the divers work. The *Black Mountain Review*. Endless correspondence, placing Williams' work, for example. Radio programs, early in 1950, at St. Johnsbury, Vermont, the openers on Williams; the manifesto, from *The Wedge*, that he himself literally follows:

> When a man makes a poem, makes it, mind you, he takes the words as he finds them interrelated about

> him and composes them—without distortion which would mar their exact significance—into an intense expression of his perceptions and ardors that they may constitute a revelation in the speech that he uses. It isn't what he *says* that counts as a work of art. It's what he makes, with such intensity of perception that it lives with an intrinsic movement of its own to verify its authenticity.

The concern throughout to get the new work out, to use it well, to make it tell.

He knows what's needed, in poetry and criticism. Something other than academic poems, forceless poems of "impacted imagery."

> This level of verse isn't an end, to be aimed at, to be "representative." And the implications of a "return to form," being in that sense a "going back," and not, as it must be, a development, invention, new use. And language, or a dichotomy of language as it now is, split & emasculated. Where criticism is a kind of witty implication of value.

Not the "New Classicism" enjoining us to "Make It Old," to accept tradition. Instead, the Williams of the *Briarcliff* letter: not Pound, developed "androgynetically from the past itself mind to mind," but Williams with his "direct approach" to the "supplying female." And language: living with farmers and lumbermen, keeping chickens and pigeons, "I get," he says, "to a sense of what language can be, what, even, it must be." "I couldn't live here if my own language wasn't whole. They'd shoot me."

A little magazine. Very simple program. Avoid literary hierarchies, and do what Williams does: put declarations and demonstrations together, criticism to open the poems, poems to exemplify not principles or standards but "attitudes implicit in the critical work." His kind of criticism. "Any discussion of poetry must come to the poem itself, and take there, if anywhere, its own assumption of meaning." *This* Pound: "Pound's discriminations were located in the poem's literal activity." Also: no " 'professorial' tone."

For the second issue, this (still current?) issue: *the university*, to clarify and attack. Richard Wirtz Emerson on the "POET AS PEDANT." (Not, certainly, Olson's "pedagogue.") Rexroth: "The absorbing of US poets by the academic world has just about destroyed poetry in my generation." 1950. Yet a decade later, Creeley begins university teaching—discounting, that is, Black Mountain, which, for him as for Olson, was *polis*. The avant-garde, a vanguard of the counter-culture.

27 June 1977

Letters. How much they tell of the *life* of poets! The need for connection and confirmation, for true generous words. For bibiliographical exchange: *i.e.*, Jung and Kerényi's *Essays on a Science of Mythology* "makes very clear that . . . centering on one's self . . . is neither egocentric nor necessarily isolate in effect." For argument: the years' long concern with measure, on which Williams insists and Creeley, with Olson's help, repudiates. Measure is metric, Creeley says, and coherence, accordingly, is exterior. Result: the notion of the "variable" foot.

Glosses the reviews of Williams' work in *A Quick Graph*. How he managed to be loyal to Williams, true to himself, and advance the cause. Particularly *Selected Essays*, that botched book. Argues the issue of measure. Notes the omission of controversial material and tries to save Williams from his publishers. At the expense of "The American Background"?

He tells Williams he values that essay "completely." One of the great essays. On "a culture of immediate references," primary culture, not Culture; but an order, such as one might achieve in a poem, "an order . . . in its living character of today." The culture of *The Maximus Poems*. Place.

The almost daily correspondence of Creeley and Olson! How much awaits us!

28 June 1977

Corman, Olson, Gerhardt. By 1950, the names begin to punctuate the letters. Somewhat later, Levertov, Blackburn. The Olson slash (/), abbreviation (abbr.) style, June 6, 1950. That winter, an Olson recording: "I've never heard a thing like it; just force/naked. Too much, it was: incredible." As he tells Williams earlier, "things move a little."

We are moving! *Le Fou*. First book, 1952. Title poem, dedicated to Olson, published first in *Origin #2*.

> who plots, then the lines
> talking, taking, always the beat from
> the breath
>   (moving slowly at first
> the breath
>   which is slow—
>
> I mean, graces come slowly,
> it is that way.
>
> So slowly (they are waving
> we are moving
>   away from   (the trees
>   the usual   (go by
> which is slower than this, is
>   (we are moving!
> goodbye

Olson is the fool who plots the lines. The fool of his "In Praise of the Fool" (later called "The Green Man"), the fool of the Tarot deck, dog at his heels, singing furiously. Letting those who want to—Pound explicitly, but the modernists, Williams excepted—"chase a king." Olson's declaration of vocation. (See also "The Fool" in *Pieces*.)

A demonstration of Olson's declarations in "Projective Verse." Olson's percussive beat, his breath, his line over against Creeley's "I mean, graces come slowly, / it is that way," the tight couplet, centered by the *plotted*, spatialized verses, with their open parentheses of simultaneous notation—a prosody to cover the real. Yet, even so, Creeley's voice throughout. Breath all right: "the HEART, by the way of the BREATH, to the LINE." Vowel leadings, too: "the HEAD, by way of the EAR, to the SYLLABLE." Coherence secured by such means as *slow, slower, slowly*. The enactment of getting underway in the last verse. The excitement of the lesson learned: "we are moving!" The acknowledgment of it, his debt to Olson for freeing him to use, as he does here, his own occasions for making poems. The community of the poem, communication, as much as a letter.

"Things tend to awaken / even through random communication"—"The Conspiracy"

In response to "In Cold Hell, in Thicket":

> He shall step, he
> will shape, he
> is already also
> moving off
> ....
> (there is always a field,
> for the strong there is always
> an alternative)

Is there "a vessel fit for moving?" Yes, the poem

> precise as hell is, precise
> as any words, or wagon,
> can be made.

To Williams, August 8, 1956: "I miss the place, of a home. . . . My so-called generation finds itself very isolate, actually split from all character of 'family,' and it is *place* that gets to be more and more what the search concerns."

29 June 1977

Place as family. "Domestic." Family = Familiar = Place: Related Cosmos. Divorced, displaced, dispirited. Needs to have "a sense of a 'new' place generally." Goes west. Likes New Mexico, as later Vancouver; the space of the one ("for a New Englander it is helpful"), the "open freshness" of the other. Feels "more relaxed on the edges." Needs a new family; quickly finds one.

Williams is his "ground." Can't get "on the same place" with his mother.

A wanderer in all kinds of spaces, in search of all kinds of places.

"Return." First published poem, in the Harvard *Wake*. The return from India to Cambridge, winter 1945. ". . . at the very beginning so to speak" (Preface, *The Charm*). No, not "the return," but the imperative to turn back, to accept a place he knows.

30 June 1977

> Quiet as is proper for such places;
> The street, subdued, half-snow, half-rain,
> Endless, but ending in the darkened doors.
> Inside, they who will be there always,
> Quiet as is proper for such people—
> Enough for now to be here, and
> To know my door is one of these.

Cambridge of Cambridge ladies, of Cousin Nancy? Not his place. Only temporary: the sufficiency of *here / now*, the *enough* he already knows enough to settle for—"Enough for now to be here."

Something smolders in this quiet poem with its space of emptiness. The sense of having the power to alter his condition? For a time, he will accept "these" people, this place; be one of them, and as reclusive and isolate.

Doors. Opening inward, closing out. Darkened doors.

> it's the blackness of our grief
> brings us back into the room
> puts the lock into our hand

"Greendoon's Song" (1948). Hasn't read Olson's *Y & X*, "La Préface," "The Green Man"; hasn't found the outlaw poet-leader. Eliot's key confirms his prison.

And his acute self-consciousness.

> *I would begin by explaining*
> *that by reason of being*
> *I am and no other.*

"Poem for D. H. Lawrence" (1948). Is this epigraph from Lawrence, who, like Olson, having being (breath) stands forth with the inviolate singularity of all things? The poem renders that positive negatively. With analytic skill. With rhythmic turns like Stein's, emotion discovers meaning. All the terms together in the concluding quatrains:

> The self is being, is in being and
> because of it. The figure is not being
> nor the self but is in the self and
> in the being and because of them.

> Always the self returns to, because of
> being, the figure drawn by the window,
> there in the evening, the darkness,
> alone and unwanted by others.

Always, this return. Inevitably, this is what happens to him. A mystery of being, like Dickinson's "certain slant of light."

The birth of consciousness: self-consciousness. In the beginning the self is "alone and unwanted by others," yet without awareness of inalienable otherness, without "consciousness of self / or figure or evening." But when it becomes conscious of itself, the self creates a figure, an abstraction, an *it*.

Non-being. "The figure is not being." But non-being is known as absence of being, is positively felt. By the self, which images its loss of being and desire for being in the figure at the window, at evening, looking out into the darkness. Self-consciousness is objectification and diminishment: isolated from source/being, without light, reduced to seeing, the distancing sense.

Alone and unwanted by others. A refrain. His burden. The condition of both the self and consciousness of self, though in the latter instance the painful necessity that moves us ever afterward to desire being. Consciousness of self: a fortunate fall, as in Emerson?

1948. Existentialism. Creeley's Prufrock.

"Living, I want to depart to where *I am*"—Lawrence.

Ginsberg: "I think there, / for I am / there . . ."

Creeley: "I think, and
therefore I am not . . ."

As soon as
I speak, I
speaks . . .

1 July 1977 These early poems in *The Charm* (1969). Publishing them now, doesn't he ask us to take stock with him, of him?

Images of road, restlessness, passion, love.

> . . . the problem is the road
> and the passion we call traveler . . .
> . . . .
> . . . What is there, after all, to explain?
> That passion is wild, the road runs, the traveler
> has come back and sits and talks and goes again. (8)

The problem, as a title puts it, is "Still Life or [mobiles]"—the latter a contrivance, easily destroyed, that the wind of passion can "catch at / against itself" (19).

> It is the long road he is coming
> where dust all day rises and the sun
> at noon is darkened with dust and in
> the dry mouth the water is brittle,
> tasteless. (12)
>
> Beyond this road the blackness bends
> in warmth. . . . (9)
>
> . . . the completeness
> of things which are warm,
>
> in the sun, in the sun's
> completeness. . . . (16)

Heritage: romantic and metaphysical: spiritual wanderer and logician of the spirit. Precise, economical, tight (formal). Simple particulars that are universal—road, dust, water. That *fable*: the dry mouth and brittle water. Like Merwin?

Love and cosmicity.

Verse: the twists and turns of his mind on his experience. Paws at it, like a cat. Worries it verbally, doubling words back on themselves, making words play out their meanings. *Logopoeia*.

The *open* open form poems of 1950–1951. To school with Olson?

His strength: truthfulness, the harsh justice of his awareness of others—and himself.

2 July 1977

> I think: poets live in a well,
> from whence the screams issue,
> a fearsome hole it is too,
> a very hell. (74)

His occasion, the cry of.

The title poem, "The Charm." It speaks, he says, in his voice, "the one I am given to speak with." About words, and the birth of speech; words born "in hopelessness"—of hopelessness.

> Where fire is, they are quieter
> and sit comforted.

The way he surrounds himself to write, alone, yet enveloped in the sounds of household activity. The difficulty of utterance: the words "are dumb / and speak with signs"; a nervous gesturing "fit . . . for hysteria." But—

> But in them I had been, at first,
> tongue. If they speak,
> I have myself, and love them. (44)

Speech gives him himself. A pentacostal miracle: "I am given. . . ." He is tongue, their instrument, but cannot make them speak. Born of himself, these "children" are indeed "uncommon."

9 July 1977

For Love. A rich title.

> What power has love but forgiveness?
> In other words
> by its intervention
> what has been done
> can be undone.
> What good is it
> otherwise?

October 31, 1955: "As the opening six lines of Book 3 of 'Asphodel'—I hold there. To all of it."

For Love: Poems 1950–1960 (1962). Poems of two marriages, the breakup of the one, the beginning of another. The extremity of it. This title poem:

> For love—I would
> split open your head and put
> a candle in
> behind the eyes.
>
> Love is dead in us
> if we forget
> the virtues of an amulet
> and quick surprise. (46)

And the last poem, "For Love":

> . . . all

that I know derives
from what it teaches me.

"These poems are such places, always they were ones stumbled into: warmth for a night perhaps, the misdirected intention come right; and, too, a sudden instance of love, and the being loved, wherewith a man also contrives a world (of his own mind)." (Preface)

10 July 1977

Poems: places, unexpectedly found, given to him. Good places—*place* is always good? Shelter and warmth not only *for* a night but *from* the night; where something willed is miraculously made right, and love, miraculously, received. A loving place that empowers creation and enables him in the projective forms of poetry to make a cosmos. See "The House," paradigm of all making.

Poems answer exigent needs: the cosmic / existential; psychological / moral; emotional / creative. In poems, he is "at home."

In the open field of Duncan's *The Opening of the Field*. See the gloss in "I am given to write poems." "Often I am Permitted to Return to a Meadow"—yes, the "I am" is granted that "return." Bachelard's reverie toward childhood: "Childhood remains within us a principle of deep life, of life always in harmony with the possibility of new beginnings. . . . In our reveries toward childhood, all the archteypes which link man to the world, which provide a poetic harmony between man and the universe are, in some sort, revitalized."

(The "essential autobiography" of Duncan's *The Truth & Life of Myth*.)

And writing itself as Bachelardian reverie? Isn't that the depth to which open poetry also answers?—"reverie which is written and indeed forms itself in the act of writing." Reverie: no idle act of mind but the full play, the liberation of imagination.

> Often I Am Permitted to Return to a
> Meadow
>
> as if it were a scene made-up by the mind,
> that is not mine, but is a made place,
>
> that is mine, it is so near to the heart,
> an eternal pasture folded in all thought
> so that there is a hall therein
>
> that is a made place, created by light
> wherefrom the shadows that are forms fall.

"A very distinct and definite *place*," Creeley says, "that poetry not only creates but itself issues from."

> Often I am permitted to return to a meadow
> as if it were a given property of the mind
> that certain bounds hold against chaos,
>
> that is a place of first permission,
> everlasting omen of what is.

The place of places: "I mean something like where 'the heart finds rest,' as Duncan would say. I mean that place where one is open, where the sense of defensiveness or insecurity and all the other complexes of response to place can be finally dropped. Where one feels an intimate association both with the ground under one's feet and with all that inhabits the place as tradition."

Why does Creeley, who dedicates so many books to his wife, pass over the presence in Duncan's poem of the "First Beloved," the "Lady"? Like Bobbie, she "makes all things possible." Bachelard: "the greatest of all archetypes, that of the mother. . . ." The Goddess.

Olson: love is form; love is a verb.

Edith Cobb: "I became acutely aware that what a child wanted to do most of all was to make a world in which to find a place to discover a self." "Genius consists in the continuing ability to recall and to utilize the child's perceptual intuition of time and space." To use oneself as an instrument, to think with the instrument of the body, "to participate with the whole bodily self."

an agony of self-realization
bound into a whole
by that which surrounds us

I cannot escape

I cannot vomit it up

Only the poem!

Only the made poem, the verb calls it
into being.

11 July 1977

Slater, let me come home. Some return other than Crane's suicide. Without love—friends, family, polis—the heart (Hart) slows, stops; the head cannot make the push beyond. Creeley's "recognition," identity theme.

We are moving, in "Le Fou," because of friends. The "company of love."

And so it was I entered the broken world—Crane's "The Broken Tower" and the "visionary company of love." So *For Love* is enclosed by that phrase, the closing poem ending

> Into the company of love
> it all returns

So much broken, even in that troubled poem, now, momently, made good, no longer visionary.

And that "Song" for Ann, made with such "care," that includes the difficulty of its occasion. How much he depends on love!

> A murmur of some lost
> thrush, though I have never seen one.

The solitary thrush of "When Lilacs Last in the Dooryard Bloom'd" and the he-bird of "Out of the Cradle Endlessly Rocking."

> For I, that was a child, my tongue's use sleeping, now I have heard you,
> Now in a moment I know what I am for, I awake
>
> * * *
>
> Song of the bleeding throat,
> Death's outlet song of life, (for well dear brother I know,
> If thou wast not granted to sing thou would'st surely die.)

So little at home. The essential landscape of "The Innocence": estranged from the evident (here/now) beneficence of the "external" world; an "I" confronting an "It," unable to fully recover the "Thou":

> What I come to do
> is partial, partially kept.

The essential personal landscape of "The End," where the "I," learning of what "people think of me" is plunged into "my" loneliness, literally choked to death.

The supreme occasion: "The poem supreme, addressed to / emptiness."

"Had I lived some years ago, I think I would have been a moralist." "The Crow," "The Immoral Proposition," "The Kind of Act of," etc. Belongs in Austin Warren's *The New England Conscience*. Casuist. See the early stories.

Marriage. "Cruel, cruel to describe. . . ."—in poems that are operations. And nothing avails—neither wit nor humor—

> As when for a lark
> gaily, one hoists up a window
> shut for many years.

Nothing so devastating and vastating as *The Island*, though "La Noche," "The Whip" and "All That Is Lovely in Men," of part I, compound his despair. And poem after later poem tells its recurrence, the despair of the unanswering "sleeping wife," the wife who is also Goddess. Here, as briefly as possible:

> In the court-
> yard at midnight, at
>
> midnight. The moon is
> locked in itself, to
>
> a man a
> familiar thing.

And:

> Moon, moon,
> when you leave me alone
> all the darkness is
> an utter blackness . . .

Nothing in part I as long, as accomplished, as "A Form of Woman," "The Hero," "The Name," "The Rose," "The Door," "For Love."

12 July 1977

In the forest again. ("The path, love is the path. / And in the forest calls, calls"—Olson, "Troilus.") Much backwards turning. So much pain, the flowers he enumerates in "The Flower." Flowers of pain, though his flowers owe more to Williams than Baudelaire.

Poems of numbers:

> "one by one // we . . ." ("Fire")
> "two by two" ("For Friendship")

Love / Place / Water

> Where it [love] is, there is
>   everywhere, separate,
> yet few [choice]—as dew
>   to night is.   (Dickinsonian)
>
> * * *
>
> Love, if you love me,
> lie next to me.
> Be for me, like rain
> . . . .
> Be wet
> with a decent happiness.
>
> * * *
>
> Love comes quietly,
> finally, drops
> about me, on me,
> in the old ways.
>
> What did I know   ("I")
> thinking myself
> able to go
> alone all the way.

The *haiku* here. And the Tao of love?

>   discover
> ways of water.

13 July 1977

Duncan's brilliant review. A reply to "The Door," dedicated to him? That remarkable poem, indebted to Robert Graves's "The Door"?

> When she came suddenly in
> It seemed the door could never close again,
> Nor even did she close it—she, she—
> The room lay open to a visiting sea
> Which no door could restrain.
>
> Yet when at last she smiled, tilting her head
> To take leave of me,
> Where she had smiled, instead
> There was a dark door closing endlessly,
> The waves receded.

Creeley cites this in his review of *The White Goddess*, and endorses the latter: "The Goddess, whether characterized as the ultimately personal, or impersonal, wife, mother, queen, or simply generically 'unknown,' is the most persistent *other* of our existence, eschewing male order, allowing us to live at last. The obedience of a poet's gratitude, for this, is the authority which you hear in his poems, and it is obedience to a presence which is, if you will, that which is not understood, ever; but which he characterizes as all that can happen in living, and seeks to form an emblem for, with words."

Duncan recognizes this *service*. Guido Cavalcanti, Dante. *Sempre d'amore*. Like Olson, in "Procnsa," but without the chiding, he places Creeley (why did he overlook Blackburn?) in the tradition Pound called "The Spirit of Romance." And how is it he overlooked Crane, so much present in the poem—in this instance the Crane of "Faustus and Helen" and "In Shadow"?

And Williams? Not enough recognized for his *service*? Recognized, in any case, as Creeley's master—master of "the operative juncture, the phrasing of a composition where the crisis of the form is everywhere immediate." Master of a generation of poets, so that "we have to do in our appreciation of Creeley's art not with a lonely excellence or an idiosyncratic style but with the flowering of a mode, a community in poetry." A mode, and an insistence? Love?

Persistent other.

> "Kore"
>
> "O love
>   where are you
> leading
>   me now?"
>
> "The Door"
>
> Lady, do not banish me
>
> . . . .
>
> . . . Lady, I follow
>
> . . . .
>
> The Lady has always moved to the next town
> and you stumble on after Her.

Stumble. Obsessive word. Is Duncan right, in the interview with George Bowering and Robert Hogg, that "Creeley's practised stumbling is an embodiment of . . . castration and impotency," that he has been crippled by a wife?

15 July 1977

"Things continue," he says in *Words,* "but my sense is that I have, at best, simply taken place with that fact." At (his) best, he finds place. And the poems continue, a continuum. Nothing occasional, all of his occasions (events), related to each other, commenting on, extending each other. What it means to track one's life. That depth. Right to insist on his seriousness. Wrong to deny "progress"? What of the rhythm acknowledged in "The Rhythm," the sense of death, of time, of aging? That he stumbles less, walks more, even dances?

That he's acquired some of the wisdom—awareness of complexity, the measure of proportion—he praises in Joel Oppenheimer (in "For Joel")? Not that he solves any problems—who solves the problem of *life*?—but learns *to live* with/in them. Learns the measures (rhythms, intervals, too) of life-and-poetry.

> Measures—
> ways of being in one's life
> happy or unhappy,
> never dead to it.

Life tracking life always beyond the fixed circumference; the Emersonian abandonment of "Circles"; risk, nakedness, "saints of this exposure."

> What
> has happened
> makes
>
> the world.
> Live
> on the edge,
>
> looking.

Or waiting, as he says of the necessity in writing to wait out the silence, to accept whatever agency there is besides himself:

> That risk
> is all there is.

And really *looking*. So you notice the overflowing life you have.

> Water drips
> a fissure of leaking
> moisture spills
> itself unnoticed.

What
was I looking at,
not to see
that wetness spread.

Looking now, giving over stasis and isolation and the mind. Finding, not that one is never more than one but that "Together / is one by one"—one beside one—and beauty comes of it, "dripping its condition."

I had thought (in "A Birthday")
a moment of stasis
possible, some

thing fixed—
days, worlds—
but what I know

is water, as you
are water, as you
taught me water

is wet.

His places are wet. Wetness is witness ("the mind / is not its only witness"). Isn't water his preferred image, the favorite element, as Bachelard would say? A poet of water, of wetness.

And appropriately so, for a poet in the service of love. Wetness is what she gives him in the act of love:

You have left me
with, wetness, pools
of it, my skin
drips

—"wetness so comfortable," he says again, and "warmth and moisture," the water that the rocks of thought *displace*; "that sense of warm / moistness, the condition // in which all grows." His ground but, without her benefaction, ground "disclosed as dirt." No wonder, at sea in love, he hangs on "for dear life to her."

16 July 1977

The persistent other, answering for the whole world (hole world, the emptiness, the space he would fill with something other than his emptiness; the silence, the "dull space" of suspension, out of which he would urge words). The reality, of his childhood, for which he thanks his sister Helen. The world she opened to him:

> wet-
> ness, now the grass
> as early it
> has webs, all the lawn
> stretched out from
> the door, the back
> one with a small crabbed
> porch. The trees
> are, then, so high,
> a huge encrusted
> sense of grooved trunk,
> I can
> slide my finger along
> each edge.

The LSD experience out of which he wrote "The Finger": "The day [in New England] broke clear and fresh and dewy, and there was all this moisture in the trees and the grass—those spider webs of moisture, and it was just idyllic."

Wetness, like weather, *out there*, necessary to place.

> The wetness of that street, the light,
> the way the clouds were heavy is
> not description. But in the memory I fear
>
> the distortion. I do not feel
> what it was I was feeling. I am im-
> patient to begin again, open
>
> whatever door it was, find the weather
> is out there, grey, the rain then and
> now falling from the sky to the wet ground.

Yes, the wetness of *that* street has radiance and still is, now, even as, inevitably, it enters the memory, and memory closes the door to it. Poetry is a way to begin again (as Williams said), to open the door, recover what the opening lines and closing lines in fact recover: not only the wetness which fills all space from sky to ground but the fact that now, as then, the landscape of being remains, never fails. The world is not all in the mind. See "To Bobbie":

> What can occur
> invests the weather, also,
> but the trees, again,
> are in bloom.
>
> . . . .
>
> The world
> is the trees, you,
>
> I cannot change it,
> the weather
> occurs, the mind
> is not its only witness.

To love, is also a way to begin again. Love and writing, the refreshment of life, Williams says.

Once he wanted to have it all in the mind, the little space. See "Some Place," where he encases himself in a house and shuts out the weather of life. As he says in "Enough," he has made "a picture // for the world to be." The world of "A Picture":

> A little
> house with
> small
> windows,
>
> a gentle
> fall of the
> ground to
> a small

stream. The trees
are both close
and green, a tall
sense of enclosure.

There is a sky
of blue
and a faint sun
through clouds.

The small, close world of childhood, centered on self. To have it all there; self-sufficient. An understandable reverie. But a lifeless picture, a representation, of what a child might see and feel: a pastoral world, which can never "be," lonely too, as yet (he knows) unstirred by the sun.

What the mind affords, in its hunger for the other, its reluctance to let it be other.

I wanted
one place to be
where I was
always.

How much he *wants*, always wants. The distress of thinking "In two / places, in two pieces. . . ." Wanting to possess the unpossessable, even with the lovely pathos of this admission:

in words

I possessed it [her body], in
my mind I thought, and
you never knew
it, there I danced

for you, stumbling, in
the corner of my eye. (see "The Finger")

Neither is enough. The work of these poems is to work through to "some other // way of being, prized enough, / that it makes a common ground." To respect the other, to let it be, as he says in "Enough," his Asphodel poem. To accept the "intervals // of a complex / loneliness," to know the beauty of that, of the fact that "Together / is one by one."

And that even though, in the intervals, ground is dirt, it is: a necessary foundation, other than self, on which to build.

> mountains come of it,
> the sky precedes, and where
> there had been only
>
> land now sticks and stones
> are evident. So we are
> here, so we are.

Place *in* the world, the human dwelling *they* build, not of words, as he does privately, but of sticks and stones. (Sticks and stones will break my bones but words will never hurt me. Reverse that.) Not a perfect place—it is built in recognition of that impossibility: of intervals, one by one, here/there; of the rhythms, the process, the changes. The desert places of "A Night Sky" made habitable; the habits of mind of "The Mountains in the Desert," foregone. "So we are / here"—here/now together—and *being* so, *are*, having being. Place: where we have being together; where we do not assimilate others to ourselves, but live our lives with, and along with, them.

The water of life spills. So it goes, of itself, just so much. You track your own precious life so that it doesn't leak away unnoticed. But you don't possess it. You yield the "I" (not the eye: the attention, the care). And you *see*, as she teaches him, that wetness is a gift, what we, having life, have in us to give others.

His seriousness. Donald Junkins says that when Creeley asks "What is the matter?" this simple question becomes a matter of ultimate concern. So he makes us moralists. "I want the poem as close to this fact [of living what there is to live] as I can bring it; or it, me." The measure of his work. And the measure by which it is so often superior to the work of all but a few poets.

17 July 1977

Words: the book I like best, not necessarily the best. As much a long poem as *Pieces* and *A Day Book*, and more consistently highly charged, with none of the vacancies words fill for him, none of hesitancies of making poems, which are in fact enacted in the later books, the risk he accepts in them that makes them greater achievements.

I like here the equilibrium, the rather high plateau of being, as against *For Love*. The way he moves out into the world. Not that he isn't "In- / side the thinking" but sometimes the door opens and he walks in the world. I like the loving recognition of "The Messengers." The celebration, the happiness acknowledged. A fragment at the end tells of dancing, not in the head, but in accord with the sounds there—the way it is with Duncan in "A Poem Beginning With a Line by Pindar" ("Oh, / how much he heard"). Another invokes "days of happiness" and pardon for "one's blunders." Such brilliant poems of acute self-scrutiny as "The Dream," "Anger," "A Sight," and "Enough" are now part of all he accepts "for no clear reason." Having "memory of water" he knows now that "Some day / will not be / this one [in "the twisted place" where he cannot speak]."

> I dreamt last night
> the fright was over, that
> the dust came, and then water,
> and women and men, together
> again, and all was quiet
> in the dim moon's light.

A paean of such patience—
laughing, laughing at me,
and the days extend over
the earth's great cover,
grass, trees, and flower-
ing season, for no clear reason.

How much this poem says about all our public and private holocausts and the belief in *polis* and "an actual earth of value" necessary to survival. To serve the Goddess, as Olson also knew, devotes one to the natural world, to the renewals and possibilities of the cosmic process Creeley recognizes in "The Rhythm." That poem *opens* the book. And a new kind of quiet reigns.

19 July 1977 Having acquired the previous work, you read through *Pieces* directly, and that in itself is a pleasure.

The special excitement: the risk, and his success in "unbound thinking." A journal. A different kind of formal occasion. Not only the Olson he remembers ("Thinking of Olson—'we are / as we find out we are'") but the Olson of "This is the exercise for this morning." Pleasure and possibility. "Words / are / pleasure. / All words." ". . . the delight of thought as a possibility of forms." Dancing, he says, "in the delight of thought, not the agony of thought as fixed pattern." The dance in "The Finger" prompts these remarks. "Man is form and woman is essence"—Williams believed this too.

Demonstrated by the way the book opens in "the literal activity of the writing itself" and creates its own track. The poems up to and eventuating (good "Whiteheadian" word!) in "The Finger" are paradigmatic. Forms are the wonders he seeks, and "No forms less / than activity." By that activity of writing come into the present, shed the past, shed prescription, become "a presence // saying / something / as it goes."

The release of it. How writing returns him to possibility and hope. Opens a path *into* his situation and thereby *out* of it. "In the dilemma of some literal context a way is found in the words which may speak of it."

Into his situation. How to deal with here/there, is/was; how to enter here/now. The solipsistic nature of his activity, the awareness of which turns his attention to things. The mind locked-in, the mind looking-out, the mind released in touch. Even the double nature of mind, in "Gemini"—estrangement within the mind. He takes us inside his head. The feel of *that*.

Other aspects of his single experience, things that must be accepted if he is to continue to live—the "family" of five single separate people so that there are five ways to say "Here we are," five locations, perspectives; the successive nature of events, time, and "time of life" (aging). Knows "The way into the form" is "the way out of the room," and when at last he takes hat in hand and goes out the door ("Hat, happy, a door— / what more"), he opens the door of "The Door" in *For Love*—or it opens—and the wonderful result is "The Finger," perhaps the finest poem of/to the Goddess, as central to his work as Williams' "The Wanderer" is to his. Central to this book, too. See "Mazatian: Sea."

Forms are wonderful. "Form is the magic of the world"—Edith Cobb, citing Albert Dalcq. Wonderful because the forms he creates have as much reality as he thinks thinking has and are objects separate from himself. He does indeed jiggle "a world before her / made of his mind."

20 July 1977

Descent. Exploration to recover the self. Undertaken at times of creative / spiritual impasse. When the center cannot hold. Pieces. "So tired / it falls / apart." Entropy.

Unity here is in the act. Don't ask what he has done but what he is doing. Among other things, getting "the sense of 'I' into Zukofsky's 'eye'—a locus of experience, not a presumption of expected value." Dedicated to Zukofsky.

Unity is of the locus of experience. The self experiencing is ground, a center of the forever-weaving fabric of attentions. Familiar insistences, obsessive concerns. Tightly woven, reflexive (recurrent). Yet a movement of thought, sequential, moving "forward" (in time) not to exhaust itself so much as to find resolution. Time itself as remedial. Thoreau's something in the lapse of time by which time recovers itself?

Is the keynote hidden in the Ginsberg epigraph? His "Song" begins, "The weight of the world / is love," echoing Williams' "Love Song." The heavy weight here.

Pieces vs. Places. The poles of experience. In *Words*, the poem "A Piece" is a place composed of pieces:

> One and
> one, two,
> three.

One and one does not make two. (Whitman: "we two together.")

> Pieces of cake crumbling
> in the hand trying to hold
> them together to give each
> of the seated guests a piece.

Relax the hand, let be.

Words work
the author of many pieces (*A Day Book*)

Words work. "How far one has come / in these seven league boots." So far the critics complain, "It's changed, it's not the same!"

Openness sets him free to wander again, no longer the romantic youth of "The Fool" in "Numbers."

Poetics:

you want
the fact
of things
in words,
of words.

Life tracking itself: "Everybody *spends* it (the 'life' they inhabit) all—hence, no problem of that kind, except (*large* fact) in imagination."

Time-ridden. Because of the successive nature of reality, the days that merely come and go, the weather:

21 July 1977

What changes. [?]
Is weather
all there is.

Because of bodily entropy: aging:

Counting age as form
I feel the mark of one
who has been born and grown
to a little past return.

The body will not go
apart from itself to be

another possibility.
It lives where it finds home.

Thinking to alter all
I looked first to myself,
but have learned the foolishness
that wants an altered form.

Here now I am at best,
or what I think I am
must follow as the rest
and live the best it can.

Summary wisdom. No longer the romantic idealist of "The Fool." None of the foolishness of "expectant dream." Comes home to the body, as in the Ginsberg epigraph. Finds that place. Yet still the Chinese boxes of the mind: ". . . what I think I am. . . ."

Four. The number of security, comfort, friends, community, peace, "celebrating return, / reunion, / love's triumph." Time translates this:

Before I die.
Before I die.
Before I die.
Before I die.

Further wisdom:

Heal it, be
patient with
it—be quiet.

The possibility of spring. Rhythm. "It is all a rhythm. . . ."

No clouds out the window,
flat faint sky of faded blue.
The sun makes spring now,

a renewal possibly of like energy,
something forgotten almost remembered,
echoes in my mind like the grass.

Echoes. Distances. Conspicuous words now.

The voice of the
echo of time, the
same—"I

know you," no
pain in that, we are
all around what we are.

Memory bends time into a self-enclosing circle, is a context of the self. The turn re-turns. Can't alienate the past.

Nowhere one
goes will
one ever
be away
enough from
whatever
one was.

Distance an old self? In this instance recover the childhood self. The juxtaposed verse:

Falling-in windows—
the greenhouse back of
Curley's house. The
Curley's were so good
to me, their mother
held me on her lap.

Again:

Smell of gum wrappers as of Saturday afternoon at
movies in

Maynard, Mass.—
Sudden openness of summer. . . .

Lost America of love. Kerouac.

The descent beckons, and he responds.

> The descent beckons [Williams writes]
> as the ascent beckoned.
> Memory is a kind
> of accomplishment,
> a sort of renewal
> even
> an initiation, since the spaces it opens are new places

As in "HERE":

> Past time—those
> memories opened
> places and minds,
> things of such reassurance—
>
> now the twist,
> and what was a road
> turns to a circle
> with nothing behind.

Nothing behind because all is here / now? A new place. "Here is / where there /is," he says in *Thirty Things*.

Memory helps to place us.

> Where we are there must
> be something to place us.
>
> Look around [pun?]. What do you see
> that you can recognize [remember].

Also: the something of shared activity: "finding place in something we both had occasion in." For example, the books of his published by Black Sparrow with illustrations by Bobbie Creeley?

"Numbers." Personal numerology. The summation of his ones and twos and threes, the algebras of existence, returning to zero.

22 July 1977

> What
> by being not
> is—is not
> by being.

Riddles of being and non-being, self and other(s)—the old insistences, philosophically, dramatically, pursued. Pythagoras, Jung, Tarot (the Fool is zero). A major poem. Thomas Duddy reads it well.

"Mazatlan: Sea." The long concluding poem. Burke would call it a representative anecdote.

Mazatlan, another Mallorca? "Domestic" crisis like that of *The Island*?

> Why the echo of
> the old music
> haunting all? Why
>
> the life and fall
> of the old rhythms,
> and aches and pains.
>
> Why one, why two,
> why not go utterly
> away from all of it.

Crane's "O Carib Isle"? The listlessness of the beach. Creative nullity? Null and void? Loveless?

> One, two
> is the rule—

from there to three
simple enough.

Now four
makes the door

back again
to one and one.

Back again, "tense-stricken," like the boy in the epileptic fit, identified with. Crane's "Idiot"?

What, in the head, goes wrong—
the circuit suddenly
charged with contraries,
and time only is left.

The Williams of "The Desert Music"?

I am that he whose brains
are scattered
            aimlessly

Hence the necessity of writing poems.

Seascape. What a vast space to make place! Attention succeeds. He is enveloped.

The air is thick
and wet and
comfortably encloses
with the sea's sound.

Bodily being. Again: "The wind holds / my leg like // a warm hand." And again: "The water slurs / and recurs. The air is soft." That much, anyway.

Daily exercise: to make himself a "locus of experience." Does this brilliantly, whatever the experience.

What does he *see* when he gets the sense of the "I" into the "eye"? A woman "lovely in all particulars." Does this prompt his restlessness? The desire for some remarkable event of weather such as John Muir reported? The "irritations" and the mind's return to them? Love's absence; bodily need.

> Here is all there is,
> but *there* seems so
> insistently across the way

Across the way!

> *Here, here,* the body
> screaming its orders,
> learns of its own.

Its own singularity, its need.

So much waiting—

> waiting, waiting
> on the edge of its
> to be there
> where it was, waiting.

And waiting as before, returned to the old unsettling concern of "manhood," of learning what he can do.

> Here I am still,
> waiting for that discovery.
> What morning, what way now,
> will be its token.

And the old concern of the sleeping wife—and his annoyance with returning to it:

> What would you have
> of the princess—
> . . . .
> You will ride away
> into the forest . . .

Thought is shapely—Ginsberg. Shapes of thought. The verses are tight and small. Resonant notations made possible by the now familiar terms.

One day's entry given over to the expedient of writing about fucking. Meditates desire in youth and age. Incites desire.

> I hate the metaphors.
> I want you. I am still alone,
> but want you with me.

Dreams of a "context of people," waking to find

> no one but my wife there, [*there*]
> the room faint, bare.

Should he go utterly away, as before? "The substance of one / is not two." But thought betrays when it presumes: "I could fashion another / were I to lose her."

Why doesn't he take hat in hand? Is the dream of a "complex of people" an answer? They are together there, a "we." And the dream of the Goddess in the last entry, that coda to "The Finger"? A marvelous transformation of the episode of the whorehouse in *The Island*? Does the possibility of sexual "ease / and delight" answer, and the fact that in bodily coming to himself he now recognizes, in the sacred orgy, his membership in a universal erotic communion?

> I was given that
> sight gave me myself,
> this was the mystery
> I had come to—all
>
> manner of men, a
> throng, and bodies of
> women, writhing, and
> a great though seemingly

silent sound—and when
I left the room to them,
I felt, as though hearing
laughter, my own heart lighten.

Isn't this anticipated in an earlier recognition?

They all walk by
on the beach,
large, or little,
crippled, on the face
of the earth.

Should anything be made of the *four* questions of the closing stanza? Does his lightened/enlightened heart (not head) now find comfort, the "secure / fact of things" in the very inconclusiveness of life? In "Numbers" he says of four:

The card which is the
four of hearts must
mean enduring experience
of life. What other
meaning could it have.

"Love's triumph."

Interrogatives keep things open.

26 July 1977

I think the achievement of *A Day Book* even greater than I did before. It is not only that he is deeper in isolation and more displaced and has farther to go in order to restore (renew) his relations to persons, places, and things. And it is not only the crisis of mid-life (age, vocation-success, settled life: how to liberate oneself and acquire energy) that is easy to identify with. It's what the prose here as against the verse more readily permits. As he says of Ginsberg's *Indian Journals*, it's the detail that lets us in to "such a specific personal *head.*" His mind is occupied with (full of) its occasion, with the context in which he is using language. He lets us see him tracking his life—or is it that near impossibility of putting the self in motion (self-action in Olson) that Emerson calls spinning your own top? He is painfully about his life, day after tedious day, and we are there, in his most private space, involved with his stance and the process of thought—the process of language as the pulse of being. How he tries to live in words; tries out the possibilities of personal pronouns, the "schizophrenia" of it, as he says. Many modes of writing, many presences as in *Presences*. Gemini. How thinking becomes self-act—or self-analysis acts on the self—and thought itself resolves and sets him in motion. "Straight forward, is forever the only way." You can follow this in the language which finally releases him as much as drunkenness or mescaline. And of course the measure of change is his recognition at the close of the prose section of the "sun's intensity at the window much like the day it all began"—recognition of his own internal change, the therapy of the daily work. Journal-keeping to that end. Emerson-the-self-therapist? And our recognition that he's come out, that clarity has replaced confusion, that the room now lacks interiority—that following Williams he now attends to what he sees and hears.

The most private is the most public (Emerson).

". . . the self image or the sorrows of Werther kind of fiction. . . . What will I do without that possibility?" Like *The Island*? But that's at the start.

From "he cannot arouse himself. Nothing stirs, really" and "I cannot take hold of things with intention." Why? Cites Olson's explanation for lack of place/polis: "now that man has no oar to screw into the earth," though it's the sexual implication that brings it to mind. Something stirs, really: his own penis. That bodily clamor, born of tiredness, worry over aging, fear of death, desire that cannot find response, moves him to sexual fantasy and recollection. The recurrent dream, the orgy (now graphic enough) in his head: doesn't it go back to the vision of sexual communion in the penultimate poem of *Pieces*? Doesn't it go forward to the essential vision of this book—that of "People," of a fully *inhabited* world of imperishable, immediate, tactile life, a shared life ("They are not isolated / but meld into continuous / place, one to one, never alone"), the life he calls "home"? A vision awakened in childhood (see also *The Island*, 151–52), the deepest place of his reverie, to which it returns.

Why he enjoys teaching and the social occasions of reading? "Where do they come from, where do they go—etc. Lovely the round and around of it, over and over and over. Delicious people. . . ." In this context recalls the "wash and fall of water remembered as a kid" and Whitman's "Out of the cradle endlessly rocking"—the energy of insistent movement. Water, and transference of energy: generativity. The icy river of West Acton, Massachusetts, remembered too.

Habits and haunts. Olson's phrase. You ground them in mother earth; *begründen*, founding, planting the oar. Not the motel John Cage thinks is all we need, attractive as that idea is in times of stasis—the wanderer's image of shelter for the night? Rather "New England—odors, sounds, senses of wetness, ways streets move, trees, the movement of the ground, senses of distances, smells, tones of voices, light. One wants to, at last, *be there* . . . simply there." As the handmade saw the Ainsworths own reminds us: "a specific locus, a situation that must have been more than coincident." A lovely place like Sascha's.

A book of echoes—"echo after echo of previous condition—in whatever person or sense of person was ever real in it."

Aware of and always attentive to children.

Aunt Bernice. Prompts his 91 Revere St.

System / Fading / Sending. Tells his dilemma in Burrough's terms. And keeps on sending.

27 July 1977 The difference in mode of Parts 1 and 2. The difference between earlier and later poems of the latter.

Thoughts of a dry brain in a dry season. Quick, wild, zany, distraught poems (notations), very punny, full of sexual innuendo, rhymes. The ironies, and despair, of "the so-called poet of love." Poems of displacement. Modulates to serious seriousness, but even here there seems to be a need for rhyme, to make things fit. The best poems at the end: the marvelous achievement—the ease, the voice, as wonderful as in the last lines of "The Messengers," doing what they say Ginsberg's voice does—

> Aie! It raises the world, lifts,
> falls, like a sudden sunlight, like
>
> that edge of the black night sweeps
> the low lying field, of soft grasses,
> bodies, fills them with quiet longing.

From "A Testament" on, so many splendid poems.

So many of them omitted in the recent *Selected Poems*. A nice project: to see what "story" the *Selected Poems* now tells.*

* *3 September 1977*. I note in *APR* that Creeley disclaims responsibility for the text of *Selected Poems*.

Against the

> Dreary, heavy
> accumulation
> of guilts, debts—
> all in the head

would summon himself to the dance: "Delight dances, / everything works." Yes:

> Trembling
> with delight—
> mind takes forms
>
> from faces,
> finds happiness
>
> delicious . . .

So he enters a peopled world. "Blesséd water, blesséd man." Recalled, he says in another poem, by

> Some small
> echo
> at the earth's edge . . .

Sound sometimes replaces sight: "The world pours in / on wings of song."

This time I am most overwhelmed by "The Birds."

> I want
> to ride the air which makes the sea
>
> seem down there, not the element
> in which one thrashes to come up.
> I love water, I *love* water—
>
> but I also love air, and fire.

And earth.

"People," "An Illness," "'Bolinas and Me . . .'" move me almost as much. And perhaps just as much, "For Benny and

Sabina," where "all / is here" and "continues taking place," the grey day quiet and wet. With how much he invests "all," like Olson. Or Crane's "A Name for All." And see "Masters of ALL" and "Colors" in *Thirty Things*, the latter's "all you people. Cars, / lights, wet streets" recalling "'Bolinas and Me . . .'"

Doesn't reverie move here?

> . . .is it
> a pasture
>
> I have in mind?
> I remember pastures
> of my childhood . . .

Duncan's poem, again. And what of "Massachusetts"?

> What gentle echoes,
> half heard sounds
> there are around here.
>
> You place yourself in
> such relation
> . . . .
> . . . See
> the things around you,
>
> taking place.

And the last stanza of "For Anybody"?

> Here in New England
> at last, *at last*—
> where I was born.

28 July 1977

That's the movement, out and back and around. As he has it in "The Picnic"—

> Time we all went home,
> or back,
> to where it all was
> where it all was.

What ice cream reminds him of in *Pieces*:

> The crowd
> milling on the bridge, the
> night forms in
> the air. So
>
> much has gone
> away.

Poet of love. The lost America of love.

Thirty Things. I count 31 poems. The extra one for good measure.

29 July 1977

"It is. It is the thing where it is"—that's not Creeley, but Williams, in the epigraph.

And much is. The round dance of cherubic children in the monoprint facing "Laughing," the one recalling Duncan's "The Dance" (with its recollections of Whitman and Olson) and "Often I am Permitted to Return to a Meadow"—companion poems: "Lovely our circulations sweeten the meadow"—the other the fairy world of "People":

> Who enters this
> kingdom. And
> the people formed
> in rock.

And seascapes: "wind on the ocean, trees / moving in wind and rain"; "the sea / opens below you, west." Vistas of being, appearing again, wonderfully, in the poem commemorating his mother's death. Landscapes of repose in "As We Sit" and "Place."

Wittgenstein in *Listen* and *Away*.

Not only in *Presences*, but early and always the intimacy with painters, sculptors, filmmakers.

The on-going tracking of *Presences* as he searches for a simpler life that can be managed. Is the return told in the last piece on Littleton, New Hampshire, with its lovely simple prose as against the more complex and playful prose of all that precedes it? And the Andersonian moment of the story within it?

Endlessly circular life. The overwhelming sense of this in the poem to his mother. And "Circle" in *Away*, gathering and enclosing so much that is precious: the woods, the sea, the "darkening body" of love (into which he would descend, as in death), "Love's watery condition. . . ." Yes:

> Old one-eye
> fish head
> wants his water back.

And the poem "For Walter Chappell" celebrating friendship, with its images of sinking down, "way / down, such roots // as rocks and trees, / the wind, seem / wise to" and seeing "it all / now" as the surf crashes through his "open" head:

> lovely light attentive,
>
> dripping fissures,
> all the world,
> the world.

All coming to this place:

> deep ditch with children
> warm nights with water,
>
> sweetening, silver light

"To 'return' not to oneself as some egocentric center, but to experience oneself as *in* the world. . . ."

30 July 1977

Say of him what he said of Williams, that it's not a question of which poems are good or bad because what matters is that "it all coheres, and each poem, or instance, takes its place in that life which it works to value, to measure, to be the fact of."

II

LATER (1978), a poem by Robert Creeley

Later. Comparative of *late,* adjective. Adverb in respect to temporal existence, far into it, when measured by a limited time? It's later than you think.

1.

The halting speech is due to the fact that what is asserted isn't "true." Even as he tries to dismiss the past, he lovingly hangs on to it. And does he hang on to it because it is a stay against the very loneliness he says he no longer need fear?

Shan't be winding. The contraction is quaint, itself an old, country usage. The overtone is sentimental. Also spares him the declarative *I shall not,* and indicates that the verse itself is an utterance/meditation of a diminished/receding "I," now referred to only as "this passing/person"—passing, it may be, out of existence, beyond that backyard (of childhood) "once and for all" (loaded cliché). Once and for *all time.*

Yet *Shan't* is perfectly right because it points the poem in the direction of return, its very negation telling the powerful hold of the past.

Winding plays off *passing* (and vice-versa); participles, both in terminal positions. *Winding* calls up *winding sheet*, and the clothes that flutter *their last regard // to this passing* pick up the resonance of death. (Indeed the clothes are subject, more active than the *passing/person*?)

Isn't it *rags* that flutter, or *flags*, as in Hart Crane?

Passing time is felt as dying, as death.

Back in blue echoes *black and blue*, calls up Louis Armstrong, and supports the blues character of the verse:

> Shan't be winding
> back in blue
> gone time ridiculous,
> nor lonely
> anymore . . .

The reason he won't be winding back into the gone time (sweet memory, and the actual place of childhood) is that he will be "Gone, / *gone*." The things and events of the past are also gone, and the insistence includes both.

And what is gone is precious. What does he remember (as Pasternak says of those preparing to meet death)? Delights of infancy, perhaps; *wee thin / delights* (just as thin and attenuated as the *e* and *i* sounds, yet sounds of infant joy, of unadulterated pleasure). And most important, as *delights, hands* insists, are the hands that held him—*hands / held me*—and the mouths, which in *held me / mouths* calls up pleasures of orality, a Roethke world—mouths so close to him he saw them as winking eyes.

Now it's because he is *passing* that the *back in blue / gone time*, that lovely blue time (like Williams' blueberry America) he guards himself against by calling *ridiculous*, is diminished to his awareness of only *that flat back- / yard* (the words themselves harsh, discrete/broken, as two-dimensional as the *a*).

What's at the center of the poem, central and deep and still clamorous, shows that he is not ready to die. That self still is, persists.

2.

This poem, too, resists death, passing time, by recovering his school days in West Acton. *Won't want* carries over the feeling initiated by *Shan't be*. The initial lines are again darkly resonant—of the Styx:

> You won't want to be early
> for passage of grey mist
> now rising from the faint
>
> river . . .

Is his reluctance to attend the rising mist that discloses (like a curtain rising) the vivid *present* details of childhood due to the pain of having childhood so much here/now? Aren't these things, present in memory, of the order of things witnessed in Hades?

The *childhood field* is, at first, as faint as the river that runs beside it. But the school bell (early, late: again the summons of time)—the school bell *rings*, simultaneously in the present and the past. Hear it ring!

> School bell rings
> to bring you all in again.

The swing of the bell is in the cadence, the ring is in *rings*, *bring*, *again*; in the *l*s of *school*, *bell*, *all*; in the vowel-leadings, too.

And its ringing recovers the past, like the hurdy-gurdy in Hart Crane's "Van Winkle," another poem in which "memory . . . strikes a rhyme out of a box." A poem, too, we remember, that speaks of

> Times earlier, when you hurried off to school,
> —It is the same hour though a later day—

And the bell not only brings you all in, but brings in all that matters. (Creeley's *all*, already in poems 1, 2, 3.) Again, now childhood not infancy, the sufficient, all-inclusive world *recognized*.

> That's mother sitting there,
> a father dead in heaven,
> a dog bark, steam of
>
> drying mittens on the stove,
> blue hands, two doughnuts
> on a plate.

Bachelard says that "when one has made the archetypal power of childhood come back to life through dreams, all the great archetypes of the paternal forces, maternal forces take on their action again. The father is there. . . . The mother is there." And since this is so, hasn't the poem begun its work? "The archetypes are reserves of enthusiasm which help us believe in the world, love the world, create our world."

He is taking the measure of life, of what is sufficient, *enough*. And it is lovely how much the dog matters, how in these poems, as in "For Betsy and Tom," he includes the loyal/loving dog that is not to be distinguished from the human and reminds us of the sentience of all things, and of our need for them. Yes, Broderick, who lights a kind world.

Hands that can grasp. (Olson: "This living hand, now warm, now capable / of earnest grasping. . . .") The warm intimate interior space of the kitchen. The satisfaction of food. ("Sit. Eat / a doughnut. // Love's consistency / favors me." *Pieces*) Mother's world, a *place* of love. Like Kerouac, up in Lowell, the "warm home time" of the kitchen. None of Olson's anxiety in "As the Dead Prey Upon Us," nor Duncan's resistance to the falconress. A thought of father, enough to indicate what *all* in fact would be; to indicate, too, that the thought itself is part of the security of home, the father's death explained (away) in the words of the Lord's Prayer.

Just the anxiety of time, of the fact that "it's getting late" ("Van Winkle"). Not much time left—not the time for indecision that Prufrock in his meditation thinks he has—

> . . . time for all the works and days of hands
> That lift and drop a question on your plate

This New England poet still has a (the) hunger for / of life. *Hands. Head.* His obsessive polar images have a New England lineage.

3.

The sequence is a protracted meditation. He calls it a poem, but it is not a single poem. What is single is the intense, complex feeling the poems explore. A sequence permits the requisite meditative sense. Transience is a theme for meditation because there is nothing else one can *do* with it. How otherwise alter it, work upon it?

He has already given us "small / spaces of existence"—intimate spaces. This book treats intimate, protected space, the "warm enclosure" mentioned in the concluding poem. It is this that especially warrants calling him a "domestic" poet.

Moved by the premonition of death, by that descent, he resorts to the work of memory spoken of in Williams' "The

Descent." "Memory is a kind // of accomplishment, / a sort of renewal" because it is the activity of imagination Bachelard calls reverie. Reverie (memory and imagination together) both renews and rounds (out) life. It marks the departure called return, *re-turn*. Bachelard says that "our childhood waits a long time before being reintegrated into our life" and reminds us that it is, as Jung believed, the work of the second half of our life ("when one goes back down the hill") and leads us *back*, to the *anima*.

When we get older we especially want the comfort of intimate space.

> Where finally else
> in the world come to rest—
>
> by a brook, by a
> view with a farm
>
> like a dream—in
> a forest?

We move toward the feminine, toward repose. We wish to enter the *gynaeceum*, the house (always maternal) of all houses, that of our childhood.

Hasn't Creely always told his story (his-story) in terms of houses—of rooms, doors, windows, etc.? He is literally a man of the house, of a space so intimate it is one with the self, the veritable center of being. So

> The small
> spaces of existence,
> sudden
>
> smell of burning
> leaves makes
> place in time

these days
(these days)
passing,

common
to one
and all.

The autumn season, one of memory—all reverie partakes of melancholy—and the odor that revives it. The initial lines comment on the previous poem, which now finds confirmation, the *smell* of burning leaves calling up the *small* space-and-world of the kitchen. With this addition, insisted on in the double verbal of *leaves makes*, that the present vivid sense vivifies the past, so that there is *place in time*: the space of true existence, well-being, in passing time (*these days // . . . passing*), actually passing as the verse counts its passing. The function of space, Bachelard says, is to contain time: to contain *place*, which is *inhabited* space. The function of reverie is to recover such places.

But the smell not only *makes* place in time, arrests it with a present image of the past, it *leaves* it in the past, back there in the flux of time. And both experiences are common to all of us. Which is true enough, but also a generous inclusion that perhaps acknowledges the fact that in reading the poem we, too, are doing a similar work of reverie.

4. 5.

A poem to *opening*, which is what the work of reverie is doing. Not just opening the boxes (and not Pandora's), which might contain the valentine of the next poem, but opening the door to the past, which quickens his very heart (*thump bump*), his "Funny Valentine." * Opening the heart. Again the

* Carl Klaus notes that this is the title of a popular song of the 1930s by Rodgers and Hart.

house, as central as the heart, a place from which to look out on/partake of a close, familiar, neighborly world, a world where dying is also a fact (*winter, west, shadows*: he never forgets the passing time, the moving sun). Yet a place full of life, of morning stir, the *door* (so often the image of prohibiting enclosure) wide open, whatever the seasons of life and death out there, life *open, never done*. Where the house is the self, the self takes comfort from such a house.

The cadence of the last three verses already pounds with the heart beat, the very heart beat (*thump bump*) that is indeed the eloquent articulation of his vital being (life and love; life = love). The heart is literally here; he gives it to us, even as we hear in *Valentine* the concluding lines of Crane's "The Wine Menagerie":

> —And fold your exile on your back again;
> Petrushka's valentine pivots on its pin.

6. This speculative poem challenges the previous work of reverie. Creeley will not let reverie cheat him of his unbearable awareness of passing time and irreversible change, of the physical disintegration of death (the dog's change in death like his own change, his dying in life), and of the fact that change denies the most precious, seemingly permanent things: self and home. Read the fourth and fifth couplets both ways:

> It's [not] me!" After all
> these years . . .
>
> . . . .
> After all
> these years,
>
> no dog's coming home
> again . . .

Nothing is retrievable, neither the dog nor the boyhood self, nor the home both shared. And *home* is the lost world (intimate space, place) that got *lost in the world* (hostile cosmic space) long ago.

Such poignance! The interjections, so sharp, evoking an actuality not to be had! And the modulation of, the echoing of

> "Hey Spot!" *The world's*
> *greatest dog* 's got
> lost in the world,
> *got lost* long ago.

His outcry not to be answered. Was the death of a dog his first recognition of death? Why did he want to be a vet? Tom Clark recalls talking to Creeley about animals: "Bob, to me, was doglike. His dogs were Boblike. Spot, for instance, could barely see due to hair over his eyes."

Too much to bear. Creeley answers by dismissing sadness as "boring / preoccupation" and adducing facts of cosmic change, change external to but affecting the self. Clouds also *pass*, making possible the fact, experienced later, that "places ride up in those / houses like clouds"; and the "rain's wet" may well bring the wetness of close happiness he speaks of in other poems. 7.

So, as Thoreau said, in the very lapse of time time recovers itself—or time too can bring things—good things—to pass.

Like the gathering intensity of 8 and 9, and the resolution of 10. The lines of these poems are longer; the poems are among the longest. 8.

There is "Nothing 'late'" about growing old because it arrives on time. It's a train you don't have to wait for. Past and future are terms of a time-line that youth, not age, enjoys. The "past" of *to be* is *was*. For the old, all the busy world of "futures" (the commodity, our own life, sold on agreement of future delivery!), the weighing of our success or failure by the powers of the world—all that is nothing to age that does indeed know not the wonder but the fact of *what's next*. Not *imperium* but *empyrean*, and maybe not that, hell.

Wonder is kid-stuff. The parody of I Corinthians 13 : 11 ("When I was a child, I spake as a child, I understood as a child, I thought as a child; but when I became a man, I put away childish things")—

> When I was a kid, I
> thought like a kid—
>
> I *was* a kid,
> you dig it . . .

—the parody nullifies the counsel of faith, hope, and charity, of awaiting the perfect which is to come. It's too late for that. The humor of

> a hundred and fifty years later,
> that's a whole long time to
>
> wait for the train.

—yes, the humor, catching up with a catch the *long ago* of the previous poem, dismisses that possibility. Is this *the* definition of *later*? Time is also measured by how you feel—so "These days" can be 1887, when he thinks of the lifespan, the birth and death of his mother.

And there isn't even a train anymore! You are left to your own devices.

Which leaves him with the unarguable facts, and explains why he says "And especially 'you'" can't argue with them.

Long ago (we know this from his sense of time as merely succession within the terms of birth and death) he put away childish things. And didn't he put away childish things in the poem on his dog? The facts are

> 1887, my mother was born,
>
> and now, sad to say
> she's dead . . .

How can he argue with a fact so intimately particular to him? This is where reverie inevitably brings him. And back to West Acton, changed ("No doubt // . . . improved" by progress!), bereft of the wonder, and wonderful love, of childhood.

He *is* one of the "'no place to go' old folks." Without the presence of his mother, West Acton is no longer *place*. (Think of the cosmic abandonment of Crane's "The Tunnel," the desire to return home to "mother eyes and hands.")

"An entire past," Bachelard says, "comes to dwell in a new house." 9.

These poems were written, not as one initially thinks at West Acton, but, as one finds here and in the explicit seal of the concluding testament, at Buffalo. The new attic room recalls the old attic room at West Acton, the "same treasures." Here reverie recovers, strengthens, sustains. This is a *pinnacle*.

The security of the room. Not a bare attic, but an attic *room*. And *scarred*, with a single *battered window* which literally *looks out*; like himself, an image of the verticality and completeness of his being. And full, full of being. Nothing *really* lost.

He, too, is *newly constituted*. To remember is to re-member.

And sitting up here, isn't he, as the inclusion of the sign "Elect Pat Sole" suggests, thinking of a Williams' poem and especially of its title, "The Attic Which Is Desire"?

Spiritual father? We see the reverie move by way of association, Pat Sole calling up

> *O sole mio*, mother

a lyric cry of the son, about his sun, his mother. Which precedes, prompts the recollection of West Acton, and the treasures, "the boxes, // old carpets, the smell." AND THE LOVE:

> KISS ME. *I love you.*

This is indeed the *pinnacle*; this is the *place*, the *small world* (of intimacy). He has "come as far, / as high, as I'll go"—horizontal distance in time negated by vertical fulfillment, a new measure of time, like the organic ripeness/readiness invoked later on. Which is why he implores the weather and the seasons.

> Sweet weather, turn
> now of year . . .

He accepts the fall. In the still vulnerable old chestnut tree, dropping its seeds, gathering *strength to face the winter*, in the *patience* of the small lawns and hedges, in the fading light of a declining season, Grandfather Creeley is learning how to die. Like Thoreau in "Autumnal Tints." (Are the leaves here by virtue of the papers blown by the wind, which echo with Eliot's winter scene in "Preludes"—echo, and countervail that vacancy, isolation, shutting-down?)

Childhood. Old age. Seasons of life. Flower-like tree. *Small* lawns, hedges. In the fall, school *begins*, three stories down, and like "3 Fate Stories" he is three stories up, out of it now for different reasons, willing now to bear all that is out there, the wear and tear of life, *the life* that he now knows inhabits *places*. Now he abdicates, in recalling, the enclosed life-denying places of "Some Place" and "A Picture" (in *Words*):

> Where finally else
> in the world come to rest—
>
> by a brook, by a
> view with a farm
>
> like a dream—in
> a forest? In a house
>
> has walls all around it?

No, he doesn't want to wall-out the all. The *man-made* (man-making?) *endurance* he wants is inescapably in and of all the world that radiates from himself:

> There's more always here
>
> than just me, in this room,
> this attic, apartment
>
> this house, this world [this house = this world]
> can't escape.

Can't escape, can't argue. Yet *can't escape*, recalling Williams' "The Desert Music," tells us that his work, to be achieved only in the poem, is the

> agony of self-realization
> bound into a whole
> by that which surrounds us

He would be a chestnut tree.* Then, as Bachelard says, his imagination "took possession of all the powers of plant life."

* Paul Diehl: Yeats' "O chestnut tree, great-rooted blossomer. . . ." Yes, and this poem is Creeley's "Among School Children." And he would have a victorious old age, like Williams, Pound, and H.D., celebrated by Duncan for their roots and branches.

> To live like a tree! What growth! What depth! What uprightness! What truth! Immediately, within us, we feel the roots working, we feel the past is not dead, that we have something to do today in our dark, subterranean, solitary, aerial life. The tree is everywhere at once. The old root—in the imagination there are no young roots—will produce a new flower. The imagination is a tree. It has the integrative virtues of a tree. It is root and boughs. It lives between earth and sky. It lives in the earth and in the wind. The imagined tree becomes imperceptibly the cosmological tree, the tree which epitomizes a universe, which makes a universe.

10. In teaching him how to die the tree teaches him how to live. Hence his testament to "a willingness // to *live*."

In the verticality of reverie he transcends time but not life. Descendence not transcendence is the primary work here. He learns again that *being* is *of sound body*, and that, as he told us in citing Ginsberg's poem,

> I always wanted
>   to return
> to the body
>   where I was born.

Putting away the preoccupations with the past and the future of the preceding poems, he now attends the now (here/now) and appreciates "the wonder of life is / that *it is* at all"—lines that echo Wittgenstein, "It is not how things are in the world that is mystical, but *that* it exists." Creeley's lines are to be read in a double way, that *being, existence* is the wonder of life, and that *that* should be is indeed a wonder. And what is the wonder of life? Not so much the life-restoring reverie of these poems, though the mind's very *wander*[ing] // *to wondering thought* beautifully defines reverie as "unbound thinking" and is part of it—no: the present fact of bodily being that permits the abandonment of reverie. As he said in "The Finger," "wonder [is] / a place to be." It is the sudden *sense*, the acquisition of

> this sticky sentimental
>
> warm enclosure,
> feels place in the physical
>
> with others

that is empowering and sustains him. Like Olson, at the end of *Maximus*, he is physically at home. Well-being is finally bodily being, the experience of himself *in* the world, the losing of the self (ego: thought) by which one finds oneself (Self)—

> finds a home
> on earth.

Yes, earth becomes home ("this house, this world"), an intimate space; *place*. He experiences cosmicity. Cosmicity as the all-inclusive feeling, and not just as Melville said, an "all feeling." Because Creeley is now secure in what Melville, who gave us "the primary imagination of the isolation of our condition," never had: basic trust. And he is at home *in* earth, the mother's lap. I think of Whitman's grass and of Ponge's *Le Pré*, and of the longest journey, begun in "Return" (Winter 1945–46), the journey to love, that, in the Ginsberg poem already cited, ends—

> ends
> in the arms of love
> at last,
> must rest in the arms
> of love

The "warm enclosure," having of course Creeley's insistent sexual reference, is the womb (tomb) of the world. In that sense he experiences being as round, and finds in the cosmos—an eroticized world—all the happiness of childhood.

Round, and circular. In "Circle" (*Away*), he writes:

> I'd climb into
> your body
> if I could, cover
>
> myself up entirely
> in your generous
> darkening body . . .

And in the poem in *Away* confessing his love of his mother, where he speaks of "endlessly circular / life," he concludes

> I am here
> and will follow.

Mother, the Great Goddess he has always followed.

The concluding poem is a testament, and like the testamentary essay, " 'I'm given to write poems,' " tells us what he has been given and will—he now realizes—always be given. "In poems I have both discovered and born testament to my life in ways no other possibility has given me." He has been permitted to come into the enabling place of love, the meadow of Duncan's great poem, the *open* field, the *mysterium* poetry not only creates but issues from. Like the grandmothers and grandfathers moved by consciousness of approaching death, he has told his story because it enables him to take "the *I* back to its center," to the place of places.

The numbers also count. They tell of completion and fullness. He does not end with zero, the empty cipher of nonbeing, as he did in "Numbers." He ends with ten, 10. A complete series. So life gathers, accumulates. The singular one, which once he felt marked the beginning and the end, now stands up against the circle, or better stands within it, the immemorial figure of being.

Are these poems, especially the last one, sentimental—"unabashedly sentimental," as he says? If they were wouldn't that diminish the quality of emotion they articulate? Or is it, that in calling this to our attention, he would have us recognize that he has come to that fullness of feeling too, that at last he is capable of it, that he is so much at home he can admit it?

5–10 February 1979
Iowa City

EDWARD DORN

12 May 1979

Through 1966:

The Newly Fallen (1961)
Hands Up! (1964)
Geography (1965)
The Rites of Passage (1965; modestly revised as *By the Sound*, 1971)
The Shoshoneans (1966)

A definite cluster of books. A widening and deepening experience, of the West. Dorn's geography; his particular landscapes: Washington, New Mexico, Idaho. Never place, never home, his lot a common one of vacant towns and desperate loneliness. Yet these landscapes are his in a way England, in *The North Atlantic Turbine* (1967), never is, never can be. "Unlocused," as he says. This book, then, makes a break, marks a turning, though the insistences of the previous work, so fundamental for him, continue.

No mistaking Dorn in his first small book, the one LeRoi Jones urged him to gather for publication in the (now remarkable) series of the Totem Press that includes his own initial volume of poems, *Preface to a Twenty Volume Suicide Note* (1961). Such sad young men! Such dismaying titles! The sorrows of young LeRoi! *The Newly Fallen*. The cover drawing by Fielding Dawson, a friend of Black Mountain days, evokes the rural poverty of the Great Depression; the format reminiscent of the thirties, too. Dorn's the more accomplished book, Jones still uncertain of his means, his prosody conspicuously contemporary, advertising the influence of such avant-garde writers as O'Hara, Ginsberg, Olson, and the "deep image" poets. None of Dorn's clarity, distinctive voice, lyric mastery (Creeley notes the "neat lightfoot way" of Dorn's line). And no political poem as good as "Prayers for the People of the World," "The Prisoner of Bellefonte (pa)," or even "The Biggest Killing," the last omitted from *Collected Poems*, and only the first retained in *Selected Poems*, that severe yet choice winnowing, having nothing (understandably) to represent the fine sequences of love songs.

24 May 1979

Did Dorn remember Joel Oppenheimer's remarks on *woodshedding* in his review of *The Newly Fallen* when he opened *Collected Poems* with the lovely poem, "The Rick of Green Wood"? Here he literally introduces himself ("My name is Dorn, I said"), tells of his northwest country life, and establishes, in part by means of the poem's balladic quality, the human measure of his care. His concern to have the cut wood dry not green in order to spare his slender wife; his concern, in this transaction with the woodcutter, to prepare for the world "that was getting colder"—all the while, as the title tells us, that even in such manageable face-to-face relationships, he is not getting what he desires.

He is ingratiating here. Without what he calls "adamant"—a characteristic especially evident in his first published essay, "What I See in *The Maximus Poems*" (1960)—*what I See*, indeed—and in essays of the early sixties like the one on Burroughs and Trocchi. You don't mess with Dorn; he knows the score, and what is more, as everyone from the beginning of his career remarks on as memorable virtue, he has figured it for himself. If "The Rick of Green Wood" shows him well-versed, but poorly versed in country things—the poem inevitably recalls the knowing Frost—don't be fooled. Apropos of Burroughs' obsessive scenes in *Naked Lunch*, he reminds us of farm jokes and the *fact* that "cornhole is a word for sodomy with animals in the midwest." Already roadtesting the language. Of fine, active intelligence, he not only lives in his occasion, but knows that he is living there under the necessity to test and clear all that forms (and informs) his condition. You never have to ask of his work, what he asks of McClure's, "So much for the effect of the verse, what of intelligence?"

Oppenheimer (a friend) says he likes the Dorn of *The Newly Fallen*. Yes, I agree. And beginning here, one will be more inclined to like him later, understanding that this Dorn, so exposed, so vulnerable in his sense of what has been lost and what threatens ("Still we have cause for terror"), is still there in the ever-tougher poet who yields less and less of his spirit and, in this withholding and intransigence and in the careful work of poetry, may be telling us how to survive.

His distinction from the start. Oppenheimer: "he/s avoided all cop-outs. . . . he/s woodshedded in illinois, the northwest, the southwest, the south, and, i take it, the value of woodshedding is that it lets you find out where you are after you/ve gotten lost." That's Thoreau, our preeminent woodshedder, who says in *Walden* that not until we lose the world (society) do we find ourselves and the infinite extent of our relations (cosmos). Well, Dorn's no woodsman and never figures as such. No respecter of Thoreau, either, maybe because Oppenheimer summoned his example? Or because, having a wife and children, he knows that that makes a difference? "That goddam sniveler Henry Thoreau," he says in the essay on Burroughs and Trocchi; grudging admiration, not for his civil disobedience—the responsible act of writing, he believes, is now inevitably so—but for his attempt as a writer to track his own life (see "The Land Below"). And Dorn never got lost, though he wants to learn the infinite extent of his relations. He simply put himself where he had found himself from the time of his childhood in Illinois, outside, at the edge, at a distance from dominant, urban, corporate, collective America. Yet like Thoreau he practices refusals, and as LeRoi Jones says in respect to uncompromising writers in *Home* (essays of this time, significantly titled), "he [was] left to rot in some pitiful mistake of a college in Idaho." So even though he moved on to colleges and places less pitiful, he makes this point in the preface to *Collected Poems*: "Throughout this period I have published through persons, and except for two cases not represented here, not with houses."

But life on the margins is after all marginal, reminding him, as he puts it in "The Common Lot," that what makes our lot common is the dreadful vacancy. In this America, he feels, even trees and children must practice forbearance. "The vacant lot is vast"; yet, as he says, "I can speak of love only at the edge."

He is full of yearning and love, and speaks of love and, almost unbearably, of its absence. Love. The most needed, the least had.

The opening poem of *The Newly Fallen*, for example. "Geranium." Belongs in a herbarium of American poems, notably with Williams' black-eyed Susan, the "Indian/dark woman," the Kora of *Kora in Hell*, who finally emerges in *Spring and All*. Or with the marigolds held high by the Black woman in the initial poem of Williams' *Journey to Love*.

Williams' book (1955) announces the journeys of a new generation of writers, those writers who found, as Dorn did, that at the end of World War II "there was no place to be," who found, as he emphatically quotes in defense of Dahlberg, that "'He was in no place and no place was in him. He had nowhere to go and so he sort of went on.'" As Dorn did, West, in exile actually, on "The New [new!] Frontier," to find, as he tells us in an essay on Douglas Woolf's novels, that fear of the stranger had replaced curiosity about him, that the loneliness was "the call of death"—"to stay away from friends now will turn out to have been the peculiar discipline of our era"—that "no one is at home here." That certainly is the message of Woolf's novels, beginning with the Emersonian entitled *The Hypocritic Days*, novels of homes that are no longer homes, that enforce flight and can't be fled because, as *Wall to Wall* indicates, America itself has become the abdicated home—home now system, system even prison—and the *coast to coast* driving does not avail in this walled-in condition (this post-Walden?). If anything avails it is the respite of temporary location—staying put—in off-the-road abandoned Western towns. And if there is any measure of human benignity it is the Indian, in *Wall to Wall*, Pedro who tells Claude, "I want to go home and live in the past a little." Worthy novels of disorientation and disaffiliation, commended by Dorn for what his work also seeks to do, to make "sociologies clear."

Dark flowers, his geranium red, to be set against the daisy, the "white daisy" of Williams' poem, and Fitzgerald's Daisy, certainly, and perhaps Edmund Wilson's, since the white flower has class, signifies social class as much as the well-dressed women who frequent the bank in the early story "1st Avenue," women whose imagined lives in the "alien world" of the Seattle hills fascinate and repulse this bottom dog and conveniently take their appointed place in his polarized view of America.

The red geranium, the "cherishable common that I worship and that I sing." *She*, out of *In the American Grain*; Pocahontas, out of *The Bridge*. Here, in Washington, the Indian presence of the rain forest, a Great Goddess / Muse evoked in need, as the reference in "The Song" to the Venus of Lespuge reminds us.

The spirit of place no longer in place, at home only in his mind, in "the great geography of my lunacy," which is, finally, the geography of most importance in Dorn until he learns (from Olson?) that earth is the geography of our being. Or, at best at home in the actual geography of pea-camps north of Seattle, to be found, as he finds Ramona in *By the Sound*, a victimized migrant. Even so, this Esquimau woman contrasts nobly with his own "pale sojourner" and could never be, in the middle-class way, "purchased by the lust of schedule" or made to seem antic astride a motorcycle. Doesn't she belong with the beautiful Indian girl of the corn dance at Taos? The beauty but not the namesake of the story "Beauty," whose movements awaken the earth and make the corn grow, "making us [outsiders, looking on, as he in "Geranium" looks on from the window of the bus] all grow into one religious bigness, rolling onward, her light brown limbs sending us hallow into silence." She is a touchstone to remember, the agency and presence of a sacralized earth. Generative: her dance eroticizes space, fills it with eros, and so makes it place, or home.

The sacred and the profane. Sacralization / desecration. His primary personal, historical, social concern.

> No one,
> has loved the west I came into, this is not
> a Shulamite maiden

No wonder we are homeless.

25 May 1979

Does he sing in hope, or against hope? How can he muster such lyric sweetness, lovely, clear, flowing, carrying feeling to the verge, never beyond to sentimentality?

> I know that peace is soon coming, and love of common
> object,
> and of woman and all the natural things I groom, in my
> mind, of
> faint rememberable patterns, the great geography of my
> lunacy.

Faint rememberable patterns. Will the remembering of poetry, the reverie of return, clearly evoke them? Will it "explain" this poet who says, "I go on my way frowning at novelty, wishing I were closer to home," specifically Burlington, Washington, which is after all not "the home of my mind"? Hasn't he, with his frown and "insane squint," established the critical remove of his work? What must he order to get underway? "Geranium" tells the displacement he feels in almost all present places. What of the past, the farm in Illinois, his mother, who in the "Farm Poems" bears the burden of victimage?

In a prefatory poem in *Collected Poems*, he accommodates their differences in the concluding throw-away couplets:

> Incidentally, for her the air
> was Red one time:
>
> this end of a dust storm
> somehow battered up from Kansas.

And in the "Farm Poems" he remembers her "year-long stare/across plowed flat prairielands." His acute social feeling comes of that time and place, of the dispossession (or lack of possession) of the Great Depression. The projective sympathy of the political poems (add "The Argument Is" to those already cited) comes naturally, genuinely of experience, not from literary example, though the echo of poems of the thirties reminds us that Dorn's politicized art has a precedent. The "Farm Poems" are remarkable, among other things, for the image of the corn, "the rich yellow dusty pollen tassles / striking my face"

> striking my face like gold we barely
> heard of, it was not
> our harvest, it was not
> our field, it was not gold fever.

No, it was not gold fever, but the fever of an intimacy not yet allayed: "soft winds blowing yellow pollen across the rows." So again we know the foreclosure of all that Crane evoked in the "hushed gleaming fields"—Ceres' blessing, fertility ripening into the harvest of human community, the peace—and polis—Dorn still hopes, in his lunacy, is coming soon.

Columbus' dream in Crane's "Ave Maria." Referred to in the closing title poem of *The Newly Fallen*, a poem gathering all the loneliness and sorrow of the book into a "peace" now recognized as conditional.

> IF IT SHOULD EVER COME
>
> And we are all there together
> time will wave as willows do
> and adios [á Dios!] will be truly, yes

The conditional here is occasioned by history, by Dorn's realization that Columbus was not a beginning but an end, that the world he discovered and squirreled away was not one of many newly fallen acorns, but the only one. So small, an acorn! A graspable image of an actual earth of value.

> You didn't know you were at the end
> thought it was your bright pear
> the earth, yes

Most likely Dorn learned from *The Maximum Poems* that Columbus thought the nipple of the pear was Eden, the terrestrial paradise. Olson had learned it from Brebner, who opens *The Explorers of North America* (1933) with this declaration: "Unless mankind is to embark some day on interplanetary exploration, there can never again be a geographical adventure like the discovery and exploration of the Americas." *Exploration*: I almost wrote *exploitation*. Which merely underscores the irony of Dorn's remark in "A Fate of Unannounced Years": "I will have to pick my cluster of grapes/in this country."

Considering this, and what Brebner calls "The Lures to the Continent," *we* are the newly fallen. Thoreau remained confident by saying that America was still new, that in his time we had discovered only the shores of America. Was I confident when I chose this concluding phrase as the title of a book? More confident than I am now, having on several occasions misspelled it the *sores* of America?

Which Dorn, with Burroughs and Mailer and so many more, already knows as the plague. From the start:

26 May 1979

> Did America say give me your poor?
> Yes for the poor is the vitamin not stored
> it goes out in the urine of all endeavor.
> So poor came in long black flea coats
> and bulgarian hats
> spies and bombers
> and she made five rich while flies covered the rest.

To the finish:

> Our days
> recur to how
> we made the world, how we desired

> to live long rather than quickly,
> but when our eyes seek those hills
> too late, from which the sun is taking
> away its power. . . .

Dorn's West, placed by references to our Mediterranean birthplace and mythic origins, is the last chapter in the decline of the West. We *have* come too late. And where dust, not love, fills space, the enveloping negation might well be read in terms of entropy.

And where the ominous smoke of the atomic energy plant in New Mexico and of the Simplot fertilizer plant in Idaho are the fixes that locate him. In "The Biggest Killing," the most outraged poem, on the present failure of political leadership, he reminds us that fifteen years ago the first atomic bomb was exploded at Alamogordo.

> No leader can be exempt from drunk blood,
> remember we passed Trinity site,
> where 15 years ago we were led by the top gang
> of all marching with their eye protectors imagine
> they covered their eyes thus those idiot eyes
> were not burned out by what they saw of their own
> creation. . . .

Now, imperiled at home by our own creation, we may find outrage acceptable and remember how early, among poets, Dorn spoke it. Shouldn't we reissue Armand Schwerner and Donald Kaplan's *The Domesday Dictionary* (1963)? Remember that the "yesterday" that Dorn says "should be one-half/ our whole possibility" is lost, that men playing "a gigantic Parker game of careers" have indeed worked this end and, with it, the wreckage of the hopes of a generation.

> . . . we are the yellowing leaves, my friends and I
> heaped upon the slopes of the New World Trinity
> where grieves forth obsolescent land-wrack to infinity.

The yellowing of the leaves of grass. The "beached heap of high bravery" and "sesames of science" of "Cape Hatteras," Crane's poem to Whitman.

Yesterday. Only yesterday. It all goes back, Kerouac explains in his account of this (my) generation, to the America we knew before World War II, that lost America; and especially the rememberers, like Kerouac, have that measure and can tell how much was lost. Not that much hadn't been lost before in our brief, violent history, but never to the revolutionary extent occasioned by the transformation of America after World War II. Dorn begins with that change, and all of his work, ever more caustically addresses it.

It goes back, as Kerouac knew, to the era of the radio, to the Shadow he evokes so well and Dorn remembers waiting for, the airways full of news of Pearl Harbor ("waiting for the Shadow / only the Shadow knows heh heh heh"). So LeRoi Jones may be too exclusive in "In Memory of Radio" when he says

> Who has ever stopped to think of the divinity of
> Lamont Cranston?
> (Only Jack Kerouac, that I know of: & me.

And it goes back to what Dorn evokes in "Sousa," the most impressive, emotionally central poem of *The Newly Fallen*—emotionally powerful because it most fully gathers and expresses the "mutilated emotions" he feels we now have.

Here, he says, is "the only May Day / of my mind," the band concert at Windsor, Illinois, when

> . . . the fresh breeze
> and the summer dresses of girls once blew
> but do not now. . . .

Sousa, whose horn "decapitates" the silence, this "semper fidelis maniac,'" is a "child" of America's childhood and his own, the America summoned also by "the ghosts of old picnickers / ambling under the box elder." Ghosts, like those recalled in the cemetery of "The Air of June Sings," a poem equally intense, pure, and unembarrassed, where he is moved to tears. The yearning of the poem moves across disjunctions of time, place, event: 1960 and the 1930s, New Mexico and Illinois, atomic blasts and dust storms. And moves in a reverie toward childhood, rising in the plea to

> March us home through spring again
> the belief, the relief
> of sunday occasion.

But Sousa, to cite Crane, can't "dance us back the tribal morn!" And the music, which reminds Dorn of "a lost celebration I can't / quite remember," fades into the present silence and sadness of Los Alamos, where with a friend he watches a protest march, where Sousa, he says, would no longer "recognize anyone." The breadlines of Salinas and Stockton now are here—the vacancy, too—but with this difference:

> John Sousa you can't now
> amuse a nation with colored drums
> even with cymbals, their ears
> have lifted the chalice of explosion . . .

Nor is song necessarily effective, as Dorn tells us in the single isolated line of his protest: "I sing Sousa," to be read also "I sing, Sousa." He does. Because song is of the essence of love.

27 May 1979 If you open the covers of the Totem / Corinth edition of *Hands Up!* two hands confront you, but if you close the covers the hands suggest thumbing one's nose.

The same format as *The Newly Fallen*. "The record of these days," he says in "The Land Below," the most ambitious poem in the book, the prototype of meditative journeys like "Idaho Out." The record of a continuing education, now explicitly in the robbing of America. An American, "finding myself in America"—*finding* in two senses, and finding, too, that "a continent is a surprise." Finding economic, ultimately ecological, dispossession is possession by a few, favored, it seems, by providence when the forest fire spares the "struggling properties" of the "lower upper/middle class" and the storage bins of investors. Greed, manifested, for example, in "the manifest destiny of Rand," accounts for the "stopped heart," the meanness in America. Dorn stands with Gary Snyder and Wendell Berry, this book a prefigurement of *Turtle Island* and *The Unsettling of America* not because it anticipates their interests but rather their subsequent drawing the line, the intense defense they've come to. "The desire to disintegrate the Earth / is eccentric," he says in "Sousa," with more equanimity than he will ever again muster. Hands Up is countered with Hands Off—with "hands off, nature / let me be," to be read, hands off nature, let me be (*Gelassenheit*). Against his tender lyrics of the land, the selling of the earth, earth only Indians in America have truly stood on.

> I am sure they tread
> upon an Earth I don't. And I would like to.
>
> * * *
>
> This world I did tread upon *is*
> in their [realtors] waxed palm. . . .

The geography that truly concerns him is not the superficial geography he knows so well, "the rickety geographies / we know better than to call home," but the landforms only the Indians have learned to live with, the veritable "bones of

America." (See Sauer's primer, *Man in Nature*, for this primary lesson of land and life.)

Like *Geography*, which follows, this is definitely a book of the West, of a continent spoiled from the outset by spoliation. *The Shoshoneans* and *Recollections of Gran Apachería* are later installments tallying the greatest human costs—the greatest enormities. Now Dorn speaks of "a hundred years of planned greed," of the homesteads that were the first subdivisions, so that in our time "strange cowboys live / in ranch style houses" and powerfully horsed "wagon wheels" pull "plastic boats behind." The story of the West, for all the grandeur Frederick Merk felt in the movement and migration of its fabulous settlement (which Olson never forgot, and who could, hearing that unforgettable teacher?)—the story from the start was a story of real estate and rape (which Olson knew but left to Dorn to learn firsthand). So, of the last frontier, Alaska, he asks and answers in *Hello, La Jolla*—another book of the far (gone) West—

> Will this be, as it is publicized,
> the last great land adventure?
> Generally that's meant real estate.

Did Dorn go West in the wanderings of his Black Mountain years with the expectation, fostered by the Turner thesis, of beginning anew on the frontier? Perhaps he did, but only to learn that however much the West lacks connection with the past, it was connected to his past in Illinois by the economic system that his mother served by going into debt ("On the Debt My Mother Owed to Sears Roebuck" resumes the Illinois history of the "Farm Poems"). Such are the economics, he says, "all are screwed / with. . . ."

What he learned inevitably by attention and by digging in one place is registered in his disgust, in the somber tone and deathward tendency of so much of the verse, in a hopelessness made extreme by disillusionment with the lies of American history. See how parodically he uses such slogans as "Wagon Wheels" and "Home on the Range." Or his demythification of the cowboy.

"Vaquero" opens the book and establishes its ironic distance. Here is the last, last cowboy, if Jane Kramer's is in fact the last. A prefigurement of Gunslinger? A cowboy of perception? The cowboy as isolated, cosmically placed figure, his agony suggested, a man against the sky. Not at all the "brave cowboy" of Edward Abbey's novel. The poem pictures him in a stylization, a study in color and composition recalling Williams' "To a Solitary Disciple." But then Dorn had studied painting, and if his poetry is an indication, favored blue. ("I have a dark blue sky / inside my head," he says in "A Song," which begins, "There is a blue sky"). So we have a blue cowboy. A Picasso cowboy, of the blue period, with that self-enclosing posture? A cowboy of another color than those we meet later, a "delicate" one who "stands quite still" in the night.

The subsequent cowboys. The "acaudate hunter" of "The Deer's Eye The Hunter's Nose," who is not moved, as Snyder says in defense of hunting, by love of animals. Or love of anything: not this snot-nosed character. Nor the cowboy who lives in a ranch-house and owns a horse he doesn't ride—more likely rides the truck with the gunrack that George Bowering imagines (mistakenly, I think) Dorn-the-adolescent riding. Not that westward moving dispossessor Dorn sees in the wagon trains of clouds: the "chunky westerner" who thinks "to remake this in his own image." Not the great cowboy he encounters in a bar and scores in contempt:

—the great cowboy
sat slightly dirty and above all

> arrogant, smoking, alone, as if
> he held uncommonly large places in his hand and
> didn't give a shit.

O.K. Not the cowboy of the six-gun mystique, or any mystique. "Out west / desperadoes are only desperate."

Like Olson, concerned with history and historiography. The poem on Meriwether Lewis' death while journeying at the hands of "money-eyed / Grinder." The poem on Ledyard and his exhaustion. Does he, a journeyer, share the sheer love of distance? Wants to know what happened to the common people ("this is all I care about /those commons . . . / [those] downtrodden"), the miners who once worked the coal mine at Madrid, the Indians, one a "Sacagawea wearing a baseball cap, eating a Clark bar."

No sustenance from the past, western or middle western, the later closed out in "Obituary." No sustenance in the present, in "forgotten towns" like that of "In the Morning," with its "rising holocaust of down people." Nothing heartening in the vista from his porch, the rising smoke of far-off Los Alamos signaling "its various technical plantations of death." Not just buying and selling lays waste our lives. Which is why, in the penultimate poem, he finds himself in America, weary and disconsolate,

> slowly walking around the deserted bandstand, waiting
> for the decade, and the facetious new arrivals.

28 May 1979

Had he ever been facetious? The sum of what he learns is in "Hemlocks" and "Oh Don't Ask Why," both among his best poems. "Hemlocks" is a reverie toward an earlier landscape in the Northwest that was, as its absence tells him, a landscape of being. A land of soft mist, where *mist* plays off *miss*, where *continuous* denotes its special value—and the way the lines of this careful impressionistic "painting" compose the atmosphere. And the way our nature is relative to Nature, to "His deep nature," in the rhythm (it is all a rhythm: Creeley) of life and death:

> mist of our green trees of Him
> who locks our nature in His deep nature
> how continuous do we die to come down
> as rain . . .

Locks tells of a determinism that denies the concern he has with changing society—that gainsays Olson's will to change. He says in "The Pronouncement," a poem composed of the immediate details of the inner and outer condition through which he moves in trying to state his case—it includes his reading of Patchen and Pound, Orwell and Gide—

> not a damn thing
> ever changes: the cogs that turn this machine are set
> a thousand miles on plumb, beneath the range of the
> Himalayas.

Hence the hopelessness and the sense, acquired from geology, that millenia bear testimony of the process of death, that the land below is a nether world.

In "Oh Don't Ask Why," a poem to his wife Helene, to whom he also dedicates the book, he admits:

> Yes, at moments I did waste
> our lives, giving way
> foolishly to public thoughts,
> large populations.

He acknowledges her love, the steadiness she brings to a marginal life whose destination remains uncertain:

> On this mountain
> or in this little spud town in the valley
> or along this highway, you held repeatedly

your eyes on getting us there,
where?

So in his present state of being—lonely, friendless, burdened by just such seeing as we find in these poems ("Carry geology in the eye // . . . to learn the nature of that terrain")—he asks her not to "ask why the welcome signs remain."

One sign promises another world, a sacralized earth, but the possibility is not assured by its recognition. The journey of "The Land Below," like the later journey of *The Shoshoneans*, brings him to an old Indian whose beautiful being overwhelms him.

> I marveled at the beauty
> of men who have long hair. Yes, it is quite
> different. Their world. I am sure they tread
> upon an Earth I don't. And I would like to.
> Not facilely, or for long, but to be with them
> for a spell . . .

Yes, to be with them, to know the enchantment of being. (Isn't this why the poem on Hawthorne follows, its concluding verse, "He was fierce / for the slight connection / back to what / there was"?) For such beauty, he believes, can never be returned to, "It never / exists again, once having been there." This is the tragedy of the West enacted by the cowboys and the Indians, as important as Hector's fall at Troy—"Hector died in battle with the natural ugliness of the world, symbolized as the state in the form of Achilles," he says in "What I See in *The Maximus Poems*." Hector and Geronimo!

A tragedy not to be redeemed by any archeologist, like Schliemann, much touted by Olson and ridiculed by Dorn, not even by Olson the archeologist of morning, whose hope of archeological recovery this somewhat Olsonian poem resists. Isn't this why Dorn, for all the Indian means to him, does not figure in *Alcheringa*? Isn't this why the second part of "Inauguration Poem #2" (in *Geography*) adopts a verse form used by Olson in *Mayan Letters*, only to dismiss the possibility of recovering what was missed? "Americans, you were that stupid from the beginning . . . // And &c is the most important gods you missed. For they / were the Manitous, they dwell in you at different times. / If they choose."

"The Land Below" is the summary poem of the volume and the link with "From Gloucester Out" (1964) and "Idaho Out" (1965). A desultory long poem of diverse materials and many voices—the voice, in fact, of primary importance, as always in his poems, modulating/contrasting with the meditative movement, the journey through inner and outer space, of mind-and-world. Such a poem permits the direct expression of many attitudes and feelings, the probing of one's condition, and the outspokenness of an intelligent and learned poet. It also accumulates, is a moving context, each element of which gathers a various significance. Several teachers appear but chiefly in respct to what he finds himself learning: Olson, Sauer, Thoreau, Williams. He has "The Kingfishers" and "To Gerhardt" in mind, but probably owes more to "The Desert Music," especially the portion of the poem dealing with the journey to Taos. He takes the American stand versus Europe that Olson does, but also declares his difference from him. Thoreau speaks his desire for clarity, and perhaps more than Dorn admits is here because he addresses the poet's problem: hypochondria. From Sauer, the love of landforms (the poem begins with an evening landscape, with "the tiers [pun] of my country"), respect for "the different tastes of bread," the "mystique of the real," an *areal* mystique that abrogates tradition, and, certainly, a profound appreciation of the Indian who answers so well to these things. This poem centers on paleface and redskin celebrating the Fourth of July, and its focal issue is fundamental: selling or revering the earth. The land below, among other things, is the land beneath the concrete. It is a gauge of life. The land of the Indian, as Crane told us in the allusion to Iron Mountain. Ed Folsom's original geographical palimpsest, the continent on which and over which and *with which* we have written our history.

29 May 1979

In and *out*. Dorn's cardinal directions. *The inside real and the outsidereal,* as he puts it in *Gunslinger*. Outside real: out *and* sidereal. Out = cosmos. To journey out, as in "From Gloucester Out" and "Idaho Out," is to move into cosmic space, in the hope of experiencing cosmicity. To be far out. The goal of journeying. Religious, in the way the corn dance was. These journeys are pilgrimages ("and / to Taos we finally came"), the Chaucerian echo here perhaps what Duncan remembered when he remarked on the wonder of *Gunslinger* being our *Canterbury Tales,* though the awareness of similar cultural sweep is just.

Inside real, outside real. And areal? Is the mystique of the real only epistemological, as in the epigraph to *Some Business Recently Transacted in the White World*:

> In speaking of what
> is Outward and what
> is Inward one refers
> not to Place, but
> to what is Known and what
> is Not known

Isn't the areal necessary to the concurrence of the inside real and outside real? Doesn't this concurrence create place? Olson's cosmos-polis; unity of self-and-world? It would seem so in Dorn's celebration of Olson in "From Gloucester Out," where he mentions Olson's play with "areal particulars."

Even perhaps in "Chronicle," where the relationship is problematical, the outer and inner spaces juxtaposed in terms of cold and warm, death and life, yet the value of the later dependent on the former: the sidereal chilling immensity of the January night sky over Pocatello ("The air, a presence / around the body") and the intimate warmth of the room where "Fred plays his cello" and the air "sings," and Dorn realizes that this human nucleus ensures survival and so

> Here, all around, is
> the world, out

Poetry/song: the music of survival.

Inner does not equate with above as in Emerson. No vertical correspondence. Inner relates to outer, horizontally, mind to thing. This defines intellect, which he says in speaking of Trocchi, is relative "to a mastering of material, i.e. what is external to man." And he is an intellectual for the reason he says Trocchi is: "He is able to place the proper weights on the scale of what we know more absolutely than one who arrives at inevitable terms casually." A careful, capable, cognizant man, not a "genius." Clarity, a classical virtue.

There is every reason for the separate publication of "From Gloucester Out." It is one of Dorn's most sustained poems of this meditative kind; only "The Sense Comes Over Me, and the Waning Light of Man by the 1st National Bank" comes to mind as equal to it. Certainly, one of the finest tributes that anyone has rendered Olson.

The title. Taken from the last line, and tells what it means to have Olson's stance, to have made for oneself a place that is a center of the cosmos. It names a place and the essential direction. *Maximus* is dedicated to Creeley as Outward, and

Olson, in early installments, learns not only to dance sitting still but to sit looking out. Of course the title evokes Olson, who is the towering (albeit often recumbent) presence in this poem of memory—of yearning and love, guilt and loneliness—the overwhelming quality, so much in evidence in the mounting intensity, already stressed in the *all* of the opening line:

> It has all
> come back today.
> That memory for me is nothing [like nothing]
> there ever was,
> That man . . .

In the subsequent portraiture size is of less importance than boldness ("on his ground"). And the loneliness. Corroborated by Fielding Dawson in *The Black Mountain Book*. A working identification for Dorn here.

30 May 1979

Memory invests a journey in the past with present urgencies. Is he for some reason, otherwise unstated, amending the earlier somewhat less-than-wholly approbative views of "What I See in *The Maximus Poems*" and "A Narrative with Scattered Nouns," the latter a story of Olson's *haunts* (home ground)—New England, Plum Island—that may be parodic of his poem on the "Lordly Satyrs"? It is certainly parodic of Olson's mythifying. Was it written before "From Gloucester Out," which tells of a visit to New England, and withheld from publication until after Olson's death? Isn't it significant that Dorn dedicates his next book, *Geography*, to Olson—though considering the political aspects of that book he may be pointing up a difference?

A journey *with* Olson, from Gloucester to New York City to the Jersey shore. Gloucester at the time of the Fiesta of St. Peter, where the band music and Italian women ("the sousa filled night") recover both the fullness of being he wants and the anxiety of its betrayal by his own imperfection. Not only by his "hesitating," by a withholding that is as oppressive to him as Duncan's in the confession of *The Truth & Life of Myth*, but by an awareness of what, perhaps in explanation, the parentheses enclose:

> (that all things shit poverty,
> and Life, one wars on with
> many embraces) . . .

Remember, in "What I See in *The Maximus Poems*": "I don't trust the universe. I would kick it in the teeth if it came near me. Because I have thus far seen the universe to be in the hands of such men." So the perfection, the "pure existence, even in the crowds / I love," is marred—

> will never be possible for me
>
> even with the men I love
>   This is
>
> the guilt
> that kills me
>   My adulterated presence
>
> but please believe with all men
> I love to be

Adulterated: growing up in, to the meanness of America, his fall from innocence noted in the allusion to Whitman's fraternal embrace.

Then, from LeRoi Jones's apartment in Cooper Square, the journey continues out into American space, into the "maze of the outlands west," where they are lost (as Kerouac was when he first hitched west in *The Town and the City*); where Dorn, like so many writers before him, and Edward Hopper, too, as he remembers in "Idaho Out," sees the poignant figures of our loneliness:

> past girls on corners
> past drugstores, tired hesitant
> creatures who I also love
> in all their alienation were it not so

Past, both verb and adjective. *Were it not so*: a Ginsberg catch, to remind us of this Paterson poet and his American journeys in the howling wilderness?

Finally, a cottage by the sea, where the sea still "whispers," as it had for Whitman, of love and death. Where Dorn would restore Olson to his proper field—"I want him to walk by the seashore alone"—where . . . . But you must either cite or read the rest of the poem! So brilliantly Olsonian in its prosody! So incredibly intensely evocative, the sudden present tense presenting Olson in all his active powers of sight and hearing, of attention and care. Senses—not impoverished like 'I' in *Gunslinger*—that connect with "the oldest brain" (the archetypal mind?); that ignore nothing, neither "delicate thrush" nor the "gesture of grey / bygone people" (the passage alludes to *Maximus*, I, 108). And a mind that "places them . . . // gives them their place / in their new explanation." So that, of utmost importance, nothing goes "unplaced / and unattended" and "there is never / a lost time." No empty bandstand, no lost America of love.

Though Olson himself remains lonely, the expletive "My God" expressing the severity of his situation but also declaring his godlike stature, the later explained by the cosmic scope of his concerns and by his egoless devotion to a sacred universe—

> he who worships the gods with his strictness
> can be of their company

This is Olson's true size, his ultimate achievement, the reason, in a subsequent letter-poem to LeRoi Jones, the gods are said to go with him when he leaves. This is the Olson of Dorn's memory, fashioned by memory:

> he, does, he
> walks
> by the sea
> in my memory
>
> and sees all things and to him
> are presented at night
> the whispers of the most flung shores
> from Gloucester out

31 May 1979

Olson and Whitman. Dorn recognizes, as Olson did, Whitman's ego. "His value is the study of the expansion of the ego," he says in the essay on *The Maximus Poems.* And in the poem he is contrasting poets who address men's "oceanic sense of their predicament"—a phrase in the essay calling up Whitman's "measureless oceans of space" in "A Noiseless Patient Spider," a poem referred to, explicitly by *flung,* in the concluding verse of "From Gloucester Out." There are other Whitman poems in evidence here—"Out of the Cradle Endlessly Rocking," with its weight of loneliness and unassuaged love, and "On the Beach at Night Alone," with its assuagement, the cosmic trust of the recognition that a vast similitude "interlocks" all things, "compactly hold[s] and enclose[s] them." So that Olson's situation in the concluding verse, even with all the distress of "whispers," is not one of dire uncertainty and isolation in "the vacant vast surrounding" such as Whitman tells in "A Noiseless Patient Spider." In that poem, the ego is separate and must do the immense work of connection, which is why it is overborne. But in "From Gloucester Out"—for the very reason that Dorn praises Olson's work in *Maximus* as a "journeying out to prepare the day for a new look at man"—the ego is no longer dominant and hence is at home in a universe whose very vastness is given, "presented," as a gift.

Still, the evocation of Whitman is not meant to disparage him but to provide a true measure of Olson. In the essay on Burroughs and Trocchi, Dorn affirms, as necessary and correct now, Whitman's declaration that "the crowning growth of the United States is to be spiritual and heroic." Olson/Maximus answers to that. He is a god in the sense of Dorn's remark in "Idaho Out"—"my gods have been men . . . / and women." One of those people who are poets because "they *are* there with all of themselves," which is what gives them force (god power), gives the poem force. "That you may believe," he says of Olson—yes,

> that you may believe
>
> is the breath he gives
> the great already occurred and nightly beginning world.

And why Olson stands in Dorn's work with Indians, the old Indian of "The Land Below" and the still older Willie Dorsey of *The Shoshoneans*. "I thought a couple of times with the Indians that I was close to gods I could respect," he says in *The Poet, the People, the Spirit*, the Berkeley lecture of his journey out to the Shoshoneans.

1 June 1979

None of Dorn's gods has been other than common, men and women, most of them unknown, raised to divinity only by his recognition. Haniel Long, for example, to whom he pays generous tribute in "What I See in *The Maximus Poems*." The author of a still provocative book on Whitman and a wonderful book on Cabeza da Vaca, who, apart from the issue of place, thereby stands with Olson. And an old-fashioned democrat full of the idealism of the fraternal heart whose *Piñon Country* shows him to have been a pioneer social explorer and critic of the West, "a radical mind with no home," Dorn says, establishing identification. But isn't *Piñon Country* also a model for *The Shoshoneans*? And isn't identification secured by Long's essential insight into the tragedy of the region he tried to make place: "Is it ever a question of race? Is it not rather of power, and of poverty?"

"*My gods have been men . . . / and women.*" The ellipsis effects a heavy stress, not an afterthought. We know that already, but "Idaho Out," its title begging comparison with "From Gloucester Out," makes it very clear. The only things that mark an otherwise tedious trip—tedious in fact, not as speculative journey—are two women met on the way, and landforms—and these are related. *Out* here speaks for liberation, and the release probably accounts for the digressiveness, though digressiveness is characteristic of a mode analogous with Thoreau's excursions, Williams' *Paterson*, Olson's *Maximus*, Snyder's *Mountains and Rivers*, Kerouac's chronicles, etc. A relaxed mode, to borrow Altieri's term; narrative, not dramatic. *Out* and *back*: the poem is unusual in this respect, fulfilling what might be called the essential paradigm of books on the redemptive power of nature, withdrawal from and return to civilization, where civilization is desecration. Its signs here the "excremental" smoke of the fertilizer plant, the atomic city of Arco north of Pocatello, and, inclusively, the Mormon imposition of design and order to be seen and felt everywhere, in the transformation, for example, of landforms "into square documents / of . . . timid endeavor." Which is why Idaho, as he says at the end, is

> . . . truly the West
> as no other place
> ruined by an ambition and religion
> cut by a cowboy use of her nearly virgin self
>
> unannealed
> by a real placement—

by *areal place*ment and all that *areal / Ariel* suggests. And why no gods appear, only human failures, like Pound ("Mr. Pound") and Hemingway.

Dorn's response to the North Fork beauty and the "pomegranate" at Florence is frankly erotic, to be measured by the memory of the deprivation of his youth and appreciated for its disinterestedness. He sees these women as parts of the morphology of the landscape, and he sees landform as woman—

> and [you] love
> its parts as you do the parts of a woman
> whose own relations with earth are more established
> than your own.

This is why, in the most eloquent passage, he says he is not ashamed of his country as "areal reality" but rather for the loveless place it has become because neither its geographical particularity nor sacredness has been respected. When he says that his countrymen do not pursue greatness, he asks us to remember "From Gloucester Out." When he says,

> An occasional woman, won't
> though I wish she could,
> justify a continent

we may remember, only to recognize its denial, Crane's belief that the continent, the areal reality, would remain virgin to the last of men.

2 June 1979

"Idaho Out," though published separately, is a central poem in *Geography* (1965), "the strong book of that period, that early sort of adamant practice," as Dorn rightly says. In size and scope, in all it gathers and manages to speak, in its use of the poem as an instrument of intellection, *Geography* surpasses the early books. It is the one to choose as "representative" of the sixties.

Three conspicuous references: Olson, Sauer, LeRoi Jones. Olson and Sauer conjoined in what Dorn calls "earth writing." LeRoi Jones—"Idaho Out" is dedicated to Jones and his wife—joined in political writing. By this time, Jones was one of the most political of poets, having, since *Preface to a Twenty Volume Suicide Note,* moved beyond the politics or antipolitics of the several literary groups with which he had been associated. Recollecting this in a recent interview, he never mentions Dorn in his disapproval of "Creeley-Olson types."

Lessons of geography are lessons of politics. Of geopolitics, in *The North Atlantic Turbine.* But both are lessons of love.

The first lesson of geography—and *Geography*—is to choose an actual earth of value, to love the earth sensuously and take her in marriage. Dorn opens the book with the largest geographical and oldest mythical perspectives. Locates us in terms of a new perspective, which, alas, may only be the newest in the history of spoliation. "Song: The Astronauts." O Brebner! To tell of the orbited moon shot in mythic terms is to evoke sacrality where rape is the object, to evoke eros when death in fact will ensue. "The immensely soft glow of it"—the lovely lyricism tells his love—

> will always be behind you
> as you stand on its face
> staring
> at the strangely
> inhabited world
> from whence you came
> from where all men with their eyes
> have been satisfied
>
> before thee

And the correlative politico-cultural lesson? That in "this Theocracy/headed by a texan" the arts of the media are designed "to keep / our senses apart," to wreck the mechanism

> whereby we track
> with the capturing powers of our own love

the expanding universe, as it goes
in our brief time beyond us. . . .

(From "A Letter . . ." to Jones, recalling the Olson who resists cosmic displacement, who speaks in "Human Universe" of the environing "earth and stars.")

The lesson writ large in "The Problem of the Poem for My Daughter, Left Unsolved," to be compared with Creeley's poem to his daughter and Ginsberg's supermarket poem. A devastating poem of profound vastation, as if all the pain of a lifetime moved this hopeless man, punning on musical scores, to say,

I do so know
all the scores by heart, by a memory
saturated with defeat . . .

Moved to this by the "shocked woman" he sees in the supermarket, a lower-class woman beat down by "a brutal economic calculus," exploited like the land (he speaks of the "exhausted mesabas of . . . breasts"), denied the very culture enjoyed at her expense, and so much afflicted by the "huge meanness / 'the measureless crudity of the States'" that she is deprived of citizenship ("all men and women / who suffer deeply . . . / cannot be U.S. Citizens"). Moved, to outrage and scorn by "a world where no thing thrives short of the total pestilence / of its spirit," by the "technologically provisioned" culture-less pop culture, the "totally onanized culture."

The poet of "The World Box-Score Cup of 1966," of *Bean News* and *Hello, La Jolla* has already found the target.

He belongs with those, from Adams and Veblen on, whose critique of American culture is instinctual-erotic, represented by the plight of women ("the women are / set loose to walk spiritless").

3 June 1979

All of the poems following "The Astronauts" and ending with "Idaho Out" are long excursive vivisections of the culture, "Inauguration Poem #2" (where is #1?) by far the most excoriating. Derisive, mocking indictments because, in his disgust, he cannot summon love, as he did in the narrower personal scope of "The Hide of My Mother," to conceal the fist in his heart.

The modulations and juxtapositions within these poems also occur in the structure of the book. Following "Idaho Out," there is the transitional poem to his wife, "Six Views from the Same Window of the Northside Grocery," a consummate poem of their "twin exile." This, and the subsequent transitional poem about the absence of his wife, "Poem in Five Parts," enclose a group of songs, some sixteen poems, which are a distinctive feature of the book. He says they are narrative fragments fed into the narrative of his life. They *are* songs, often celebrating women; relief from the long poems, redemptive to that extent, even though he seems to be undergoing an emotional crisis, to be losing his wife. Private woes become public issues, just as public ills become private woes. Yet these poems, and a few more songs later on, are often exquisite, equal to the high accomplishment of poets they sometimes call to mind (Williams, in "Daffodil Song" and "Christ of the Sparrows"; Creeley, in "My Wife Is Lovely," "The Exploration," "A Wild Blue, Yonder"). Then, in "Song: Heat," love and politics join: the work of politics is to restore love. In the poems that follow this becomes revolutionary work. "We Shall Refrain from Them," "The Smug Never Silent Guns of the Enemy," "Fort Hall Obituary," "Mourning Letter," "Eugene Delacroix Says," "Song: Venceremos"—these are not so much jeremiads like the earlier long poems as poems of revolutionary ardor, political poems naming the enemy, defining his puny patriotism, attending his victims, extending sympathy to South American compatriots (the guerrilla poems prefigured), who are told, in Olsonian fashion, to do what Dorn would have all of us do

> halt
> before the incursions of general infection
> from a stronger world
> dance,
> and in your side stepping
> the spirit
> will tell where.

All of which culminates in "The Sense Comes Over Me, and the Waning Light of Man by the 1st National Bank," a fierce poem made so by the accumulated awareness of past and present losses. Finally, closing the book, a coda of four poems, reminding us of the value and loss of our primitive (primary), mythic, erotic heritage; of the marriage we have forsaken.

4 June 1979

You measure a poem like "The Sense Comes Over Me" by the more than usual candor and depth of recollection of the past—the measure, likewise, of "The Early Days" in *By the Sound*, where he recovers much—"the poverty, the smells, the shame, what I remember of girls I wanted, too late"—that burdens the poem. These are essential accounts—accountings—of the "absolute meanness," the "utter defeat and utter hopelessness," he had known, still knows.

"We needed love. We couldn't have it." ("Driving Across the Prairie," 1969)

The point is not the originality of his views but the intensity of feeling, the powerful presence of past experience.

Poverty in Illinois in the 1930s:

> this is no judgment, this is
> the weight of dissimilar things bound together

by a strictly regulated common deprivation
the low and the high, no middle, held in a smiling
equilibrium
you may eat only the shit I give you . . .

Incomprehensible poverty, pig-shit its smell, and "a woe of that lowly order" that became "my sign and weight in that land." The self-pity, too, "of my wounded middle years" with their "ceaseless speculation over / the ways of love." The focal episode of climbing the water tower to show off for a girl and finding there in the "pictographic scratches" the history of the thirties and the reminder of the suffering of his mother and stepfather. His "unruined and damned hieroglyphs," he says,

Because they form
the message of men stooping down
in my native land, and father an entire conglomerate
of need and wasted vision. All the children
were taught the pledge of Allegiance, and the land was
pledged
to private use, the walnut dropped in the autumn on
the ground
green, and lay black in the dead grass in the spring.

The walnut tree is the most resonant image of the poem, evoking an unattended natural fruition and bounty, growth and instinctual fulfillment gone to waste, "the principle / residue of my past, and the past / of my gutless generation." It appears in an earlier song of labor unrest in Pocatello, as a solace:

Furnish my soul with the hope
Far away and by a river
In the darkness of a walnut stand.

Darkness here may carry over to the "darker borders" associated with the "ways of love," and the stanza may evoke home (more visionary than actual, but we always place home in the past) because the present in Pocatello is "no home, no back."

Gutless generation. The judgment is harsh, and unrelieved. A present confrontation in the White House by a younger generation may spoon some of the pus out of his brain, may fire his teaching of home truths in the classroom, may inspire the eloquent declaration that the West is not "a Shulamite maiden" (who would marry Simplot?) and the warning of coming strife. But none of this alters the fact into which the poem subsides—that his generation has been preceded and "there is / nothing so lame and halt as lateness."

Yet books are acts, and his is timely. Is there comfort in this? Or is the lateness, as he said earlier, historical, informed now by the fact that what transformed our Garden of Eden into History has brought with it the flowering of the police? That it is too late to do anything, that history has caught up with us and we have been caught by history—that the geography of our lunacy, comprised like his of beneficent American "myth," does not conform to, is irreconcilable with the actual political geography? And is it, as in "Ritual Party in an Alley," that, as he also found in writing *By the Sound*, we have defeating rites of passage? Is it, finally, in a poem responding to the cost of the civil rights movement ("For the New Union Dead in Alabama"), that he has found nothing to nurture the spirit in the "grim / territories of the west," only a *reality sandwich*? That he has been gelded by "our gelding cutlure"? And that having lost the Rose of Sharon in "the tortured night / of this banished place," he can, in the extremity of erotic anguish, only deny us what we have denied? Can utter only this Blakean-inspired prayer?

oh rose
   of priceless beauty
refrain from our shores
suffocate the thin isthmus
   of our mean land.

cast us back
into isolation

Doesn't Ralph Ellison ask, as John Callahan reminds me, the question that shows how different our politics is from that in any other country? "And could politics ever be an expression of love?"

5 June 1979

Down and out in the Northwest. By the (Puget) Sound, just above Seattle, on the Skagit River. A temporary location, mostly marked by weather, the cold mist and grey gloom of hopelessness. And by second growth. So: "the thick clogged second growth around the feet of the greater trees caught the whole element and made of it a black mesh, forever dripping." Weather is primary, not to be trusted. Nor the abused, lumbered-off land, and many of its occupants. ("Natural resources," he says in *The North Atlantic Turbine*, "generate the unnatural.") *First Facts*, Olson would say. Like the meanness Carl Wyman knew as a child on the farm. There's a mean thing here, Tom Joad says of our promised land. "I grew up with death," Dorn says when claiming his nativity. Part of the naturalism of a book of naturalistic lineage? "Populist modernism" is LeRoi Jones's term. The writers he collects in *The Moderns* (1963) are interested in people who "exist outside the mainstream of the American social organism," and environment for them is not merely scenery but the totality of all that surrounds us.

23 June 1978

Wyman. Carl Wyman. A why-man, a searching questioner to whom things must answer ("You know, Billy, how I have to explain these things to myself"). College-educated. Bookman. Probably a poet—has a poet friend whose bluster and insensitivity measure his own unassuming quiet compassionate understanding. As much as Mary, his wife, a "Canadian," an "oddball." Yes, as McCarty thinks, "slumming." *Different*. For one thing, better off, free to come and free to go.

Dorn all right, one step removed. His voice, in the even low-keyed precise spare—yet sometimes poetic—prose. His tone, acumen, unsentimentality. Slowness, too. Nothing goes fast with Dorn, he's meditative, gives you the whole trip. His experience, raised to essential autobiography?

The Wymans came to the country. Now, a year and a half later, they are leaving. Why? The novel "explains" this. "The Wymans came to the valley because of what they thought was a pressing need to leave the city although as time passed they saw this pressure had been largely of their own." *They thought*; then, *they saw*. Time: 1957 or '58. Their coming to the country, the new life they try to undertake there—is this representative of a new impulse to flee the city for the land, flee civilization for nature, system (welfare system in Seattle, as Ramona experiences it; middle-class security and self-enclosing lack of contact) for freedom? Withdrawal, to a redemptive countryside? But hasn't Wyman been there before, on the farm in Illinois? Hasn't Billy, in Wisconsin and Alaska? Hasn't the West, this land of stump-farms and abandoned homesteads?

Locate anywhere then, for example, up here in the Minnesota "woods," and "America" surrounds the small center. Systemic poisoning. Take this Washington "frontier" town of four taverns, with its floating population of construction workers (dams), loggers (Weyerhaeuser), migrants (commercial farms, chicken factories), with its union hall and employment office and welfare agencies—this life is marginal but neither free nor sufficient, self-sufficient. No one, understandably, valuing his humanity would choose to be a "bread-man," would accept the "unthinkable contract" of the "good steady job" in which one barters self for money. ("Men's hours are their souls"—Duncan.) Yet city versus country doesn't spell choice, or only, as Wyman finds, since everything depends on jobs, the choice between the good steady job or dereliction and submergence, the later a desperate clinging to an "old possibility" (the American dream) as one sinks further into the *difference* that closes out all possibility. "For the man without means to seek a private space for himself would be a nightmare if encountered in a dream. Even the middle-class man who has at least some encouragement for his aims instinctively knows that the world has already gone a long way in contracting for the curtailment of any outward movement." Space (Olson spelled it SPACE because it was large) no longer promises freedom. The uninhabited land may be uninhabited but it is owned: look at any plat book.

The Rites of Passage: A Brief History. History in brief. Process, not geography (*By the Sound*). A *rite de passage* marks a crisis in the life cycle, a change in status, a growth in being, requiring a symbolic death and rebirth. Usually, most importantly, from adolescence to adulthood, as in *Winesburg, Ohio*. Brief histories, of the Wymans, the McCartys, the Henderssons. Passages of the most sobering kind, to diminished life, to compromised allegiance and disaffiliation. The myth enacted by the rite is the "old possibility," probably possible only briefly in American history. Of the many evidences of its passage, the crippled Wobbly walking down the street head-down into the rainy wind; the Henderssons, McCartys, and Wymans trying to live in "the cold heart of that raining country."

"Billy, Carl said, You can't really live this way now, you know."

26 June 1978

How many times do we have to hear this story? It is myth, truly, passed on, as myths are, orally. Or as Billy passes it on to his kids, by buying them a horse. Will they graduate to motorcycles and ride the Alcan highway, lured by the "old possibility"? I have known them here, life savings invested in a school bus and four trail-bikes. Will they also fulfill the boyhood dream by landing in jail, to bear thereafter the mark of *difference*? Why is it the dream lives longest with the sons of impoverished farmers, with marginal people, with the floating populations of western towns, the people Dorn is often drawn to (see his first story, "C. B. & Q."), the sons and grandsons of Poker Flat?

Is the dream the inevitable inheritance of Dorn's western materials or was it the force that turned him westward? Or was it that this dream, inevitably entailing disillusionment, was at the heart of the heart of the country, inseparable from the meanness, that ineradicable sense of things, the injustice learned in childhood, linking his destiny with the wanderers, the strangers, the outcasts, the different ones?

Yes, we are (still) two nations.

Dorn passes on the myth by telling of its passing. Will this be the last generation to heed it, to believe it, to invest it with its life, to suffer it? And if not, with what consequences? In Billy Hendersson he creates a folk hero who bears its burden—a more credible and more fully realized character than Kesey's McMurphy. (You can gauge Dorn's greater art and insight against *One Flew over the Cuckoo's Nest*, and learn something, too, about the fate of books.)

27 June 1978

Some people have blue flush toilets and others sit on privies under umbrellas. That's a *difference*. And difference is important. There's a chapter with that title, and a conspicuous use of the term. James McCarty uses it to put down Ramona, his Esquimau wife; it's the cover word for the promiscuity he imputes to her. Its chief use is socioeconomic, having to do with the difference, say, between a commercial farmer and a migrant, or a hardhat at the union hall and a derelict at the state employment agency. With the fact that impoverishment *makes a difference* (between what is trivial and important) and that people are irreparably marked by difference—Ramona who thinks of herself as different, Billy whose prison experience has made him different. Do the well-off feel different? Not Gloria, in all the confidence of money. Difference belongs to the marginal perspective of this book. Dorn knows it's difference where the meanings are; he has learned this hurt internally. He is not experimenting in misery. This is an inside narrative ("You're what's thought of as an intelligent man. You're not bad . . . you try to see the right side of things from the weak, helpless men's point of view"). Hence the understanding, the imaginative realization of the main characters, and the sharp rend(er)ing in the stereotypes of the victimizers—the Women for Good, the blue and brown "costumed" interviewers of the employment office, the engineers ("experts in khaki pants"), Farmer Smith, Dr. Quackman. Mary's belief that "the world's even more distasteful from the other side [urban middle class]" also informs the book. It situates the Wymans in the middle but not in the middle class. In an interview Dorn insists that it is not a middle-class novel. Elsewhere he says, "I was never middle-class nor were my parents, I mean our safety was never public. Our poverty was public."

28 June 1978

Ramona and Billy. The different ones and the great ones, worthy to stand with the precedent folk characters of our literature. Folk characters? Larger than the others, more resonant, exemplars—in this instance, of ways Carl doesn't take, or is it of a resignation he doesn't have, a willingness to follow out a destiny to its end? James doesn't belong with them because he too readily submits and accepts bondage; of middle-class background, dereliction is his way, his life trajectory is downward. (Neither Carl nor Dorn especially likes him.)

Ramona. (Not Helen Hunt Jackson's). You've probably seen her on the streets of Cass Lake. The drunk foul-mouthed Indian woman, too drunk to get into the "Indian" car ("the old car with no fenders and one headlight"). A "primitive." Change "Esquimaux" to "Indians," you've heard this: "We have a lot of trouble with the Esquimaux. They're pretty shiftless. Can't keepem from killing the reindeers, they won't send their kids to school. Seems like they don't wanta learn. They still trade their wives, can't teachem nothing about how to live." (Said to Ramona by a lecherous white man.) You never saw her at home in her shack so you never noticed she (transpose Ramona) is beautiful. "Yes, the radiance of her smile. And how she really did love to laugh. Stars in their systems were hardly more in accord than those two pastimes of hers."

Schoolteacher down from Alaska, tubercular, hospitalized, deprived of her children by welfare workers. Knows that difference, too. Ends up in a pea-shack, as Dorn says the Esquimaux and Indians had, "by a slow, irreversible reduction of the logging industry, until there was nothing more for them to do but commit themselves."

What's remarkable? "Have you ever thought that those people have constructed a very damned unalterable determination to live. Good God, they cling to life as though it were precious when all their experiences, not violent, or *interesting* at all, but dull, and uniform, and subtle, tells them it's cheap." And then, of the Indians who always bring their grandmothers with them to the migrant camp: the old grandmother "will probably smoke a cigarette when she can get it and sit without saying a word during the long winter, old, crippled sometimes, wrinkled always, silent much of the time because the old sage form she is a part of has run out." To which is juxtaposed: "And that true smiles and happiness can go on will one day be the defeat of the system from top to bottom."

But will this human warmth displace the cold air? Is poverty as warm as he finds it here, and will it "rise"? Be exact: he says, "tends to rise." It's a very cold rainy country, to leave behind, if one can. Isn't the culture of poverty Oscar Lewis extolled also a poverty of culture? Yet, don't discount the humanity Dorn insists on, how the Old Man (white) stayed with the Indians for the reason Dorn, with his inimitable deadliness, supplies: "They have no religion of elaborate delegation to dispose of such things as homeless white men. A general irony it is up to the ethnologists to probe."

29 June 1978

Billy. Depicted by speech, brilliantly, like Ramona, and Albert Wonder, the evangelical chicken farmer, and most of the others. Note the "sophistication" of the transients' talk on pages 81–83; had to include it. Folk tradition = oral tradition. Depicted by two actions. First, his emergence as a hero in the unemployment agency (rightly called), where his towering rage, all in CAPS, provides the only decent human measure and response to the cold weather of Dorn's acute phenomenology of unemployment. Then, later, his large presence still in mind, reduced to life-size, at the union hall, when we find him out of work and dunned by a creditor, and begin to learn the story of his life and why, when no one else does, he speaks in outrage.

It's Billy's story from this point until the end, a story of victimage, relieved sometimes by picaresque comedy, always by lack of self-pity. His story counterpoints the representative action. He tells it in the course of a deer hunt, and ironically playing off *Huckleberry Finn* and *The Bear*, it turns the America Dream inside-out. No great hunter, Billy hunts in desperation. To get meat for the kids, whose reddening gums distress him. What he finally gets by shining is a lost steer, which he rips off. The rip-off, the emblematic defiant act of a dispossessed "hero." Won't we always remember Billy, as we see him at the end, limping out of the supermarket with a case of instant coffee under his arm? But who needs a case of instant coffee? "I intend to go on collecting these wages for the rest of my life."

Billy! Who lit out for the territory, having had, in Wisconsin, too much civilizing from a sexually eager Aunt Polly! "She used to try to get me to read certain books. Now I understand they were pretty good, but I couldn't see it then. They were, well, you know, they were all the English Works, I remember one, it was called *The Return of the Native*. Before I read it I thought it was about Africa, you know, the return of the native. But it wasn't. It was about England. It was good too." Took daring to write that. Billy! who says he "thought Alaska was a new world, but it was just Wisconsin again"—delivering prescriptions in Sitka, learning it was a "land of business men" and money made *the* difference. Who fulfilled his boyhood dream in prison—no con, just conned—and learned what it meant *to be different*.

So in "The Tunnel," it's got to be Billy who is trapped in the escape hole and suffers our explosive technology. (His injury comparable to McMurphy's lobotomy?) Return of the native, return of the repressed, return of the depressed? And it's Billy who goes on returning to rip it off. Not Carl, who turns away from the chicken factory, the loveless America of the loving gospel preacher, sickened by learning that chickens, so used, develop the neuroses that develop in "a housing project or in suburbia."

"People of Earth," in *Hello, La Jolla* (1978):

> You should check your calculations.
> From a distance, it looks like
> a chicken farm.

Billy says to Carl: "It's the same difference . . . we see the same things."

30 June 1978

> In this space [pea-shack] large families live. Of course. People who do that sort of work, and who are expected to live sequestered from normal society, have large families.

> . . . the people of our narrative were forced into a kind of spiteful enjoyment of the spare time that came upon them.

> *Spite is the vitality of the powerless; it is a way of not being resigned, of keeping a lost fight alive by preventing the dominator from enjoying his domination.*
> —Paul Goodman, *Nature Heals*, p. 125

> Occasionally there is a bright kid walks in to take a 'quick' check on the job situation and when he finds out there is nothing, walks briskly out as if he would not deign to waste his time there, and as he goes he casts a quick disparaging look at the older men sitting

in the rows of seats, waiting. Though none of them say it or even think it, they all know this child will learn either by becoming a breadman, or after a few more visits, he will take a seat too.

When the rain failed in that land of perpetual rain, Smith drilled an easy well for aerial irrigation, and if that well failed he charged it to the government, his enjoyment of such leniency the government makes to large farmers in distress was complete. And in the worst of seasons this same man who enjoys that government which makes for him a private little welfare state because of his problems, sees fit to be benevolent to a group of tortured and beaten men who have nowhere else to go.

Oh lands of abundance. They are more cruel than those lands in which there is a scarcity.

Still, how will it be explained that in the union hall there were no really tattered men and in the unemployment office there were as a rule *only* tattered men. And thin men. Ghostly men. Men, some of whom, were ashamed to be on the street. But who were only arbitrarily made ashamed, be assured, for any man within certain limits may be substituted for any other.

Instead of endlessly disposing of people as materials, it might do well to show them, for instance, the workings of a hydroelectric power system. This would not be too difficult since the system is near at hand and the largest class of ignorant workers have time to waste. Obviously, apart from the very interesting business of how water produces power, it would relieve those workers of the necessity to perform the rite of acknowledged cheating, for which they are in every respect expected to hold the bag. It would relieve the pressure, relieve and correct their sense of false presence, which relief is needed, false pretense being one of the most prevalent of modern diseases. In effect, this

> planned policy to sequester men from the work they are on the other hand forced to do, is one of the primary aims of the modern state: it is a planned murder beside which war is of little consequence. But in a world in which populations grow much faster than real work, such disclosures become pointless.

The local is the universal. The Third World. This is not a story of Oakies. Rather, a later chapter of a chronic condition, of the way men and women fall out, float, become sequestered, become thin and ghostly, dispossessed as were the Indians before them, those ghosts, Lawrence said, who would come to haunt us.

A Bibliography on American for Ed Dorn. First assumption, "that *politics & economics* (that is, agriculture, fisheries, capital and labor) are like love (can only be individual experience)." Postscript, "the real *power* contemporary to one is *kept hidden*."

1 July 1978

Ghost of the father, beaten into thinness, finding it hard to do his job. A book about getting and losing jobs, and none agreeable because jobs are excremental and money is shit. Dorn's vision, so sharply economic and political, is excremental.

He says in *Love Songs* (1969):

> And I've known this for a long
> time, there has been no
> great necessity to say it. How
> really, the world is shit
> and I mean all of it

So that even in the poem to the American Goddess Cocaine in *Gunslinger* we hear an echo of Swift's "Goddess Cloacine." And Dorn's devil, Robart, is acquisitiveness personified, his minions, the nasty Atlantes, who only say shit (out of Luther, out of Brown's *Love Against Death*). And in *Apachería*, there are the relentless soldiers running down the Apaches, running into our time, their blue coats turning "like everything else in the present century / to something khaki looking vaguely like shit." The Gross National Product?

The origin of this vision is the meanness that has become the meaning of America. Learned on a tenant farm ("that damn meanness he connected with everything in his life. His father forever so tired and skinny looking . . ."). His father is the first, the primary image of dispossessed man. About whom, in recollection, fury gathers: "An absolute meanness of interest they were unaware of. Utter defeat and utter hopelessness. The feeling of being isolated like a small band of slaves inside a completely legal transaction. . . . The meanness they lived in ruled them." And with it the shame fixed by identification with his father caught, unaware, defecating, the father already diminished by his mother's digs at him, his very helplessness the cause of the boy's hatred. Now, in the therapeutic movement of recollection, all this acknowledged as the reason for his revulsion at killing animals. "Was his father then the rabbit you could knock in the head and walk away?" He would not do "their goddamn hackwork."

The crux of the discussion of killing in "The Deer." Reason enough for Carl's overriding sympathy with Billy. And isn't Billy's injury excremental, itself the worst of bad jobs?

Reason for the attention he gives the Old Man, otherwise nameless, a stand-in for the "few unattached white men who inhabited the camp . . . like ghosts. Their presence there could hardly be explained—they seemed derelicts of the spirit who had wandered off course and found it impossible to get back." This grandfather points the spiritual way to disaffiliation. He is no longer transacting business in the white world, has returned to the native. He is one of those people who have "compromised their allegiance to the thing that might destroy us all." He belongs, as Dorn says he does in the lecture on the Shoshoneans, with the Indians because, like them, he has no country; and he belongs with the old Indians, with Willie Dorsey of *The Shoshoneans*, the beautiful ancestor, "the spirit that lies at the bottom."

"Billy, Carl said, You can't really live this way now, you know."

"If anyone needs reminding, possible means 'able to be.'"

2 July 1978

Not just the marginal vantage but often the intellectual style is Veblenesque. As early as "1st Avenue," where the social situation is Bill Elephant's (his accident is as bad as Billy's) but the head we're in is Dorn's—"What is the dark? America, it is all that is hidden under your hat." And 1st Avenue is America, the first survey of: "A dead atmosphere. Ahead, and in back, there were no butterflies all at once swimming into view, large and black-oranged fringed, like a weightless tiger, the great lightness, the delicacy, the great possibility lighting here and there."

Back home in Illinois (in "Driving Across the Prairie," 1969), nothing redemptive, no love. His sister embarrassed by his long hair and the red handkerchief on his wrist. A dangerous way, he admits, to save himself from all this town still represents. From people who've added nothing to the cosmology the Indian left and remain unaware of it, when he wants "to be able to look back into the faces of the old gods." And wants (as *Apachería* will bear out) to stop the *mind* that makes the "crippled stem of this country."

"The Stripping of the River," the last poem in *Collected Poems*, is about that crippled stem, the great continental river-tree of our life, tributary now to both coasts, at the expense of "our green heart" and "our true richness."

5 July 1978

Reading *The Shoshoneans* again yesterday. Here, an Indian land, twice-removed, but still within the open reservation of the Leech Lake tribe. A book about "America." If you want to find out about America, consult the minorities, read their books—read this book, where, at the end the Indian finally is permitted to speak for himself. This significant gesture accompanies the message, is the message: Indians, the Ponca in this instance, want to speak for themselves and want to be heard, as Clyde Warrior, the telling part of his speech canceled, wished to be seriously heard by those concerned (officially) with the "War on Poverty." (Didn't General Sherman bluntly put the policy: extermination or pauperization?) By speaking out they want to begin the essential transformation of powerlessness into power. Not POWER to dominate others but to determine their lives. Local responsibility and decision, *polis* really, genuine community. Nothing necessarily "Indian" about that. Powerlessness is a sign of the times, of the "sociolatry," the religion of society in corporate industrial states, as Paul Goodman says. As much as growing up absurd and the missing community.

Warrior says that Indians, like all of us, want to "maintain the world they live in" and to be "included in on the act of America." He says the indignity of Indian life is one with the indignity of being poor in America, like the meanness witnessed in *By the Sound*: It is "the powerlessness of those who are 'out of it,' but who yet are coerced and manipulated by the very system which excludes them."

Isn't there a contradiction between maintaining one's world and being included in the act of America? Perhaps decentralization and grass-roots democracy resolve it? But hitherto, the act of America has denied both, has worked the terrible homogenization that LeRoi Jones is cited as saying requires that people get rid of what is most essentially themselves and accept in turn "the cheap and dishonest mentalism of the 'American Dream.'" Acculturation = Americanization. Randolph Bourne said the process left behind the detritus of cultures.

Does the glacial imagery apply? A large and relentless process. But isn't it quick? Gertrude Stein says that it takes three generations to make an American. Willie Dorsey's "white Indian" great grandson is a case in point. But does it take that long to unmake an American, to disorient and demoralize? Acculturation and deculturation are not of equal weight in our usage: we seldom mention that the latter is the price of the former. Not Dorn, who takes the perspective of deculturation: "I am no more acculturated than he is [a Paiute boy, a "professional," met in Maggie's Bar in Reno], although we are of course quite differently deculturized." Isn't the resistance to deculturation an element of Willie Dorsey's remarkable presence?

A young man here, working out his own entrance to society, will not accept the message of this book. Is he more realist than I? Is he like the Indian grandfather who knows the reality and instructs the little boy in the ways of survival? He says there can be no separatism, that the system is too powerful to admit of any other relation to it than acceptance and accommodation, that everyone's destiny is *necessarily* within it, and—there is observation to countervail the cynicism—

almost everyone wants what it offers anyway, that there is no world of their own left for Indians or other minorities to maintain, that, as Ellison has it in *Shadow and Act*, history cannot be unmade and lost cultural traditions restored. Running through his vehemence is the belief that American society isn't without some merit, that integration into American society is worth more than the Paiute boy allows. He grants what Dorn, in my mediation of him, says; even honors his courage and need to say it; but he finds the saying of it futile. He cannot recover the spirit that moved him in the sixties, and this book belongs to that stirring time. Power, he believes, will simply have to exhaust itself in the exhaustion of resources. Maybe the eighties will be better.

6 July 1978

A travel book, at one point, fittingly parodic of travelogues ("And as you leave this 'Biggest Little City in the World'"). And to be put with other travel books in the long tradition of the adventurous muse, with the documentaries of American rediscovery in the thirties (certainly with Agee and Evans' *Let Us Now Praise Famous Men*); and put against the enclosed and self-reflexive travels of *On the Road* and Kesey's Pranksters, though they testify too, and in Kerouac's case there is the matter of fathers.

From Pocatello out.

A tour of the Basin-Plateau, not the prairies, and not in the protective company of soldiers, either. That much farther on, and the landscape that much bleaker, limiting. Nothing grand like the buffalo hunts of Irving's romantic account (though he knew genocide and named it in the Pequot Wars). The "bitter landscape" of Nevada. Moonscape of America. Journey now, as then, through a landscape of attitudes, working out—confirming—an attitude to "America." And like all our journeys, over Indian land, this one, like some others—Thoreau's, to Maine and Minnesota—in search of Indians, who are neither easy to find nor easy to know, and never, never to be labeled. The least conspicuous figure in the landscape. The police very conspicuous, the country now one constabularly, everyone trained to pick out strangers. A hostile environment.

To enter the open field of experience: always undertaken at risk. A black man and a white man traveling together, the photographer as "dangerous" as the professor. Though never described, probably in "beat" clothes, closer in dress to Indians than to tourists; certainly not "respectable." Suspect. The anxiety of it, a deep current of the prose, of places like Reno and Elko. Yet one of the reasons they can enter the Indian world: quick identification, followed by the equally important assurance of generous, receptive attitudes. How otherwise enter into easy talk with Old Pancho or enter the penetralia, find Willie Dorsey? Dorn tells of Leroy Lucas' willingness to participate in the sun dance in order to photograph it. Isn't participation, unmentioned, the price of the encounter at Duck Valley? Not only the willingness to give an Indian a lift but the explicit determination to find the Indian in one's occasion and to follow him. Lucas performed the strenuous curative ritual of the dance. But what of the long night of steer-riding, drinking, and sleeping it off in the car? A necessary ritual of entrance.

How to find the Indian? I haven't found a Chippewa after more than twenty summers here; I mean in the way of casual encounter, as you find any one in your neighborhood, in the daily course of experience. Knew a "Christian Indian" once. Helped me clear; later went off to Canada to preach a fatalistic gospel. Know some white experts and have learned something from them. And after all to live on the Red Lake Trail is, willy-nilly, to learn from what's at hand about shell- and grit-tempered pottery and chalcedony points. To learn about a culture safely in the past, to dig that, as my wife literally digs middens. But not the culture of Tract 33 (on the "Indian" side of U.S. 2), that veritable development of suburban tract houses * and asphalt roads, entered, I'm told, at risk.

And what of the closed reservation at Red Lake, where the Indians at Panemah Point spoke—perhaps still speak—only Ojibway? That was mediated for me by the white community manager during the heady times of OED and by an Indian librarian on his way to becoming a "culturalist." He invited me to send books, but never acknowledged the crates of them I collected and sent for several years, my meliorism accorded the silence Chuck Storm later told me such "liberalism" deserved. But can't you help anyone any more? Is it *always* patronage? Why can't others recognize, as Dorn says of himself, that one may be deculturized, albeit differently and, in my case, also in different degree? Had Dorn washed Willie Dorsey's feet, would he have appreciated that as much as the gift of cigarettes?

I read this book and follow its map in amazement. I lived for a while in this landscape. Several times, in the comfort of a pullman, like one of those casually interested travelers Dorn mentions in *By the Sound*, I followed the Snake River, on the way to Boise. I was stationed later at Wendover and almost daily flew the Basin-Plateau. I never saw an Indian during that

* Have developers taken over this term in ignorance of its irony?

long time! Didn't know what I was flying over, wasn't looking for anything but landmarks, the railroad tracks almost due west across the desert. "The Sundering U.P. Tracks"!

7 July 1978

Not to be above it but of it. To find anything you have to be looking (out) for it. "There were Indians. I looked at them by now almost casually as my special subject, other men seemed part of the blurred background." Proprietary? Not as it may seem coming on these sentences in the first paragraph of the book, for the encounter with Willie Dorsey soon to be related is the culminating experience, earned by all that the book subsequently tells of the journey. And placing this experience at the beginning not at the end means that he will not let this transfiguring encounter relieve him.

To find an Indian you must go where he is: in (some) bars and taverns, in front of general stores, in enclaves no longer marked by railroad tracks but by dead cars, on highways and dirt roads, in reservations, and if you are lucky (deserving) in an abandoned-seeming clapboard house, in the uncut grass, beyond three gates. You must not only look for him but know how to look at him, to recognize him. And contact makes the shock of recognition.

Contra anthropologists who have made Indians question-shy: "Sometimes I noticed the Indians I met didn't register at all when the first thing I said to them was in the form of a question." Not that he dismisses anthropologists, or only the value some find in assimilation. He knows their work and acknowledges it in footnotes; he has done the necessary scholarship. But he goes about his special subject differently because he has had different teachers, chiefly Olson and Sauer, and because the meanness he has known has made his subject very special to him.

Ten years or so after *A Bibliography on America for Ed Dorn*, this remarkable result. Did Olson notice it, appreciate Dorn's appreciation of his (so often pedagogical) gift, the deed with which he transferred his interest in the West to his student? This bibliography / methodology "abt man in Amurrica" (Olson's *Guide to Kulchur* but not Pound's Culture) really concerns the West, which for Olson and Dorn is a metonymy for America. The West is his *local*, the place he digs in, the littlest looked at that thereby becomes big. And he chooses to treat one Indian tribe, as Olson suggests, and one of those he names: "the Utes (whose language is of family of Nahuatl, thus showing Aztecs passed down Rockies.)" Did he remember this when he found the "beautiful ancestors" and heard Willie Dorsey's song—"this man's low, incantatory verbs spill[ing] down across the plateau and basin, between the mountains into the final plexus of the great Uto-Aztecan image of the world he sings in his daughter tongue"? And did he remember the instruction about axes of reference that in his practice became part of the discipline that brought him to this moment when "one can hardly think to be merely in Idaho or Nevada"?

Millennia, Person, Process, Quantity: Olson's axes of reference. They sharpen the attention with which Dorn saturates objects, provide the context in which he sees them. He has the "millennia sense" that comes of knowing geography, ecology, anthropology, a sense of time not limited to the linear, one-dimensional, progressive notion of history, the track of manifest destiny on which Geronimo rode to defeat. And it makes for good sense: for his recognition of the well-watered plain of Duck Valley, the good quality of the hay, the pleasure Indian boys find in doing the real work of cutting it, and the fact, we might not wish to admit, that "the change over to an agriculturalist economy can't be easy, even for a gathering people" because as much as hunters they have the habit of nomadism, a "habit of considerable millennia" not to be broken in a few generations by official decree and harassment. Culturation, not acculturation. What Sauer's *Man in Nature: America Before the Days of the White Man* is about, the incredible human achievement of habituation to the land, that long inhabitation of place that makes an Indian unwilling to forsake it, set against the implicit consequences of what every child already knows: *after the days of the white man*. After history, as Levi-Strauss tells it in *Tristes Tropiques*.

Person. Equated with psychology in Olson's diagram, where Dorn is placed at the intersection of the axes. At the center of the field, a centrality Dorn insists on in the title of the essay on *The Maximus Poems*. Heeds some of Olson's declarations (in "Projective Verse") and demonstrations (in *The Maximus Poems*)—such things as the need to attend the things of one's immediate occasion and enact the experience of it fully, in its multidimensionality. Journeying as a mode of such field work, though he journeys for other reasons, too. The leaps and shifts in exposition, a means of "cover[ing] the real." Speech, the great power here of the speaking voice. The essay on *The Maximus Poems* itself an example, what I see now, here in Sante Fe, with my immediate concerns (no quarter given, take it or leave it). The splendid landscape of the second paragraph. And those "very nice bells coming from Christo Rey"—is he mocking the bells of "I, Maximus of Gloucester, to You"? He might very well be. Consider the fierce rejection of "By ear, he sd" and what seems to be his association of this doctrine with another, "the getting rid of the lyrical interference of the individual as ego." Nothing so indiscriminate as the ear, not one of his "princely senses." Detests objectivity, he says, but he's not about to follow

Whitman. No orientalism either—contemptuously rejects it, disparages it. Why? When the recovery of so much he, with his fellow poets, wants, involves the chastening of the ego, the "Western Power" of consciousness ("I don't find the 'ego' at all obnoxious, but am aware of it as an undesirable word now")? Because he doesn't trust the universe, will not put his guard down; and because the ego *is* a creative power, and a radically critical one, like Redburn's in Launcelott's Hey, necessary to oppose an easy acceptance of "uniformity and placid reason," necessary to the necessity of standing apart. Doesn't eliminate the ego, just its lyrical interference. Clarity, again.

Maybe what Olson says of Creeley's narration applies: the story swings on him to be measured by his measure, "the highest circumstance I have ever encountered." The encounter with Willie Dorsey, which he tells with such close attention to "the psychological double mirror," overseeing his own act of seeing. (The complex conjunction of outer and inner may account for the deservedly high praise he gives Olson's "The Twist" and "The Librarian.") If *Person*, as Olson says, is to be "serious in . . . attention to the importance of life as it is solely of interest to us as it is human"—Olson says this of Jung, naming it religious—then Dorn's contact includes this dimension. Isn't he speaking of it when he says, "what is real and birth-giving, the non-argumentative edification of human event"? Isn't it the measure he applies to *The Maximus Poems*? That Olson is "journeying out to prepare the day for a new look at man, and what I have thus far read thrills me as a song about man, from a spirit which has an unerring knowledge of what is decent and lovely and dignified in man." A song about man.

The "highest pitched" for Dorn involves for us not only Willie Dorsey but Dorn himself. His human beauty, here overwhelming, even more so when he tells of Willie Dorsey on the Berkeley tape, where the passion is so clear, so clarified, it sings. The highest pitched is song. The ultimate measure: "Simply that men are lovely when they sing. . . . Each utterance is particular, that's what saves us all. We must have that."

Companion book to Jones's *Blues People* (1963)?

What Dorn says of Leroy Lucas' participation in the sun dance may be said of him: "He was there prepared to do more than look, was very much an emissary of himself." A remark, incidentally, establishing the measure of the "systematic carelessness" he finds almost everywhere.

> There are no hierarchies, no infinite, no
> such many as mass, there are only
> eyes in all heads,
> to be looked out of
>
> * * *
>
> both:
> the attention, and
> the care
> howevermuch each of us
> chooses our own
> kin and
> concentration
> (*Maximus* I, 28–29)

Process. Not much about how to do things, not as much as in *By the Sound* (silage, chicken farming, tunnels). Just the process of how to find out about now without disturbing the peace (the police). *'Istorin*, finding out for oneself; recording it. The description of Reno an equivalent of Olson's Pausanias? The expert use of significant detail. Reminds me of Edmund Wilson, whose *The American Earthquake* and

8 July 1978

Travels in Two Democracies are exemplary new journalism, like the best current examples born of social crisis and contradiction and the need to witness. His studies of the Zuñi and the Iroquois, too.

Quantity. Olson says it used to be called *environment* or *society*. He doesn't elucidate. Perhaps he suggests enough when he says it's the present time, characterized as it is by increase in the number of things, by the extension of technology and "the increase of human beings on earth." Quantity as a factor of civilization, modern culture, cities: the dominant, prevailing culture within which—against which—the deculturized (dispossessed) must learn to survive. A prominent factor for Dorn, necessarily; setting off his special subject, almost always evoking derisive treatment. The "neo-wild West," for example, an incredible overlay of attitudes and things (stereotypes, plastic, money) that prompts the following: "Aren't we just kidding ourselves when we speak of Indians, or Civil Rights, Justice via the courts, like due process? What do we think we mean? And when culture is brought forward, like a pizza on the tray, whatever combination you want, that's really loading it! You know what—I'll bet you money there are people in Reno who are 'interested' in Indians, dig their folklore and so on." Commoditization. Like Wendell Berry's "nature consumers," consumers of "Indians," ritual, and so on. Both poets are revulsed by it.

Probably Reno gets what it deserves. The biggest *little* city, indeed! Just as small towns are small. Those "slot machine types," for example, whose "controlled cast of facial muscle [is] altogether unlike the laughing picture of my Moapa girl" (no women encountered, only Mrs. Dorsey and Marsha glanced at, yet the Indian woman, like Ramona in *By the Sound*, is his muse, her laughter a form of song). Slot machine types: "California women pulling, pulling off the machine." A body image to go with others. Reno as "gastric," its diet nickels; the "turgid meatus" of its streets, the "effluvia." But then the atmosphere is saturated with money, with shit.

A constant target, stereotypes of Indians. Yet he employs stereotypes when describing the California women. And the "Siamese twins," those elderly couples with time and money, in wrinkle-free clothes, "the women gray-haired (dyed to silver) with spotty tanned skin, the men like they had been put together with enriched flour in the backroom of some Bank of America branch." (Compare with his loving portraits of Indian elders; consider a view he endorses, that a man "should grow by virtue of his own roots.") He casts a cold eye; "arctic direction" not "indirection," to modify Donald Wesling's good phrase. The meanness prompts but doesn't excuse this. Not even the more fully explained response to the Chinese, to the patriarch of the restaurant, whose inquisitiveness about Dorn and Lucas evokes a high pitched moment of another kind: "I wanted to scream, Listen, you miserable beady-eyed rodent!" But he knows, "It's not good. All men get twisted here."

Oh the meanness of Quantity! "Who can summon the exactitude to care in an environment which is truly mean—even if caring becomes then the more crucial?" Quantity: "No Indian's condition will be improved by a 'forwarding' of him into (with all the concomitant loss of his language and land, given up to a rapacious people) the world that so persistently surrounds him." Or others of the "countless peoples" for whom this world has proven to be impossible, undesirable to accept.

10 July 1978

Perhaps if we learn to find and see an Indian we will find the lost America of love? If we feel the meanness, understand the destructive policy (always, Crane said, iron dealt cleavage), realize the unequal conflict, appreciate the great human beauty of Willie Dorsey and Willie George. And, as he says of Willie Dorsey's oneness with the earth ("In him we are honored to witness the total exclusion of the private"), "If we happen to find ourselves in the frame of a human integrity of that order"—perhaps, then, "we can go openly toward it."

Yes, perhaps. If we accommodate the most unaccommodating position, which is to let be, to grant the sovereignty of separate existence, of ways of being not our own. But as Dorn says, "*To be* is nothing. . . . This goes for all Americans, the entire hemisphere." And he knows that we are as likely to acquire the necessary spiritual discipline as alter our historical course; that Vietnam is the present demonstration of what we are.

Olson said in the second postscript to the *Bibliography* that we need another set of muckrakers. Dorn is not one of them because he lacks the necessary political faith in America, in the possibilities of legislative reform. His vision, unlike theirs, is of enormity. Not having a country any more than Indians do, he belongs, he says in the Berkeley lecture, to the Fourth World. What moves him most in this extreme situation is survival, the power to survive. The epigraph from Theodora Kroeber speaks to that determination. It calls to mind the Cholo widow in Melville's story. It is what the Indians have to teach us.

There is no program here except (*except!*) change of head and heart, involving another "conceptual alignment of human activity." Dorn is not a muckraker because he is deculturized, disaffiliated, a stranger in the land. In the impasse that he reaches here he does not tell us, as he does later, that he stands with the Apache, that he has come to accept the extreme solution of resistance, of guerrilla warfare, "the frenzy of survival rushing from our pores," as he writes in "And when, above Janos." The recollections in *Recollections of Gran Apachería* are both his and theirs, deadly recollections of a policy for a century now essentially the same. As in *Our Word: Guerrilla Poems from Latin America*, he implicitly sanctions revolution. Our Word = Our World = Third World. And Our Word is a pledge, these translations an act of solidarity with his comrades, the poet-often-student-guerrilla fighters who wrote them.

Perhaps he agrees with them that "the pain is of great antiquity / but not eternal." Looking at the photograph of Geronimo's band taken on the way to Florida, to which these guerrillas (surrendered, never captured) were removed, he tells us that

> They look better than we do.
> They will look better than we look forever
> We will never really look very good
> We are too far gone on thought, and its rejections

From 1967:

11 June 1979

> *The North Atlantic Turbine* (1967)
> *Twenty-Four Love Songs* (1969)
> *Songs: Set Two* (1970)
> *Recollections of Gran Apachería* (1974)
> *Slinger* (1975; *Gunslinger*, 1968, 1969, 1971, 1972)
> *Manchester Square* (1975; with Jennifer Dunbar)
> *Hello, La Jolla* (1978)

Impasse makes the break. Anger and hatred follow. How do you define a political poet? Are political concerns, views, content enough? Or must one, like Amiri Baraka (no longer

LeRoi Jones), not only speak in behalf of collective interests but actively, in ways more pragmatic than poetry, promote them? Put one's poetry explicitly to that *service*? Not only draw the line but take a stand there? And if one doesn't, like Dorn, then isn't he, in the exasperation of not having that release, pressed to find a fuller range of adequate verbal means? Aren't poems like "Ed Dorn Sportcasts Colonialism" (the world box-score poem) and "The Cosmology of Finding Your Place" examples? The humor of the first exceeding itself, mordant, deadly, because the point of this harangue is not, as he says, to get speech into the poem—he had done that, always tellingly, before—but to show us how the inexact, hyped-up speech of sportscasting—of the mediating media—is a big sell; that were this athletic contest of haves and have-nots actually the case, this in fact is how it would be broadcast; that parody now is truer to fact than fact, just as in Pynchon fiction is truer to history than history; that language has been corrupted, become moral mush, everything that Orwell said resulted from its present political use; that in entertaining it—letting it entertain us—we have become decadently interested, the detached and unserious viewers of events, watching the war in Vietnam on TV.

The humor of the second is one with incantation in helping us identify with the draft resisters in whose behalf this poem was written; a poem equally outrageous in its conception—finding one's place at the bottom!—and in published form, with its various typefaces and undulating verse form, visually provocative, appropriately dada-esque.

Does the fact that Dorn read this poem on a political occasion (I first heard him read on such an occasion) alter the assessment of his politics? Weren't many of us political to that extent then? Didn't we, as he advises in *The Poet, the People, the Spirit* (the title is exact in triangulating a politics, and Berkeley was the place to receive it), do what he expects the poet to do: withdraw affect, compromise allegiance, look at people, not the apparatus of the state? And didn't we disclaim revolution, thinking that change of mind and spirit—what Charles Reich belatedly popularized as a change of consciousness, not quite what Emerson, attentive to generative ideas, called the silent revolution of thought—was more radical and "far more subversive," subversion being the root of the matter? *1967*: don't forget Vietnam, how it had necessarily preempted all of our attention and energy and incited our resistance, how much it and its aftermath account for Dorn's work in this decade. Why you detect some Burroughs in the routines of the broadcast and recall Mailer's oral masterpiece, *Why Are We in Vietnam*? (1967).

Modulation and counterpoint. Hello, La Jolla really begins with a poem like "A Theory of Truth" in the long initial sequence of *The North Atlantic Turbine*. Access of intellect, born of dismay. In the prefatory statement of *Collected Poems*, substitute intellectual for theoretical? "I have known my work to be theoretical in nature and poetic by virtue of its inherent tone." Even the love songs, with their welcome respite, are not like the earlier songs—intellectual again, even "metaphysical." *Recollections of Gran Apachería* grim, the stark tragedy to remind us of more recent genocide not now in focus—the characteristic of the Vietnam War, he says, was just this lack of focus—and how we will someday recollect it with the historical and moral acuity he brings to the *Apachería*, a word we are meant to trouble over, its immediate association, according to Bob Lewis who asked a Mexican friend, with *carnicería*, meatmarket, butchery, slaughter. *Gunslinger*, comic dramatic narrative of the epic West, where the evil (entrepreneurial) forces of American history now, on

Indian reservation land, battle other evil forces to no conclusive, heartening end. *Hello, La Jolla*, at the end of the line, its wit corrosive sublimate. Increasing distance, and ferocity. The theoretical concerned with the intellectual, with mind and its processes, so that the events of *Apachería* and *Gunslinger* are brought to our attention as eventuations of kinds of mind. Only the small gentle poems of *Manchester Square*, and only a handful, these as sharply observant but somehow gentler, the satire, say, of "Carlos Place" reminiscent of Eliot—"The Retainers, shuffling their gung ho / with their gung fu, then, bored with that / they throw their eyes like dice / across the grey felt of a tabloid"). Dorn, as he says in the title of the first poem, "Home Again," not unhappy, as the last poem tells us, because England is surviving its own history, and

> . . . the green hand still
> gently rocks the cradle.
> This garden is going to be
> difficult to destroy.

Sure, he may say in *Geography*, "Socialism is shit turned only half way round"; but he also cites, as if in anticipation, Donald Davie's "Once an imperial nation, / Our hands are clean now, empty," and now tenacity, care, gentleness, survival matter, virtues not of revolution but of persistence. Revolution belongs to the Third World, persistence to ours. Is this a translation in political terms of the generational conflict?

Yet mostly a record of meanness that, accountably, sometimes makes him mean. "The man who doesn't belong in a community is probably the man to pay attention to," he concluded at Berkeley. "He's the man who knows where he's come from."

A man without a country. Exiled into language.

The North Atlantic Turbine. NAT = NATO? The chart of currents on the cover, to call up Olson, especially the poem on Juan de la Cosa, where the beginning is celebrated; perhaps Sauer's *Northern Mists*, the Sauer of the West, like Dorn, having turned East? Turbine = currents = the magnetic forces of history, as in Lawrence's account of America. A perverse energy, as Crane has it in "The Dance"? Adams' dynamo? Lines of economic force, of the trade, Thoreau said, that curses everything. The meanness is not just American; it belongs to Western civilization, originating in the imperialism fostered by the opening of the seas. That's the point of the whole book, and he's American in making it, and most when he says

12 June 1979

> the new
> world was an evil world—
> it should never have
> been discovered.

Aklavik and Inuvik, in the most northern of Canadian territories, the last native communities are its outposts just as much as South Africa: one tied in by liquor, the other by investments; the Esquimaux of the one resisting, as they can, the pull of acculturation, the Blacks of the other, knowing it well, now (1966) resorting to assassination. Reducing the complicated history of the turbine to simple good versus evil, to the necessity, pushed by Dorn, to destroy it. And don't forget the sundering U.P. tracks that carry its force across the continent, "right through the heart," dividing the races of—is it Melville's phrase?—"cosmological america."

Where is that picture, was it from the *Illustrated News*?, the one of Dorn in sportjacket and tie, ensconced among his

13 June 1979

books, sherry at hand, smiling, undoubtedly pleased with his reception in England. The Fulbright lecturer at the University of Essex, 1965–1967. As he says, a lover of "the dazzle of learning."

Not incongruous, if you consider the congruity of costume, the fact that he likes to dress and dresses his part. The studied casual elegance of the photo by Mary Canary on the back of *Apachería*, or the studied comic one, standing beside one of those binoculars you pay to scan the landscape with, in *Roadtesting the Language*. Michael Rumaker remembers him wearing a shiny red leather jacket. In "1st Avenue," he characterizes himself by rummaging not for useful work clothes as Bill Elephant does but for books and the kind of fur-lined flying suit you turned in at the end of the war.

Maybe the most important aspect of this "overreached book"—his judgment—is the fact that in writing it he discovered he was a poet of the West, that however much the "atrocities of [his] own hemisphere" justified disaffiliation, it was still his hemisphere, ground he knew and could measure accurately. Both "alien's take" and "unlocused" point to the familiar difficulty of foreign residence, to the inadequacy of what is also so wonderful to have, the heritage of English culture that makes England, as Hawthorne said, *our old home*. "I am at home here only in my mind / that's what heritage is," but "my heart and my veins / are burning for home." This book gives birth to Gunslinger (in "An Idle Visitation"), who appears here in order to restore to the poet—probably not "I" who is not yet prominently "I"—his "missing heart," to remind him of "the girl you left / in Juarez, the blank / political days press her now / in the narrow alleys. . . ." *Alleys*, as in earlier poems, like pea-shacks.

So lovely she is England
with her swollen bellies

Landforms of love. Olson: *Love is form* = landforms? Because the "topological [is] a prime and libidinal character of a man"? I like best, in "Oxford," Parts II and III, exquisite lyrics to the sandstones and limestones, the latter exactly named, "Comforted by Limestone," not a psychic landscape like Auden's "In Praise of Limestone," yet generously recalling it—as "An Idle Visitation," in the reference to "the footstep in the flat above," recalls Eliot. Comforted by earth itself.

Erotic landforms, yet cultural restraint and propriety. The "first note" in the opening poem of that name, where the Dorns, entrained, do not yield to their desire to make love. And "Fornication," the first part of "Oxford," naming the moral equivalent of the political judgment he makes in observing the well-kept women from abroad, "care packages" Oxford-bound, "imperialism / implied by their shapely legs." Anti-types to the rose, the girl in Juarez. So this formulation of his previous concern:

This is no rose,
this is the turbine. Continents
break before it

14 June 1979

"We share orogeny," he says of England and America, but "we [Americans] have had to put up with used shit / from the beginning." In sum, a refuse theory of history. We applied inherited ideas and ignorance (along with our own) and never "dismount[ed] the old model." So there's no comfort in the old equation of America versus Europe, since the versus doesn't count for much; and the only way he can be an American is to identify with the Indians, which is to abrogate history and inherit (inhabit) the original geography, the space that was SPACE, because it was before the time of realtors. But Faulkner knew that was impossible.

No comfort, as anyone who goes abroad knows, in an alien's take on your own country, in the French commentary on Watts, matched though it is by news from home of Harlem. He *has* retained his ear for news of atrocities at home, but this merely adds its oppression to the already loveless (there is only one "song") and death-filled wintry climate of his experience. "Black comes into your senses," he says, "more than green."

Retained his ear for speech, exploits it more. A texture of speech—the full range of the sixties. Voices, prefiguring *Gunslinger.* The poems longer, serial, more expansive, utilizing the spatial possibilities of open form. Frequent broken/junctured lines, declarative thrust. A harsh prosody. His equivalent of the violence he says is now communication?

The memorable poem, for me the signature: "Wait by the Door Awhile Death, There Are Others." A meditative journey, wholly inner, through much that has preoccupied him, even as seldom in his work, entering his dreams. Kinds of death: dullness, disaffection, bodily entropy (aging: nearing forty), homelessness, cosmic abandonment. All that time in England, at the university, having to listen to colleagues talk of "the american situation"—having to stand at the "mahogany sideboard of tastes" and run through the "whole menu" of political events (how we do in fact convert history to cocktail chatter, which is just what the poetry refuses to do), having himself to look serious—

> Look like I *have* a home, pretend
> like anyone in the world

> I know where that is. And could
> if I choose, go there.

Weariness of spirit more than body, recognition of finitude. Tarot: among signs, the ram, "the reflection of Isis"—

> I wear
> a tiara. I can think of people
> who won't believe that.

Yes. No, not this poet of the rose, whose "I," in a dream, is Sophia Loren, "a mature venus"; whose speculation on body and self becomes Whitmanesque and Creeleyesque

> The body. I am
> however, the host of my body.
> I invite myself to enter myself.
> I have gone there sometimes with great pleasure.

Who finally dreams of a man named Pedro, "a man without a country," abandoned to the sea, without the necessary "references." "He is the man we would all save with our tongues / because we are secretly him." Save? as poetry saves when it reminds us of the very body of the world that nurtures us. Or, as he has it, only of what once was, "that time / the world seemed open what a satisfying meal / that was." Body and soul; self and world. Wherefore no cosmicity?

15 June 1979

Twenty-Four Love Songs. His "ramifications." Venus versus turbine. Eros versus meanness. Within thc longer journey home, this journey of love, of estrangements and reconciliations. A sequence of lyrics, having a common open multiphasic prosody (with nice variations from the norm) and a common theme. "Metaphysical" in quality, in its conceits, its union of sensual and intellectual; reason enough for omitting the weak, easy-cynical #20 on reprinting. Appropriate because that tradition is notably common to America and

England, and the poems (an American speaking) work to harmonize the discords of his marriage to Jennifer Dunbar, an English woman. To find the *clef* as well as the *cleft*. Song and sexuality, the generative word. These songs make love, sometimes visually enact it.

One of the splendid achievements of this generation of poets. Shelved next to Donne in the bookstore!

The longest journey, telling "the runic secret of homeward," the western journey that began with the rape of Europa, for time, history, and death, as myth has it, begin with the erotic act. Nothing parochial, the myth not adventitious: to be read in this context.

> It is deep going from here
> from the old world to the new
> from Europa home
> the brilliant scrolls of waves
>   wave
> the runic secret of homeward
> when Diego de Landa
> the glyphic books destroyed
> there were old towns
>   in our hemisphere sadness
> now as then
>
> no sense in old towns chontal
>   got to have
> newtowns of the soul

The echo of the first line. Is it Creeley, some poem on place? The hardest journey, the return? The oldest journey: Greek, Norse, Spanish. Rape, destruction, then as now; sadness, too. Europe begins with Europa, and continues to reenact her story. But Europa also projects Venus, the "brilliant scrolls" calling up the erotic seas of Crane's "Voyages" and Williams' "St. Francis Einstein of the Daffodils," its beckoning Venus-

Liberty discounted? Is the loss of Venus our runic secret, the secret of our ruin, as Olson has it when he says that Venus does not arise from these waters, fish do? Doesn't the poem beginning "The agony of beauty" remember this context and play off Olson's "The Ring Of"? And the Newton in "new-towns," does that pick up the favorable presence of Einstein, the possibility of change, in Williams' poem?

In any case, she is the goddess he brings home, service that merits his place, as Duncan would certainly recognize it, among our troubadours. A voyage to pagany made good, with good results, the excremental smell (and vision) ventilated (and clarified), love and poetry, as Williams said in "Riposte," natural elements that cleanse and dissipate evil gases:

> Back Home, Back Home
> the day wakes up and once
> out the door into what's
> left of the fresh air it still
> comes clear
> how lovely
> love is there

Home: inside and outside, human and cosmological joined, the indefinite pronoun referring to a twofold clarification, to the apprehension of the presence of love, itself the very earth and the love of woman that reveals it to him. She is the day that wakes up, just as in *Gunslinger* she is the

> Goddesse, excellently bright
> thou that mak'st a day of night.

And who, as the *Love Songs* also tells us:

> You tell us men are numberless
> and that Great and Mother
> were once synonymous.

16 June 1979 #9 ("EYE high gloria"): the expanded eye—and "I"—of drug-awakened consciousness. Eye-high-gloria: equivalents. Opening the nick in time (Cezanne? Thoreau?) by means of jazz and pot; entering an ecstatic condition of congruence and warmth. A morning glory of a poem, the unpunctuated flow, pushed by participles, all the *ings*, "rime   ing." Enactment.

Prelude to *Songs: Set Two: A Short Count*? To that sequence, that journey out, beyond the borders, to love and nurture? That foray, guerrilla-like, on the cosmos? Drug-induced. Acid, as in Book II of *Gunslinger*. Difficult poems of erotic-cosmological experience when "the gnosis / lets go into hold of creation," when the lovers come through (*we* have come through: D. H. Lawrence), are delivered into life, animated by the World Breath.

Set Two = set to? The Empedoclean notion of love and strife, of wholeness and sexual differentiation. The demonic as well as blessed phases of experience. These visions one with the normal polarization / valorization of his work. Acid gives him a world of love denied in the present world of strife; extends his allegiance to the cosmos. The red-white-and-blue landscape of the last poem not America, but the very world in space. *That* is "His new england." Is the "blue space" also his mind? His mind a / the cosmos?

"His new england"? Olson's? "This volume / is to honor / the Scald." Olson died in 1970; his gift: an actual earth of value.

19 June 1979 *Recollections of Gran Apachería* and *Gunslinger*: books of the West, phases of western history. Poems of the American (Western, European) *mind*. Companion volumes, really. Both works of imagination, neither dependent on immediate expe-

rience. The historical imagination/remembering of the one; the imaginative dramatic projection of the other. A scale of performance: from personal speech to impersonal drama, from tragedy to comedy. The farthest out, or the farthest in?

Why is *Recollections of Gran Apachería* dedicated to Creeley? I would have thought either set of love songs, some of them Creeleyesque, more appropriate. Because, as he said in a lovely admission at Iowa City, with Creeley in attendance, finally he had a book good enough. Yes, this book is a masterly achievement, inimitably Dorn's, exemplary of one of his ways of taking up history. *Gunslinger* is an example of another way. Both diverge from Olson's practice.

Apache means *enemy*. Turtle Island published this book. The forces are joining. The comic book format: a comic book for our time! The drawings by Michael Myers comic (rightly) at our expense, showing how much our very presence—and our things—desecrate the desert landscape, clutter its space.

Recollection, of what has been omitted from our histories, or accounted for without sympathy. Not just Dorn's recollections but the Apaches', as in "And when, above Janos," where *they* remember the most terrible trial of survival, the killing of their own children. Or our recollection, as in the final almost unbearable poem, "La Máquina a Houston," where *we* join the man with the camera photographing the Apaches on this stopover to death-by-exile, our minds filling, as the poem does, with the lamentation of the three thousand dogs, some of whom followed the train until exhausted.

The history of the West, of manifest destiny, is one of the railroad. In *Gunslinger*, too. Coming and going.

A comic book of the tragic, in the sense of fated, the subject beyond tragedy: genocide. Ahab's iron rails. The determinism of American history, determinism, the machine.

The "First Lines," a catalog of the initial lines of subsequent poems. Reminds me of Whitman's "Inscriptions" and his own litanies. The last first line: "The train has come to rest and ceased its creaking." These lines are also the threads of the "corrupted cloth" the *Recollections* "unweave." Olson wove history in *The Maximus Poems*, Dorn unweaves (deconstructs) it, though his book is well-made, carefully ordered (woven: *poco a poco*).

Some poems have titles, and sometimes they are ironic.

A hagiology? Victorio, Nana, Geronimo, Juana, etc. Chosen for *Selected Poems*.

A demonology? General Crook, who put the Apaches to work cutting hay at one cent per pound (Dorn omits the fact that women and children did most of the work). Captain Crawford, whose photograph does indeed resemble Poe, but who may not, as Dorn has it, have been "sated with German Romanticism / his eyes . . . sunk deep / in centuries of masturbatory introspection." The historical accounts I've read do not support such extreme characterization.

20 June 1979

Polarization and stereotypes. "Assorted Compliments" samples some. Yet Dorn himself employs them, for example, "Whiteye." Maybe Crawford. Isn't the common feature of *Apachería* and *Gunslinger* the reduction of a complex history to its melodramatic outcome, where the forces of good and evil meet, here Indians, who do become guerrilla fighters, and the military? The repudiation of stereotypes (generalization and symbolism versus particularism and image is the equivalent in poetics) is a test of Dorn's democratic politics, since stereotypes, as Elinor Grumet reminds me, always are primary manifestations of the sociological conflict of races and minorities. Stereotypes image our paranoia; and victimage,as Kenneth Burke taught us, is an inevitable social phenomenon, a consequence of the hierarchical nature of language.

Perhaps the characterization of Crawford has erotic import? Isn't his masturbatory introspection and the German Romanticism that nurtures it to be compared with the child rearing of the Apaches, the child's exposure to the external world, which is why their art is of "cosmic physical proportion"; the child's freedom ("the children of both sexes / had perfect freedom"), which is why, if Wilhelm Reich is right, they are self-determined, capable of rebellion when their survival is threatened? Such child rearing suggests matriarchy, and only a suggestion is needed to put in question the patriarchy of the military. Or, in *Gunslinger*, Robart's trainload, who have no Lil, no poet to sing the praises of the goddess.

Dorn tells us at the start that the Apaches "were noble / not in themselves / so much as in their Ideas." And their leading ideas, he says in the poem on child rearing, "come directly from the landform."

This exposure to the world, this training in "pure observation," this turning *out*, accounts for their ability to live in the here/now, for their freedom from the "pathological" "predictive Mind," the "Alien Thinking" of Western man. The poem treating this most fully is called "The Whole European Distinction," and it is juxtaposed to "Creation," which relates the Apache cosmogonal myth. And note

> Woman created first
> out of a direct act of labor
> not from some spare part
> Night girl is the nucleus of the universe.

Mind, that Western invention, or discovery as Bruno Snell has it, versus *muthos*. Olson's ground.

> Above and below
> a sea of light

See Nut, in Olson's Dogtown poem. Native thinking is mythological thinking:

> I am Thinking, Thinking
> Thinking, Thinking
>
> I am Thinking Earth.

And they were overcome by Mind. By "frag mentation." Their world, cosmos, unity destroyed.

Historical background in "When the Boundary Commission"; historiography in "Reservations," the largest poem, very much at the center. Americans have inherited the European "inability / to live on Earth with other kinds / and certainly / not with kinds other than themselves." (Melville: "The Anglo-Saxons—lacking grace / To win the love of any race; Hated by myriads dispossessed / . . . —the Indians East and West.") So "foreign Policy / has always been an Internal policy." Vietnam. Regeneration by violence. Meanwhile

> turning back the sunlight
> promoting the early return of the glacier

not knowing, imagine, "What a crisis is."

21 June 1979 Dorn's long poem. A SPACE(d out) EPIC, as Georg Gugelberger says in a fine review of *Slinger* (the *American*

Book Review, Summer, 1978). Not just the prominence of drugs—pot, acid, cocaine; not just, say, an epic of the time and place that produced the Castaneda books, but a poem, Dorn says, in which he tried "to approach the cultural phenomenology of the late sixties and the early seventies on the broader base that poetry has to have." Epic as a poem of culture. And an epic of space, as Olson spoke of space, and as American long poems sometimes have been. *From Mesilla Out*. A journey, again, over familiar ground, that never reaches its goal in Las Vegas, though Howard Hughes is found. Now the quest may be an epic one of consciousness (to use Crane's characterization of his long poem, of modern epics), the goal attained in acts of imagination, or whenever the mind, which in respect to the habits of thought that Olson repudiated in the "old discourse," is overcome, finds itself *out*, in the sense that Dorn gives that word. What happens to "I" in the poem enacts the transformation of ego that Olson proposed, the transformation of the mentalistic habits he despaired of: the description inherent in symbol and metaphor. Dorn, I think, is impugning neither the "eye" nor phenomenology, as Gugelberger believes; he is impugning what Olson does, the sovereignty of description over act; act, as Gunslinger instructs us, making us one with event, not estranged from but immediately of the world.

Creeley writ large? A postmodern epic.

Long poem. Five parts, if you count *The Cycle* separately; four books. Quaternary, after Jung? The seasonal round? There is a "Winterbook," prefaced by a notable poem on the return of spring ("Life surges with the Sunne out of decline"). But the diurnal is more prominent than the seasonal: a *day* book, of day, sunset and sunrise. "Dear lengthening Day / I have loved your apparencies since you created me."

Long in the sense of lived with/in for a long time. A spacious verbal space.

Maximus and *Gunslinger*. Duncan (letter, 24 October 1977): "Ed Dorn was Charles' great hope in the new generation. All the more striking that Dorn proposed a major shift from the Olson insistence upon the ground of actual event: the fictional bravura of *Gunslinger* comes as an antithesis to Olson's thesis in a dialectical move." Yes, and *Gunslinger* displeased both Olson and Creeley. But granted that Maximus and Gunslinger resemble their respective authors—no question of Maximus in regard to size, or of the Gunslinger of "impeccable personal smoothness"—they are still alike in several important ways.

Maximus emerged in a situation comparable to the emergence of Gunslinger, that is, both belong in the tradition of American character Constance Rourke treated in *American Humor*. Both are mythic figures over and beyond their special prominence because their allegiance is to origins. Maximus inherits the Mediterranean work of his namesake, and especially the middle name Cassius, which identifies his opposition to Zeus, to the patriarchal. Not having that nominal advantage, Gunslinger is a *semidios*, born in the Near East, the bearer of more than 2,000 years of experience, that is, of *all* of Western experience. He still worships the sun and the Great Goddess. As he says of the poet we may say of him: he's "marvelously heliocentric." This relates him not only to the Olson-Maximus of *Maximus III* but to Davy Crockett, who one cold morning liberated the frozen sun and walked away with sunrise in his pocket, an "archeologist of morning," where Gunslinger, now a western hero witnessing the decline of the West and not confident of redeeming it, is not.

(The battle that ends the epic is anticlimactic and of little consequence, and Gunslinger sleeps through it. His farewell to the community of consciousness that the poem gathers together is sad, picking up much of the loneliness Dorn has felt and speaking as well for his own departure from the poem.) Like Maximus, Gunslinger is a pedagogue, and his horse is one of the horses of instruction, named Claude Levi-Strauss for the very good reason that the central issue of desecration/sacralization is correlative with a central issue in studies of myth: *culture versus nature*. A poet-pedagogue needing a Pegasus, and poetry the means of instruction. But also, like the stagecoach, as against the train, outmoded, ineffective? The stagecoach in *Looking Backward*? Looking backward? Without Olson's confidence in feedback? In using history to change history? Like Davy Crockett, Gunslinger is a cosmological hero, whose motto might be this injunction to Everything on the open road:

> Here Kums the Kosmos
> Don't just stand there! (lookin dumb
> Stick out your thumb.

Like Olson, in "From Gloucester Out," someone whose self is related to the cosmos, in touch with the *outsidereal*, his *insidereal* thereby in proper balance. Someone who has fulfilled the potential Dorn says the poet has to be free of evil, to be connected with "the whole burst of glow in the cosmos." Which may explain the distance between Gunslinger and Robart, the purely spectatorial nature of the confrontation?

Robart, after Howard Robard Hughes, is Gunslinger's opposite. Mentalistic, patriarchal, evil. Satan, not merely Howard Hughes; the entrepreneur above the law, the embodiment of the conspicuous evil of America: acquisitiveness/greed/shit. Hughes, as much a mythic figure as the cowboy; a throwback, too, even though his speech has all the flavor of an advanced technological and media-minded society. And in this book where language does so much of the work, where it is foregrounded, Joycean extravaganza, and gives much of the pleasure, the contrast of archaisms (used chiefly in respect to Gunslinger and his company) and technico-communications and pop jargon makes the point as much as anything. Throwback? Well, Hughes believed in an "outdated entrepreneurial philosophy of single ownership." Like some of the people on the Illinois prairie or in the Snake River valley? Did Hughes come pleasurably to mind because in his later stage as drug addict he was kept by the "Mormon Mafia"?

Anyway, all that is evil clusters in Robart, or almost all, since the populace of Universe City (and university!) is like the mob in *Huckleberry Finn* and prompts a similarly ferocious scorn from the author. They are the sick citizenry to which Gunslinger addresses the curative "Cycle"—"the Great Cycle of the Enchanted Wallet / of Robart the Valfather of this race / . . . the Cycle of Acquisition."

Our saga? Picking up the theme of American criticism, the creative life versus the acquisitive life, formulated melodramatically by Van Wyck Brooks? Now Swiftian in its revulsion, its parodic extremity, a work of hostility equal to that of the late Twain ("The Man Who Corrupted Hadleyburg") and of Melville in *The Confidence Man* (a book acknowledged, as Steve Clay notes, by the borrowing from its opening sentence in the poem on cocaine). The comic book drawings of the original publication.

Among other things a scatological imagination of demonic deity running the universe. Atum? Creation by masturbation.

"He's got a Starfinder in the head of *H*is cock // Or used to have." The enemy of the imagination and the Great Goddess. Rob-art. Like "Big Richard" who held the pot,

> He cons the present to hustle the futchah
> By a simple elimination of the datadata

Etc.

22 June 1979

The comic. Consider

> Entrapment is this society's
> Sole [soul] activity . . .
> and Only laughter,
> can blow it to rags . . .

The mode is political. As Robert Kelly says, Dorn wishes to "jolt us into reorientations." Not just change the mind by altering its attitudes—as Baraka tries to do in the proletcult, episodic play *The Motion of History*—but remake the mind by showing us, as E. F. Dyck argues, the breakdown of classical logic. The first may give political satisfaction; the second is too long-range for that. And too subtle? Demythification and remythification, foregrounded language, and all the rest of the ingenious intellectual play are for a special (privileged?) audience? For his "true readers," as he says? It is fundamental work. And isn't politics at best the business of the present, most effective when it attends to the arrangements that help us, as Paul Goodman said, to live on a little?

The comic perspective, as Kenneth Burke describes and uses it, is inclusive (both/and), humane, benign, eminently social. But in Rourke's *American Humor*, the humor, as with Crockett, is often a matter of stance toward a fearful natural environment more than toward society, or if toward society, of the oppositional kind of "The Dandy Frightening the Squatter." Dorn's concerns are both cosmic and social, and in regard to the social he is often vindictive. His comedy is not ameliorative; it is either/or. It distances us from society rather than brings us back to it.

The loveliest passages are often set-pieces: the poems to morning at the beginning of Book II, "The Lawg" (on spring) in Book III, "Prolegomenon" (the Great Goddess) in Book IV. The most pleasing and available character is Lil, the Great Goddess herself, of many avatars, including the most obvious, Mae West (Maia West?). Of course the reference to women's liberation (*"if she was a woman / then she is my sister!"*) isn't needed to tell us that she is Cocaine Lil. And in the remarkable poem on ȻO-KÁNG that follows she is Miss Americaine, the fullest flowering in his work of Geranium, the feminine Indian presence of the land to which he is most devoted. If anyone is a pure product of America, this Inca maiden is.

Is this to say that only cocaine brings him home? That in a country wasted ecologically and in everything "sickening" ("The Fenomena is stark, energetic / full-of-shit . . ."), only drugs promise an America of love?

23 June 1979

For him Olson's hoped-for cosmos-polis remains cosmos versus polis. Because he lacks place. He demythifies history (the myths/lies of America) primarily in behalf of those myths that help us repossess relationship to Mother Earth. When he speaks of America he means this hemisphere, and he speaks its principal languages, as in the concluding verses. His loyalties are fiercely held. He has had enough shit. If he could he would work the radical alchemy this declaration suggests: "The sun is the gold, in a way."

31 January 1979

He apologizes for the amount of "calculated" white space in *Hello, La Jolla* and says that we may consider it an invitation to fill it in. With what? Our own comparable verses, observations of our culture. Many volumes of verse have as much unfilled space. No need to apologize for that unless the page is a "field" and these small, hard, bitter, sardonic bullets (*projectile* verse, indeed! the poet his own muzzle and charge, as Olson said) are believed to be as insufficient to its challenge as the insufficiency of wit is to its object. "Calculated." Like these deliberate, intellectual verses. No lyric force. No song, no body, Bruce Wheaton says, just rational speech. So, no need to employ the page as a field. "A for Ism." Not only the concrete for the abstract, the particular for the universal, as Ed Folsom said in his introduction to Dorn's reading—and to which Dorn assented. "A for Ism" = aphorism = Gk. *aphorismos*, definition, short, pithy sentence, fr. *aphorizein* to make out boundaries, set aside, cast out, define = a terse and often ingenious formulation of a truth or sentiment usu. in a single sentence (Webster's Third). Aphorism suits an economy of mind and spirit, minimal engagement and measured energy, the need, accompanying the sense of being turned off, to draw the line, *to make out boundaries . . . cast out*. Aphorism puts one outside, is the retaliation of an outsider. Didn't Dorn get too much satisfaction in reading his aphoristic verses—satisfaction, too, in scoring us for finding them funny? *Aphorism closes rather than opens the field*. It expresses an extremity of disaffiliation. Yes, because, as *disaffiliate* reminds us, a primary meaning is dissociation from a gangster-ridden organization. "A for Ism": that is, telling instances of the Ism of our time, our very culture, *Americanism*, the very much lost America of love for which it is now so hard to summon any love.

Consider Raymond Williams' useful summary distinctions on the individual and society in *The Long Revolution*.

> To the *member*, society is his own community. . . . To the *servant*, society is an establishment, in which he finds his place. To the *subject*, society is an imposed system, in which his place is determined. To the *rebel*, the particular society is a tyranny; the alternative for which he fights is a new and better society. To the *exile*, society is beyond him, but may change. To the *vagrant*, society is a name for other people, who are in his way or who can be used.

Consider *vagrant* and Dorn's early comments on the American West and the stranger (concluding with: "All homes have become questionable, a man holds as many strings as possible").

> When we think of the vagrant we think naturally of such people as tramps and the fringe of society to which many criminals belong, but the condition of the vagrant—the essential negation of relationships which he embodies—is not confined to these obvious examples. In some societies it is possible to live out this condition with considerable material success, and there are signs, in some modern thinking, that the condition of the vagrant is the only available condition of man in society: whatever a man does, this is how he feels, and, given a particular social atmosphere, there is no need even to pretend otherwise. . . . The one thing the vagrant is certain of is that all the others who are not vagrants are fools, killing themselves for meaningless meanings, pretending to meanings.

Aphorism. Author-attitudes and literary styles, as Paul Goodman knew so well.

Aphorism: :*Epigram*, a short poem treating concisely, pointedly, and often satirically of a single thought or event and often ending with a witticism or ingenious turn of thought (Webster's Third).

> *To be good at sports*
> *you must be spiteful*
> *and horrible.* (26)
>
> * * *
>
> The most oecological way
> to kill the fleas
> is to kill the dog.
> ("Distraction Control"!)

Epigram, often in the form of the couplet or quatrain, but better defined by its tone. (*Princeton Encyclopedia of Poetry and Poetics*).

> When I slam the door on your finger
> I'm just milking your venom.
> ("Spuw Slang")
>
> * * *
>
> Even if you didn't know a thing
> you could read Chichén Itza.
> ("A Tour of the Capital")
>
> * * *
>
> These dispatches should be
> received in the spirit
> of the Pony Express:
> light and essential.
> ("PREFACE")
>
> * * *
>
> A poet's occupation
> is to compose poetry
> The writing of it
> is everywhere
> ("A for Ism")

The poetry he composes in this volume, whether long or short, is aphoristic, epigrammatic, closed, and corroborates his acknowledged interest in the eighteenth century—an (the) age of epigram. And corroborates what Barbara Herrnstein Smith says of "Epigram and Epigrammatic" in *Poetic Closure,* especially in the epigrammatic pages (208–209) where she notes that "the epigrammatist does not have 'Negative Capability.'"

1 February 1979

Never a theoretician, he nevertheless works out a poetics in "A for Ism" and updates "Projective Verse" in the interest of his own present work. Defines his differences from Olson.

A poet's occupation.

> *Oh poet, you should*
> *get a Jobooski.*
> ("The Russian Quote")

Olson's advice, and as we take up this book he lets us know that he is gainfully employed (not gainfully unemployed). Olson might not have liked this book anymore than he liked *Gunslinger,* but Dorn contends (declares) that he is doing (the?) essential poetic work. I read *occupation* as *vocation,* though it may be read otherwise, for example, in a military sense.

To compose poetry. Compose—played against *writing*?—is a charged word. It bears the weight of "composition by field" and the distinction between "literature" (past writing) and "poetry" (the vital imaginative sallies of the present time). The classic instance of its usage, the touchstone for this generation of poets, is Williams' introduction to *The Wedge* (1944), where, in time of war, he defends his vocation.

> The war is the first and only thing in the world today [he begins]. The arts generally are not, nor is this writing a diversion from that for relief, a turning away. It is the war or part of it, merely a different sector of the field.

Yes, probably having this in mind as well as Williams's specific instructions for composition—taking note also of Williams's recognition that the relation of art to society is complex and "the poet isn't a fixed phenomenon, no more is his work"—Dorn occupies a different sector of the field. In his lecture at Iowa, the burden of which is the clarification and divestment of Olson's influence, he makes these salient points: that Olson did not give him the eighteenth century, which is now his preoccupation; and that Olson did not often front immediate cultural reality, but, like many writers, put it off in order to do his own work. But Dorn's work is to front (confront) that reality. This is one possible reading of

> The writing of it [poetry]
> is everywhere

Everywhere—even La Jolla—provides the occasion for poetry. Not just Gloucester, not only *places*—but every *where*. And in his defense there's Williams's famous passage:

> When a man makes a poem . . . he takes *words as he finds them interrelated about him* and *composes* them . . . into an intense expression of his perceptions and ardors that they may constitute a revelation in *the speech that he uses*. (my italics)

That certainly applies to these poems. *The words as he finds them*: the writing (on the wall?) is everywhere. And he *composes*, but whether he "reconcile[s] / the people and the stones"—the work enjoined by Williams in "A Sort of a Song"—is questionable. No *ardors* here. He *disturbs* us.

And for cause.

2 February 1979

The eighteenth century provides Dorn the example of the epigram and the example of the use to which he puts it. In that century writers did the work of investigation that he recalls us to in endorsing Ed Sanders's *Investigative Poetry*. Sanders, he reminds us, was one of Olson's favorites; and Olson is one of Sanders's favorites (*Investigative Poetry* is dedicated to his memory). So Olson, curiously, is a model of the very thing Dorn finds lacking in him. Perhaps the epigraph explains this.

> Investigative Poetry: that poetry
> should again assume responsibility
> for the description of history

History replaces his-story. (And description replaces enactment? Life isn't, as Olson would have it, preoccupation with itself, life tracking life? One tracks history. "Man is; He acts"—but his act is of this investigative kind.) Or history doesn't replace his-story, only on the condition that the acts of attention that comprise one's story involve historical events. Dorn is not giving us his-story as in his earlier work, but "data clusters" relating to the immediate cultural occasion. Like a few of the verses in Creeley's *Pieces*. Sanders says that *Howl* is "a work of American history." If so, so is *Hello, La Jolla*; "indictment verse," like *Howl*. Lacking, of course, the bardic breath and hysteria (pun on history?). Controlled by the epigrammatic form, by the "Straight Information" that Gunslinger says is his ammunition.

And this guy, Dorn, is a dead(ly) shot.

The lecture at Iowa that mystified us was as calculated as the white space of this book, as deliberate as each carefully formed sentence. Dorn was not about to tell us where he had been, but only where he was, and the lecture prefaced his reading of the poems in *Hello, La Jolla*. He triangulated his position and acknowledged his own ambivalence about it by reading chiefly from Sanders' alarum, "To the Z-D Generation," on the exigence of investigation, and by questioning it with the skeptical response of Jeremy Prynne, whose trust in the zealous, even when poets, is probably less than Dorn's, and the corroboration of Tom Rawarth's gossip about the doings of poets at an international gathering at Amsterdam.

What is Sanders up to? He wants to correct the drift of a particular civilization, as it happens. He wants to investigate the investigators (exterminate the exterminators), to wage a war of truth against the secret agencies (we know their names, their acronyms) by "J'Accuses" (Zola) and "Encyclopedic Paradigms" (Diderot), and by keeping the issues alive. He would enlist 10,000 Z-D's (Zola-Diderots) and so "save America."

No question that what he asks us to investigate exists and America had better be saved from the drift of that. But isn't it questionable to think that 10,000 investigators, even if all were poets, would/could correct the drift? Dorn brought Sanders' mimeographed "To the Z-D Generation" to our attention as a secret document (a few copies were available to prime the duplicating machines); there was about his oblique lecture as about Sanders' paper the very sense of conspiracy that defines the "enemy." How portentously he noted a remark on difficult times of transition by Antonio Gramsci, a revolutionist imprisoned by the fascists, known for the reflections of his *Prison Notebooks*.

Sanders conflates the graphic possibilities of open poetry and comic book. He is a master of popular culture. At the expense, sometimes, of seeming parodic even of that, infantile, regressively sixtiesish, obsessed. Dorn, too, is such a master, but *Recollections of Gran Apachería*, for example, uses the comic book format to other ends, to impugn the means and mentality of popular culture, to make us aware, by contrast with the poems themselves, of another discourse of high seriousness that might well be lost in the drift of our particular civilization. Seldom does a comic book package anything so little comic as the story of the Apaches. But Sanders?—you'd think his was the only language available not just the only one he finds serviceable.

To some extent Dorn endorses Sanders' insistence on investigation. To a greater extent he endorses the conspiracy to which it is directed. Like all of us he has the justifiable paranoia Pynchon depicts (awakens) in *The Crying of Lot 49*. That history—the drift—does not make him hysterical is only explained, perhaps, by his deep resources of mordancy.

He is an uncomfortable man because he cannot follow Sanders or be the investigative poet *within* society he would like to be. He has studied the eighteenth century, as we know from the verse of *Hello, La Jolla* (and such verse as "The Cobbett Quote" and "The Baron Macauley Quote," and his Gibbon-ish use of footnotes). But neither his elegance nor his eloquence will make him a Charles James Fox, the great opponent of George the Third's tyrannies he so admires. He lacks footing: lectures and poetry readings are not substitutes for parliament (even Congress), and this may be the reason why I feel that such artfulness as he brings to them is wasted.

Neither will the *Bean News* make him a Freneau.

Olson relinquished a career in politics to become a poet whose project was to initiate another kind of nation. It is not possible, is it, given the fact of conspiracy in government, for a poet to relinquish poetry for politics? Of poets who have had careers in government, who is there besides MacLeish? Is Baraka an example of the possibility of another kind of political footing? Why didn't Dorn mention his early friend? Is Max Weber's "Politics as a Vocation" the last word?

3 February 1979

Don't let the breezy "hello" of *Hello, La Jolla* fool you. Take "The Sanders Quote":

> *Ye writes where ye can. With*
> *your bloody fingers on a prison wall*
> *if necessary.*

Or "Beyond the Air Bag":

> Sensing that Mediation is soon
> to be carried too far, the majority[a]
> [a]which includes everyone *
> are very queezy about being "read"
> as *ready* for the neutron bomb.
> The immediate floating of the
> ideological Razor,
> "kills people, saves property."
> creates a calculated tension between
> what is human, and what is desired.
> Desire
> is irrepressible.

The heavily footnoted, heavy-footed *Alaska: In Two Parts* (the title may be read in two ways) brings Billy's frontier up-to-date. Honest Americans are asked to show their honesty by emigrating. And the open road is not open, only the scrawl of the writer who writes while driving, his eyes "fixed to the road." Of course we are at the end of the open road. San Diego always was. Back in the 1930s, Edmund Wilson called it "the jumping-off place" because of the incidence of suicides and because here "you seem to see the last futile effervescence of the burst of the American adventure." Dorn closes his book with "Sunset":

* Dorn does not place the footnote here, but here is where he reads it, as part of the poem.

La Jolla is glittering this evening
They say we might get the green flash.

The prefatory verse says that we should receive these dispatches "in the spirit" and "in the spirit / of the Pony Express." The latter spirit is "light and essential." The Pony Express is invoked for one reason, certainly, and probably for another. Commenting on this verse, Dorn said of the Pony Express that "at $5.00 an ounce, the only hedge against junk mail we had." But I like to think—since there is no other evidence—that the Pony Express is an instance of something else he said when speaking of the Preface: "A country is changing, but still has its past coming through the filters in a nice way."

ROBERT DUNCAN

24 September 1979

A *R.D. Book*? Isn't *The H.D. Book* a model of inquiry? of "tribute and study"? of open criticism? Admirative, as Bachelard says. Admire first, then judge. The lesson of Duncan's practice and of his comments on the reception of H.D.'s *Trilogy*—on the unresponsiveness (response is responsibility) and easy strictures of critics like Randall Jarrell and Dudley Fitts. These comments in late installments—the last obviously first, having moved him throughout his long demonstration of the learning, understanding, risk of participation refused in our time by "orthodox" critics.

His corpus strewn with the bodies of critics, the "inert mediocrities" who dominated the period of his emergence; with those, he says in the preface to the revised *Caesar's Gate*, who objected to his "sentimentality" and "philosophizing," vices, he adds, first noted by Olson in "Against Wisdom as Such."

You might say that the entire *H.D. Book* answers Jarrell's remark that "Imagism was a *reductio ad absurdum* upon which it is hard to base a later style"—that in answering, it gives a corrected version of the poetic ground, the great enterprise, common to modernism and postmodernism.

The H.D. Book works out and exemplifies a poetics of inclusiveness—of the outlawed and out-of-bounds—and justifies Duncan's heterodox practice in verse and prose; does this as in mid-career he searches out in others a poetics necessary to self-making, the "soul's way." And it not only answers the strictures of New Critics but of an ally in what he considers their great adventure, Olson, whose admonishment against the magic of poetry in "Against Wisdom as Such" jeopardized his poetic life by calling in question its very source.

"The voices of disapproval remain, for they are part of what the poet knows and feels. Deeper, they have been incorporated in the poet's psyche, taken-to-heart. The old arguments against the cult of beauty, against Imagism, against the ecstatic, against the occult and mytho-poeic crowd in to impersonate the poet's own duality between doubt and conviction in writing."

25 September 1979

"Against Wisdom as Such," *Black Mountain Review*, 1954. First received by Duncan as a letter, in a correspondence notable for generosity, Duncan, we find, having encouraged Olson in the trials of composing the early *Maximus* poems. Criticism so much to the point of all he valued—he had already taken H.D. as a master—that he was profoundly disturbed, as he continued to be to judge from the frequent references to Olson's letter and the prominence of Olson—no contemporary so conspicuous—in his work. And challenged, adversity provoking the adverse (see the etymology of *verse* in Part II, Chapter 8 of *The H.D. Book*), calling out the warlike, the *brown warrior* in his very name, his commitment to the Heraclitean principle of creative strife.

He tells us that he could never have written the "small . . . proper book," the appreciation Norman Holmes Pearson asked him to write to mark H.D.'s seventy-fifth birthday (September 10, 1961; she died later that month). He was too deeply implicated in H.D., so deeply that only the work of "essential autobiography" would begin to fathom their relationship. (Is this tribute to H.D. equivalent to her *Tribute to Freud*? her *End to Torment*? Or perhaps in another sense than McAlmon's, another *Being Geniuses Together*, Duncan's genius nurtured, sustained, and ripened in devotion to hers—and those of her confreres?) What is remarkable here—in contrast, say, to the direct attack on Robin Blaser for the disservice to Poetry of his translations of Nerval or on Hayden Carruth and Adrienne Rich for considering art as property rather than communal resource—is the restraint, the withholding of motive until late in the book, when he keeps the book open by turning back on it, making it itself the object of attention. The motive? Resistance. He would "take up arms for her honor," fight for her (their) cause; the book itself would be a challenge worn on his sleeve.

And hasn't its periodical publication over the years kept that challenge alive? (Hasn't the difficulty of finding the installments been challenging?) And kept this life-enabling book open, as open as his verse, always incomplete, there for revision, in answer to his compelling need to remain open, to keep his life unfulfilled? ("Let me not come into fulfillment until the end of all things.") And doesn't its size measure his challenge and in that degree answer Olson?

Had Olson undertaken a comparable book, wouldn't it have been *The E.P. Book*? And Creeley? Certainly, *The W.C.W. Book*. Who but Duncan would have done—could have done—an *H.D. Book*, have chosen a poet of such (seemingly) little standing and raised her up among the acknowledged masters? H.D. is to R.D. as Virgil and Beatrice are to Dante. "Thou art my master and my author." *Author*: not only writer but originator, mother, source, as the dream of stroking her back has it and poems in *Roots and Branches*, correlative with beginning *The H.D. Book*, also tell us. And this before her death transformed the occasion of the book; much earlier in his career, in the 1940s, when he discovered *Trilogy*; even earlier, at the very beginning, as we find in the memory opening the book, when his life and his vocation, the soul's way of poetry, were decided by hearing a high school teacher of English read H.D.'s "Heat."

"I go where I belong, inexorably"—H. D. in *The Flowering of the Rod*.

An inevitable book.

26 September 1979

A model of entering, of making another's work the ground of one's being. Reading / writing: rites of participation. "Participation is all." Ground work. Does this title of Duncan's forthcoming book play on *Grund / begründen*, as Kerényi plays on them in *Essays on the Science of Mythology*? In its root sense *verse* is ground work, and so is the work of *gestalten*. And he has set himself to work the common ground to a communal end ("all mankind's experience . . . taken as the true ground of reality"). But isn't the essential ground work for him the recovery of source that Jungians refer to in *participation mystique*? "My initiation of self as poet in the ground of the poet H. D." We witness the "life of [a poet] crossing and interpenetrating [the] life of [a] poet." In an open form, itself a demonstration of this weaving—the following out of threads of association, the knottings that for him are one of the metaphors of organic proceeding, unfolding, processual form. Nets. Constellations. Catches (where lyre is net, as in Robert Eisler's *Orpheus the Fisher*). He fishes the sea and the sky, a fisher of Man. His gathered/clustered words are catches of imagination, of cosmic music, too.

"The net is not the world; it is the imagination of the world."

He speaks of H. D.'s art as tapestry, and explores his own dream (of art) as an unfinished hooked rug. So he weaves his life into and out of the fabric of hers. This is *The R.D. Book*, his source book, glossary. What *Bottom: On Shakespeare* is to Zukofsky, as he himself remarks. If you would open his field, enter his ground, you must read it. No critic will better it. It shows what he thinks (he has thought widely and deeply; his ideas have grandeur) and how he thinks (along lines of association that can be endlessly advanced because he begins again and again by returning to their source, by saying, so to speak, their seed-word). Like *The Truth & Life of Myth*, a later work employing this (Freudian?) method of exploration, it gives "essential autobiography." That is, as he says of the *inbinding*, it involves "a process returning to roots of first feeling" and so, as he says of the redeemed soul, recalling Orphic mysteries, requires that he drink of the "fountain of memory," recover the generative-erotic source, childhood, the soul's initial place. Essential autobiography belongs to the soul, to the psyche. And to eros. Psyche and Eros, "primordial members" in the myth, the story of "what Man is," that he wishes to trace, tell, enact. His essential myth, treated in both *The H.D. Book* and *The Truth & Life of Myth*.

Essential autobiography accounts for the life of the soul told by poetry. That is why he tells it by reconstructing the composition of his own poems, and why his introduction to *Caesar's Gate*, with its reproof of M. L. Rosenthal, isn't petty. Poetry is so much the essential life of poets that essential autobiography is essential to explaining it.

Isn't essential autobiography all that really concerns him in his recent introduction to Allen Upward's *The Divine Mystery*? Isn't he especially sympathetic with the "changeling" (I almost wrote "foundling") whose "true self is hidden in a story-world," who, in his work, "remains true to his origins," who, like Jane Harrison, does not abandon so much as redeem the narrow religious views of his parents?

(And isn't the fact that Pound reviewed Upward's book essential, too?)

The Truth & Life of Myth. Myths tell us who we are, "the true story of who I am." Life tracking life. His-story. And more: that he subscribes to a universe of agencies, potencies, divine powers, to a living cosmos, divine not fallen; and in consequence has both an ecological and ecumenical faith. He speaks of the sense of "universal humanity" to be found in "the mixing-ground of man's commonality in myth."

Open. Never closed. Because *The H.D. Book* demonstrates what it proposes: movement toward the achievement of form in the intuition of Form, the totality of inclusions never to be reached (like Whitehead's God?). Form, the fullness of time, a temporal matter spatially-conceived, *all there at once*. An evolution of forms where Form informs the forming. A life of forms, then, in which his own life and forms participate: that dance. So that the round dance, which is as much an insistence of *The Opening of the Field* as the terms of its title, is an image of community, of the total living Form of both Poetry and Society. This is why his poetics is a politics, why he believes the good of a poem can never be more than the good of society, why his thought reaches its apogee in "Rites of Participation" (Part I, Chapter 6), which begins, "The drama of our time is the coming of all men into one fate, 'the dream of everyone, everywhere.'" (The last phrase is H.D.'s, from *Tribute to Freud*, where she extols Freud's discovery of dreams, the common property and universal language of humankind that would enable us to understand and perhaps save ourselves.) Poetry is a rite of participation serving the commune of all that lives—and "everything," as Duncan exclaims with Pythagoras, "is sentient!"—the end coded in the primal cell. And the rite of participation is a *right* to all that poetry (Poetry) has been and can do that he would not be denied by Olson, who recognized the occult in Duncan's early work but not the whole of which it is only an indicative part—which, in fact, is what *The H.D. Book*, where Mme. Blavatsky is considered as fully and seriously as Freud, sets straight. As Olson should have known since, as Duncan says, he "calld us to dance the Man" and made second birth, the search for Self (soul), our true work. Poetry is soul-making, the poet's work, Duncan's, H.D.'s, Olson's, necessary to the human history called Poetry because the story is one of survival, of "the evolution of forms in which life survives." And *that*, as Duncan tells it, is the great story of modernism and postmodernism.

So our concern is not only or primarily with art but "through art to find what life might be." Art—the collective consciousness, the WORD that Bill Rueckert puts at the summit of NATURE and CULTURE—art is the ever-generative repository of our imaginative achievements where life can be recovered because language is also a community—"a community of meanings as deep and as wide as the nature of man has been." To limit language to discourse and meaning to a property of a system is to imperil life. There is nothing grandiose in speaking of Poetry as the story of survival. There are forms of decadence and forms of growth, as Louis Sullivan knew, and in the service of a more abundant life, the artist is asked to find forms of growth, of survival. *The Pisan Cantos, Paterson,* and *Trilogy* are exemplary for this reason.

A writer lives in the writing, has life there, as in this instant/instance. A reader, too, if he reads as well as Duncan, accepts his rights of participation.

How salutary the conjunction of art and life! In art itself "to become impure with life."

27 September 1979

The H.D. Book, incomparably rich (impure) with life, bringing to notice so much that is hidden and excluded, corroborating George Butterick's statement that the postmodern categorically includes more. Inclusiveness necessarily begets impurity, but those who welcome it do not consider it impure.

A great book of criticism, a critical achievement to stand with Olson's collected prose writing, both epical in Olson's definition of epic as pedagogical, having at heart "the teaching purpose, the paideumatic." The most fully developed organic poetics, pushing the *projective* of "Projective Verse" into occult and spiritual realms proscribed but sometimes entered by Olson, opening the *field* to the mysterious universe of latent or hidden meanings, not only to a universe of energies but to a universe of correspondences that petition us to be read. (In keeping with the cartographical sense of projection, Olson plots and maps the universe, he makes his *mappemunde,* a map of the Self, as Charles Stein shows, where Duncan no Jungian, though on that account not exempt from Jungian interpretation, "reads" the universe in a more Freudian fashion.) A superb essay on rhyme, on modern aperiodic forms (not only irregular but open: without period), on their weaving, constellating, aggregating, on the organic correlations of physics and physiology, genetics and evolution. An indispensible book on modern and postmodern poetry, where the counters of critical discourse are again made resonant, more so, or more usefully, than in Brown's *Love's Body*. And a grammar of poetry to put beside (aside?) *The White Goddess*. A revisionist history of modernism, especially of Pound, Williams, H.D., and Lawrence, writers who went in search of strange gods; of Imagism (the image as eidolon, and so still efficacious in *The Pisan Cantos, Paterson, Trilogy*); of the "female genius," the hardships of H.D., Virginia Woolf, Dorothy Richardson, Laura Riding, part of the recent history of the transformation and restoration of the Great Goddess; of the occult, theosophical, gnostic, kabbalistic, romance, and other outlawed traditions as the ground(s) of modern art. In sum, an account of the "spirit of Eleusis" and of the recovery by a saving remnant of "the mothering Life or Great Mother."

Ground work: chthonic: the old order.

He himself begins at the time of World War II where these modernists began at the time of World War I, bereft of Persephone (Kore), desolate, in the waste land. And isn't his work, already proposed in "Persephone" and other mythically allusive poems of *The Years as Catches*, to bring Kore out of the hell of war-ravaged civilization into the meadow, the open field of restored life to be opened by an open, inclusive poetry? Doesn't Williams, whom he treats so well in *The H.D. Book*, chart the course? From *Kora in Hell* to *Spring and All*, the later the first adumbration of the open, inclusive form Duncan seeks.

And doesn't war evoke one of the profound informing dreams of his work, the Atlantis dream told in "Occult Matters" (Part I, Chapter 5)? "I belonged . . . to the generation that had been destroyed in a cataclysm before the world we lived in began." ("At dawn in Oakland in the cold of the year I was born, January 7th [1919], with the sun before rising.") His fearful dream, like that of the Eleusinian mysteries, tells of emergent life out of death (the birth that cost his mother's life), only Kore is not vouchsafed him. "In my life dream, I have not seen the Maiden, for I stand in her place or in her way."

28 September 1979

No ideas but in things. You read the universe, the meaning(s) in things, as Levertov says so well in "An Admonition." You can constellate it, as Duncan proposes in the exalted opening to Part II of *The H.D. Book*, because the universe itself rhymes, because, as Fenollosa says, "metaphors do not spring from *subjective* processes" but follow "the objective lines of relations in nature herself." *This* makes it mysterious, to be searched out; is why, as with Emerson in *Nature*, Duncan evokes the stars and gives us a cosmic field of endeavor, suggests not only the "occult relation between man and the vegetable" (Emerson) but, all-inclusively, an occult relation to every realm of the universe.

"The imagination of this cosmos is as immediate to me as the imagination of my household or myself," he says in "Towards an Open Universe" (an important gloss on what *open* in open poetry means), "for I have taken my being in what I know of the sun and of the magnitude of the cosmos." No idle assertion! This, finally, is what it means to follow a sound, an image, a line, to create a form in that obedience: to find oneself in "a cosmos in which the poet and the poem are one in a moving process," are indeed participating, like dancers, in the cosmic round of on-going creation. To follow in this fashion pushes Fenollosa's notion that the syntax of a sentence follows the syntax of nature to its ultimate Orphic conclusion: "Poetry enacts in its orders the order of first things." It, too, is a rhyme—the rhyme of creation itself.

And the *structure of rime*? Isn't that to be found in the universe?

Duncan restores much that Melville called "flummery": to "Live in the All," the Goethean injunction translated by Carlyle (a Duncan source), "To live . . . in the Whole," the privilege of creation, which Melville, acutely aware of the sovereign imagination of romantics and transcendentalists, derided as being in on the creation. Poets often claim prerogatives of kingship and use imagination as a scepter. Duncan, too, early on, up to *Caesar's Gate*. But in his mature and enabling thought, the poet lives in the whole (field) and creates in service to, in behalf of the whole creation. He is an agent of life more consciously aware than most of us of this agency, and more conscious than many poets that he is necessarily derivative, that he depends on, and therefore is at the service of, language and tradition, of what has been created. Still, the primordial is not behind but before him, and the act of poetry opens into it. He does his work in the light of Whitehead's philosophy, not Kant's. He knows with Whitman, the

> Urge and urge and urge,
> Always the procreant urge of the world.

29 September 1979

Correspondences, not in the dualistic, hierarchical sense of higher and lower, spiritual and mundane, that finds its counterpart in the structure of Emerson's poems and makes their activity (Imagination = "Reason") one of transcendence. Field work, ground work, rather. Not an *Augenmensch* like the Concord see-er, reading the world upward into symbol and idea (Idea), but a weaver who connects, juxtaposes, overlays its images; a listener who, hearing resonances, responds. His practice is closer to Emerson's in prose, which, as David Porter has recently shown, is the open form(al) outcome of Emerson's descendentalism and constitutes his legacy to the insurgent tradition of American poetry.

Emerson. A source not recognized by Olson, banned by him at Black Mountain!, which may account for Duncan's mentioning him in his essay on *The Maximus Poems*. Dewey, too: *Art as Experience*. He knows the American lineage, his ground, just as he knows the American history of occultism. "I point to Emerson or to Dewey to show that in American philosophy there are foreshadowings or forelightings of *Maximus*." A poetry of energies, of act. But in *The H.D. Book*, where William James figures, the important aspect of the tradition is *experience*, its fullness, its inclusiveness—what prose in its spaciousness better permitted Emerson to accommodate. "It is 'the total world which is' that concerns James; and in his sense that What is is multifarious, in his insistence upon the many strands [all the realities of fact and fiction, vision, dream, madness, vagary, the supernatural, etc.] we must come to see before consciousness have something like the fullness demanded by What is, James is kin to Emerson before him and to Dewey and Whitehead after."

Olson introduced him to Whitehead, where he found the remark he often quotes: "We may not neglect the multifariousness of the world—the fairies dance and Christ is nailed to the cross." *Multifarious* and *multiphasic*: "A multiphasic experience sought a multiphasic form." So he seeks "those forms that allow for the most various feelings in one, so that a book is more than a poem, and a life-work is more than a book."

The discipline of totality, as Olson speaks of it: "And the reason is very much tied to field—to that which I have called the virtue of totality: that experience is such (is so rich), that the more kinds of experience one includes, etc. . . . This constellating of experience and attentions is such a breeder of values that one can say that just here is the gain which has undone all hierarchy."

Kin to Whitman, too, whose inclusivity of Self is also a democratic, a political value, and whose witnessing reminds us that the witnessing of such experience is a distinguishing quality of our literature. "By good art," Pound says, "I mean art that bears true witness," truth to the "wholeness of [one's] experience."

An *open* universe is both on-going and all-inclusive; an *open* poetics, opening to What is, permits the poet to search out an idea of humankind "big enough to live freely in."

Has anyone since Whitman done as much as Duncan to further Emerson's aesthetics of liberation? Does anyone since Whitman stand so much with Emerson in having "the very heightened sense of relatedness of everything" that, Duncan claims, "sets poets apart"?

1 October 1979

Such pedagogues! In poems, too: Olson, in "The Praises"; Duncan, in "Spelling" (trespassing on Olson's etymological territory!). *Mutheologoi*, concerned, as Duncan's title puts it, with *The Truth & Life of Myth*, Duncan's book, of the size and import of Olson's *The Special View of History*, to be compared with it. (He had heard these lectures in 1957, and of the qualities or basic conditions remembered the primacy accorded love: "It is with EROS that mythology is concerned."

And didn't he go farther than Olson in securing that primacy, not, as with Olson, by amending Hesiod, but by evoking the Orphic theogony?) As different, though not wholly differing, as their books, so that what Duncan says in *The H.D. Book,* where he so often challenges and corrects Olson, is true and turns the lesson of "Against Wisdom as Such" back on Olson: "Our wise is not more or less than our ways." His wise was unavoidable, as "Occult Matters" shows, his inheritance, poetic ground, essential autobiography he could not alienate. He knew—and again Olson is part of the context—"that the sum of our wisdom was what the dead knew. Wise with what was dead in us." Wise with what was hidden. In a chapter acknowledging Olson ("A psyche will be formed having roots in all the old cultures; and—this seems to me one of the truths I owe most to Charles Olson's poetry—the old roots will stir again"), he concludes by citing the criticism of "Against Wisdom as Such" and declaring in behalf of the wisdom of his way, "There is something about looking behind things." Then, the assertion: "There is the fact that I am not an occultist or a mystic but a poet, a maker-up of things."

Olson recalls, in an advertisement of *The Years as Catches* (1966), his first meeting Duncan in 1947, and then con-fusing past and present, says:

> Right, from the start. A *beautiful* Poet. The Wings of poetry. And since, each gathering light, illumines more. Ancient, permanent wings of Eros—& of Orphism . . .

Is he repudiating "Against Wisdom as Such"? If so, isn't it because not only in his own development as a poet but in Duncan's relentless instruction he had learned to appreciate the many ways of poetry?

In *The H.D. Book* Duncan places Olson within the more inclusive traditions of modern poetry that he had explored in his own education as a poet. And he does what he did in "A Poem Beginning with a Line by Pindar": puts Olson in the context of his own concerns, in juxtaposition with his—and Olson's—masters. One of the things both book and poem emphasize is survival, endurance, and courage in the way of poetry. And, as he tells it in terms of H.D.'s career, how wayward the way is, how easily one is sidetracked by the social groupings in which one finds oneself. As he perhaps had been when he was associated with Spicer and Blaser and was writing "Medieval Scenes," personal history, "feverish youth," recollected in "Shadows" ("Passages 11")?

Did their differences really matter in the face of apocalypse? After all, didn't they share a common adventure "in a time when only one vision—the vision of an atomic disaster and the end of the species—haunts the world," as he says in *The Truth & Life of Myth*, and "men labor to exorcise all the old stories"? How wonderfully Duncan has it in his dream of the last day, itself a single installment of the book and a dream of the importance of his Atlantis dream and like it derived from the earliest stories his parents had told him. The world is coming to its end in fire, and he finds himself called to redirect the spring of all the mythic lore that has fallen from the heavens, and at the spring he meets Olson, at once a Doctor and a Zaddik, an Einstein who "knows the numbers of the cosmos" (as Olson does in "The Praises") and a Freud, "the new Master over Love in H.D.'s life." Their work is to "restore the Milky Way, the spring of stars that is our mothering universe" (to "arch again / the necessary goddess," Olson says in "In Cold Hell, in Thicket"). Yes, but what is so lovely is the recognition and what it acknowledges: "As I saw it was

Charles—it was in his glance, how those familiar eyes beamed with the thought of our task together at the spring." The Doctor, he admits, had "a key to the old science of the spring." And then at the end, when Olson's eyes again beam on him, he recognizes him as "at once my superior and my companion in the work at the springs."

At the end was a father.

2 October 1979

In the beginning was the mother. That, in respect to himself, was the fact about *muthos* he had most to teach Olson. He had also to teach him the legitimacy of correspondence, the manifold nature of the image and the extent to which Imagism was the product of the renascent theosophy and psychology of the early twentieth century. And that poetry was rite, as much *dromenon*, the thing done, as *muthos*, the thing said. Saying was an act of arousal, enchantment, magic, a rite of participation enabling him to play a part in creation but also to make-up things and live with/in the realities of the imagination.

As he had insisted before in the biographical note to *The New American Poetry*, where he acknowledges a phase of his poetic growth omitted from *The H.D. Book*, the period at Berkeley, 1946–1950, when Spicer, later displaced by Olson, had been his mentor.

As for *muthos*, the mode of his inquiry, essential autobiography, verified the fact that for him in the beginning was the voice, in the beginning was the mother, the mothering voices. Like Phanes, in Orphic cosmogony, he had been enclosed in an egg, "in a shell of murmurings," had been "rimed round, / [a] sound-chamberd child." His mother, as "Tribal Memories," the first of the "Passages," also tells us, corroborating the first installments of "Beginnings" in *The H.D.*

Book, was herself Mnemosyne, mother of the Muses. In Chapter 2, he summarizes the initial chapter on the agency of women and voices in giving him his poetic destiny—the women, Miss Keough, his high school teacher, Athalie and Lili, his Berkeley classmates; the voices, Miss Keough's (and H.D.'s), his (and Joyce's), both teaching him resistance, that "the authority of the poem was a voice of the spirit" and that to heed that voice meant not taking orders from anything else—parents, university, the military. (The initial chapter unites poetry and love against the powers that make war. Like Olson: the necessary stance is resistant. Like Frank Lloyd Wright, of whom he personally reminds me: his genius is boundless—"the deepest drive of the artist, a yearning to participate in the primordial reality that challenges the boundaries of convention.") Then he adds, only to treat it later in "Occult Matters" and *The Truth & Life of Myth*, "In the very beginning, in the awakening of childhood back of this later awakening of the man I was to be, there had been my mother's voice reading the fairy tales and myths that were to remain the charged ground of my poetic reality." Which leads him on to Mnemosyne, to poetry as re-membering, to the notion (rejected) that poetry may be the mother of those who have destroyed their mothers, and, finally, to the notion (accepted) that "Poetry is the Mother of those who have created their own mothers."

"In the beginning I heard of guardian angels and of genii, of visions in dreams and truth in fairy tales, long before Jung expounded the gnosis or Henri Corbin revived and translated the Recitals of Avicenna." Isn't this directed at Olson?

4 October 1979

The Truth & Life of Myth is a reverie toward childhood. As Bachelard would have it, the conjoined activity of imagination and memory. It enacts Duncan's meditative/creative practice. It tells us, as the opening poem of *The Opening of the Field* does, that sometimes he is permitted to return to the source, to the mother and the fountain and those moments of childhood that he says are "created as Edens, the mythic seed of a power in the story to come." Not easily. He must find the "opening" word, "the releasing pattern of an inspiration," and now overcome the hesitancy of believing that he had already done this work—and too much of it—in *The H.D. Book*. But he hadn't come so far, and now presses on: "I too must go back . . . to childhood, where the germinal experience of poetry and myth lay." He would fulfill the dream he speaks of in a line sounding again the title of the opening poem of *The Opening of the Field*, "Sometimes I dream of at last becoming a child."

He recovers an episode of the mothering voices that surrounded him in childhood: hearing his mother read to him and his sister the famous poem of Bashō on the frog, the pond, the water sound, and, in investigating his act of memory, seeing the very scene, the picture window, the rectangular pond and its fountain. At this point, without explanatory transition, he mentions the story of Psyche and Eros and tells of searching for it, as he has the Bashō, in his childhood books. But when he finds it, it does not, like the Bashō, awaken childhood memories, and he notes that this story, which he had heard as a child, "belongs to my mature and studious reading."

The transition to the placing of the story of Psyche and Eros, he says a bit later, is an example of how mythic content comes to him and commands the design of the poem. And after a few pages on myth that are not as digressive as they seem because they prefigure his idea of the Passion of form-making, he picks up the story of Psyche and Eros again, where it is most present in his work, in "A Poem Beginning with a Line by Pindar." Then, telling how this "fable embodying the doctrine of the soul" wells up and takes over, he suddenly breaks off to relate his present intense experience, the weeping to which the very writing has brought him. The recollection (of the recollection) of his mother reading, of the fountain in the garden—this now associated with the flowing fountain of the primordial—brings him near to weeping. It is only when he considers the other associations that he weeps: the recollection of weeping in George Herbert's poems which he read in 1945, thinking then that Herbert wept, not as he did for unrequited love, but for man's sin and Christ's redemptive suffering; man's sin which he now confesses as his own, the "refusal of love in the desire to have love"; love, the very recognition of which also "moves us to tears." This remarkable passage concludes with a restatement of this powerful recollection, only to add another quite as powerful, the reference to García Lorca ("Garcia Lorca stole / poetry from this drinking fountain"), Lorca who figures most in the introduction to *Caesar's Gate* in respect to Duncan's early perturbations over homoeros. There he asks if "the singer steal[s] the water of his song from the fountain of generations?" and considers his childlessness, the fact that some poets give up the bearing of a son in the bearing of their art. But the burden of all this—and it addresses both "A Poem Beginning with a Line by Pindar" and *The H.D. Book*—is the following: "In my manly years, I weep for pain and in the pain of others, and for grief; and I weep for the power of works of art that break the reserves of my aesthetic and stand in the immediacy of first experience, and I weep for the courage of noble men."

6 October 1979

The Truth & Life of Myth addresses the mysteries of love. "It is with EROS that mythology is concerned" (Olson). At bottom, myth treats, as Duncan believes with Freud, the strife of Eros and Thanatos in the creative will. Like N. O. Brown, in

Life Against Death. And doesn't he, like Brown, belong to the Freudian left, with those who believe that eros will countervail the entropic forces of our time?

Thinking of writing "A Poem Beginning with a Line by Pindar," he thinks of Poetry as a fountain. He thinks not only of Psyche and Eros, who figure in that poem and in his recollection take him back to childhood, but of his creative work in making that poem, the passion, the suffering, of form-making, which is why he weeps for the courage of noble men (Pound, Williams), men who risk what Olson called "nakedness" ("the immediacy of first experience," the primordial), who even in old age leap into life. Which may be why that poem ends, recapitulating "Often I am Permitted to Return to a Meadow," with a vision of children dancing, their dance itself, as the *Kabbalah* has it, an initiation into creation *and* destruction.

Doesn't this explain how these recollections come together? At the very end of the book, in speaking of Christ's injunction to enter the dance, he says, "Each child, taking breath, leaps into life with such an anguish." The child's birth—and the later entry into life as Duncan depicts it elsewhere in the spirit of Hart Crane's "Voyages I"—already involves and so informs the anguish of art. Only suffering works the transformative miracle of Psyche's soul-making; only suffering works the transformative miracle of art. Both involve passion and must undergo the Passion, the anguish of which is "a truth of poetic form."

Christ supersedes Psyche and Eros. His Passion fables the artist. The first Eros is the wrathful Father, the Old Testament God, and the second Eros is the Son, who is loving. Or, the Father is Chaos, the "First Person of Form," and "the poet . . . like the Son, in this myth of Love or Form, must go deep into the reality of His own Nature, into the Fathering Chaos or Wrath, to suffer His own Nature."

"Love is form," Olson says. Born "of yourself, torn."

This myth belongs to both his-story (Duncan's) and to history. It is the truth of history, as, in re-membering it, he traces the vicissitudes of the loving Christ in church history and poetic tradition. In fact, both personally and historically, he re-*embers* it, kindles its presence. So he restores his Christ, the "ever-remembered Lord of Sensualities," as he says in "Another Animadversion," where he insists on the Incarna tion and the Passion as true signs of divinity.

7 October 1979

The recovery of the sense of the truth and life of myth accords with the work of reverie toward childhood. The opening word is (always) μυ, mu.

> μύζω (A) To make the sound μὺ μῦ or μυμῦ, to murmur with closed lips, to mutter, moan . . . (B) to drink with closed lips, to suck in.
>
> Liddell & Scott, *Greek-English Lexicon*, 1897 ed.
> (Duncan's initial epigraph)

"The first *muthos* was simply the interjectional utterance *mu.*" Jane Harrison, *Themis.*

Muthos, utterance; the sound of our anguish on first (and forever afterward) taking breath.

Why is it I recall "mimic murmurs of the sea" ("The Venice Poem") and "mimic flowers" ("The dancers / mimic flowers—root stem stamen and petal" in "The Dance")? I know they are among Duncan's most significant lines.

Bachelard, having cited Henri Capien's "Orbs of words, murmuring memory," turns immediately to the importance in reverie (remembering) of our "mother tongue." Later on, in *The Poetics of Reverie,* he notes that "the subconscious is ceaselessly murmuring, and it is by listening to these murmurs that one hears its truth."

In "The Homecoming" (1947) Duncan recalls Friedl's presence as that of the Great Goddess—the poem is clearly connected with "The Venice Poem"—and says:

> Every man is some woman's son
> who moans and becomes like Venus in her sleep.

H.D., in "Doves," one of Duncan's greatest poems, telling his love, restoring her to the "first world" before words, is "Mother of mouthings":

> Mother of mouthings,
> the grey doves in your many branches
> code and decode what warnings
> we call recall of love's watery tones?

Isn't it in "Epilogos" (*Bending the Bow*), a poem incorporating Keats's "Ode to Psyche," that the mimic murmurs of the sea and the mimic flowering unite?

> When I say *Love* the word comes out of me
> like a moan—life-sap. . . .

Mother of mouthings (*muthos*), mother tongue, vernacular. Vernacular, a common ground of Duncan's association of Dante and Whitman. Dante says we derive our first true speech from our mothers and nurses. Whitman says that it is "in embryons and childhood . . . we always find the ground-work and start" of language.

And there is Whitman's "Word out of the Sea," as "Out of the Cradle Endlessly Rocking" was once called, a poem that bears comparison with Duncan's "The Venice Poem," which in turn might well be read in the light of Duncan's Freudian reading of Whitman's poem as word out of the womb, where the mother is the sea, not the sea the mother. Yes, the sea in Whitman is primary for Duncan, who cites from "With Husky-Haughty Lips, O Sea!"

> The first and last confession of the globe,
> Outsurging, muttering from thy soul's abysms,
> The tale of cosmic elemental passion,
> Thou tellest to a kindred soul.

There is the terrifying sea of "The Venice Poem" (the Venus poem) and the birth of Venus—

> She rose out of a great rustling of waters,
> transformed in the sea roar
> within the shell.
>
> What is happening?
> music, magic,
> emerging
>
> out of the shell-coil ear
> the mimic murmur
> the remembering

Remembering.

> . . . the soothing voice
> in whose ambience first
> faith was full. . . .
>
> My mother's voice singing or crooning in a humming sound hovers above or around and passes into a silence of concentration which it becomes or survives, in which I work. (*The Truth & Life of Myth*)

The concrete image moves upward
  into the coherent
  only in sound,
  in the tone leading of vowels,
  in the humming, the hesitating.

9 October 1979

"The structure of my life like the structure of my work was to emerge in a series of trials," he says in the introduction to *The Years as Catches*, his earliest poems, reissued in 1966. Trials = tasks. The tasks of Psyche, after the loss of Eros. "These are the old tasks. / You've heard them before" ("A Poem Beginning with a Line by Pindar"). Among them the harrowing of hell.

Coming into manhood in a time of war, coming to poetry, too, outcast, driven, always in extremity. Tormented, as ever Hart Crane was, or Whitman, by the passional self; by the loss of love, by an unloving mother and distant lovers, by the need to find a poetry equal to his need, his yearning, his longing.

I sang and tried to fill the void.
The poet's art is a passionate fountain.

The presence of the meadow is known only by its absence. "I have forgotten the green and the opulent meadows."

Birds, fish, or self, all swift utterd things,
  [I hear Nina in *The Sea Gull*]
give agony, turn on the heart that is motionless
and warn it of distance, uncover the treacherous
lovely cold of the empty. . . .

The polar landscape of Crane's "North Labrador." Here, too, words "go utterly, utterd unheard, / into the ear of eternity" and love is the "unanswered hunger," "the restless immovable word that is lodged / in the unopened ear of beginning."

In the beginning lamentation, elegy, grief.

His work begins with the black, then opens into the green, and then earns the green, again and again, in the ever-presence of the black, knowing that strife rules the cosmos. In and of the green tradition, yet critical of it when it forgets the black, including Poe in his great Whitman poem.

Right from the start. Already a poet of high accomplishment. And all the essentials (myths) there awaiting their further opening.

When he gets beyond the Bardo state of *Caesar's Gate* (poems of 1949–50); when he begins to live with Jess Collins in their household (heart, hearth) in 1951. When he finds the more inclusive formal means, the confirmation of "Projective Verse" in 1950, the subsequent exercises after Gertrude Stein, the experimental formal play of these "Imitations" and of *Letters*. The loosening-up, even the limbering-up, if you remember that *melos* is limb and makes up the melody, not the symphonic melodies of "The Venice Poem" (1948) but the more atonal melodies that accord with the multiphasic dispositions of spatial form. "The Venice Poem"—a long poem of considerable merit, with echoes of Eliot's *Four Quartets*—this poem, he would say, is a hive, with that kind of formal perfection, to be visually represented by closed parenthesis ( ). But as Olson has it in "La Préface," his opening poem, "The closed parenthesis reads: the dead bury the dead, / and it is not very interesting." The allusion to Eliot's *The Waste Land*. The parenthesis must, as Duncan agreed, be opened.

Duncan's remarks on this stage of his development in the preface to *Caesar's Gate* acknowledge both an erotic and formal transformation. (His poetics is one of transformation, under the necessity, for one thing, of transforming lust to love. An erotic poetics. A poetics of eros, to help him with Psyche's tasks.) In the seven years between "The Venice Poem" and the inception of *The Opening of the Field* "the force of the poetics I had pursued," he says, "had overtaken me." And what had occurred—represented here as a fearful journey of poetic trial (and error)—was the "transformation of a continent into a life"—the continent, in *Caesar's Gate*, being a psycho-sexual wasteland, the Asia to which his work-and-life now gave him "passage." Passage to India, the first of many passages?

In another account of this development (in the context of *The Truth & Life of Myth*) he considers it an awakening. (Sleeping and waking are insistent terms in his work; "The Structure of Rime," in *The Opening of the Field*, begins with an injunction to wake up.) An awakening, prompted by Helen Adam's reading Blake to him in 1953. This, he says, both broke his "modernist pride [in] artistic achievement" (the formal hive and the will to achievement) and taught him that the myths he employed were more than psychological correlatives—"not only a story that expresses the soul but a story that awakens the soul to the real persons of its romance." Awakens the soul to its destiny in the "field of ensouling."

In recollecting this he cites Blake:

> O Earth, O Earth, return!
> Arise from out the dewy grass;
> Night is worn
> And the morn
> Rises from the slumberous mass.

—recollects the summons to open the field. Just as in his Whitman poem, he remembers with equal vividness reading Whitman:

. . . my own being at thirty-seven
in the opening of the field of grass you made for me . . .

And in his lecture at Iowa recalls listening to Olson's lectures on Whitehead in 1957, when he was beginning *The Opening of the Field.*

10 October 1979

"The Venice Poem" ends with his birth out of the fat form of the Venus of Lespuges. Zagreus? She *is*, he says; of first things; "Not Chaos, / but First Form," whence the "flood of first forms." And when he despairs he turns to her:

There must be a moment when that faith returns.
The artist searches out the deepest roots.

The Opening of the Field revives the Great Goddess, now Kore, queen of life and death. Turning to her verifies a claim made in "The Venice Poem:"

There is nothing unfair
he has not created
brooding upon the primitive source.

Where *brooding* tells us he has invoked Mnemosyne, the great speckled bird of "Tribal Memories"—mother of memory, and memory the means of his return to the mother.

Returning to his deepest roots: that turning marks the watershed of his career. The blurb on *The Truth & Life of Myth* is exact: "*The Truth & Life of Myth* stands as a major part—along with his work-in-progress *The H.D. Book*—in a projective imagination of the nature of Man and his Reality which has occupied Duncan's creative energies in three volumes . . . .: *The Opening of the Field* (1960), *Roots and Branches* (1964), and *Bending the Bow* (1968)."

Waking and *opening* and *making*. Making-up is essential.

making up, making my way
out of myself into the depths of my self

Once making up begins . . . the dreaming/reverie begins, and the voice of the poem "comes from a will that strives to waken us from our own personal will," and that entrancement (entrance-ment) "gives the poet both a permission and a challenge," the permission of the event and the challenge to remain wakeful to all the requirements of "the striving form." Isn't he explaining the opening of *The Opening of the Field*, as again, in the following? "The poet is not only a maker in the sense of the maker of the poem, but he makes up his mind, he makes up a world within a world, a setting of elements into play, that carries over into a maturity the make-believe of childhood, where, too, certain misunderstandings and mistakes led not to disaster but to fruitful pastures."

11 October 1979

The Opening of the Field. A constitutive metaphor. Annunciatory. Of act: this book opens the field. Declares the demonstration. Open Poetry: Field Composition: Projective Verse (opening *that*, too; advancing it; offering, among others, the instructive poems of "The Structure of Rime"). Field of *meanings*, woven of them, including the forbidden, the neglected, the unexpected. To have a poetry admitting them, the more inclusive kind he calls an ill-kept garden in his Berkeley lecture; the "field of rank growth beyond the projects of city-planning . . . beyond suburbs, that describe the limits of orderly discourse" that he remarks on in "Changing Perspectives in Reading Whitman." Beyond boundaries, out-of-bounds; fields of feeling, of fantastic life. The larger fields of Man, of Poetry.

Also plays off Olson's "In Cold Hell, in Thicket," especially the recognition of the *selva oscura*, the dark wood of the self, the wilderness of unopened life, and the need, by way of art, to break into the clear(ing), into the field: "there is always a field, / for the strong there is always / an alternative." H.D. confirms Olson when she says in *Tribute to Freud* (1956), "the *hieroglyph of the unconscious,* and the Professor had first opened the field to the study of this vast, unexplored region." *Field* is the unconscious, the dark, the chthonic, the cave, what in the earliest poems he speaks of as "the cave-home of our childhood" (and there, "the roots of sorrow"). The opening he seeks permits him to explore this ground, the field of his life, the field of life, and the field of fields, the cosmos. Here he begins the psychic journey of his subsequent work.

The field is earth itself (Olson: "an actual earth of value"); the "water fire earth and air," the natural elements that are "guardians" in "The Structure of Rime IV"; "that old, old Garden which is the Mother's heart." To open the field transforms the chthonic darkness, liberates the (re)generative natural forces, restores the Goddess (as in the *Anados* of Kore described by Jane Harrison).

> This is the Book of the Earth, the field of grass
> flourishing.
> This is the region that feeds forth souls under the old
> orders
> returning to the dominion of its King and Queen.
> . . . .
> This is the Book of the Provider.

To open the field restores the excluded gods, perhaps in the Heideggerian sense of disclosure. Saying as "opening the clearing," leading us "into the open," permitting the hidden to disclose itself, being to appear.

All to this end: "The grass must give up new keys to rescue the living."

12 October 1979

Could a poet so much concerned with renewal, with life-nurturing and -sustaining organic, generative powers, ever forget Whitman? And not, in our time, strive (Hermes-the-thief that he is) to find the keys to pick the locks of our prison? ("We think of the key, each in his prison": Eliot.) But keys are also new perspectives and methodologies—new generative ideas, as Susanne Langer says in *Philosophy in a New Key*. And keys are meanings: new meanings—and *renewed* meanings—for what was first tendered in *Leaves of Grass*. So he advances the Whitman line. The organic, green tradition. Truly: to such final recognitions as "the amoeba is my brother poet" and "'Everything is sentient!' / Everything has power over your being."

The new keys open to/ belong to the *old order*, as Jane Harrison speaks of all that preceded the Olympian order and, subsequently, was taken up again in the Orphic religion. Though Duncan here calls up other mythologies—Norse, Christian, Kabbalist—the mythic ground of the field is chiefly that of the Eleusinian mysteries, the "*ancient chthonic, & mother-daughter rites*" noted by Olson in "Apollonius of Tyana," who approved Apollonius' slighting the Olympian gods; the mysteries so important to Pound's *Cantos* as Leon Surette shows us in his brilliant book, *A Light from Eleusis*.

We are asked to go back to the ground and learn again (to respect) the mysteries of organic life, of generation, growth, and death; to acknowledge in the decay and growth of vegetation ("*burnt leaf of november and green of may*" is the refrain of "A Song of the Old Order") our dependence on the rhythm and the round of life. Christ's word to John, "If you have not entered the dance, you mistake the event," may be read as applying to this dance.

What is the mystery? That "at Eleusis Kore brought / out of Hell, health manifest." It is the transformation homophonically rendered here by *hell* ⟶ *health*. The mystery of the middenheap (Whitman's compost), of "rot" and "root," as the vowel-leading tells us; of the necessity of corruption, evil, and death to flowering, light, and love. To say that "this is the Book of the Earth, of the field of grass flourishing," says more than the mere apposition says: it says that the dark earth underlies (underwrites) the field. And this is true of his book, which includes the shards and rottings of his experience and the pestilence of the age. The title of the poem, "Nor Is the Past Pure," puns on *pasture*. The meadow to which the initial poem tells us he is permitted to return is not, this poem reminds us, "permitted without corruption." And he is not, in its evocation of childhood, permitted its innocence and security. He is not permitted, as he wishes to be in the penultimate poem ("Ingmar Bergman's SEVENTH SEAL"), to take refuge from the horrors of our age by returning to childhood. As an initiate of Eleusis, having seen Kore, "Queen of the Middenheap," his task is to participate in communal rites (the dance of poetry) that help us bring life out of death. The Eleusinian mysteries give him both the ground of his poems and their commitment.

14 October 1979

The dance. As much as for Olson the metaphor of poetry-as-act, as *kinesis*. Not for Duncan as for Olson most appreciated in the single dancer, but a communal rite, always, whether of the children in "Often I am Permitted . . ." or the adults in "The Dance," a communal round, a circle that figures the natural law, natural rhythms, and the living cosmos. The round dance of Jess's drawing on the title page (which seems to emerge from a black abyss and have its being in a leaf), "a ring around of roses," where *roses*, as the pun suggests, is the flowering of *eros*. The very circulations of being: "The Dance / from its dancers circulates among the other / dancers." And the beat of their feet ("Lovély thēir féet póund thē gréen sólīd méadōw"), like the "god-step" (the dithyramb that "makes Zeus leap or beget") that initiates "A Poem Beginning with a Line by Pindar," summons creation, transformation, the natural including poetry which Duncan considers "a natural thing." (See "Poetry, a Natural Thing" and "The Natural Doctrine.")

> The dancers
> mimic flowers—root stem stamen and petal
> our words are,
> our articulations, our
> measures.

The variations of the refrain enact an essential transformation of the poem (another is the work of memory, reviving his pristine vision of the meadow):

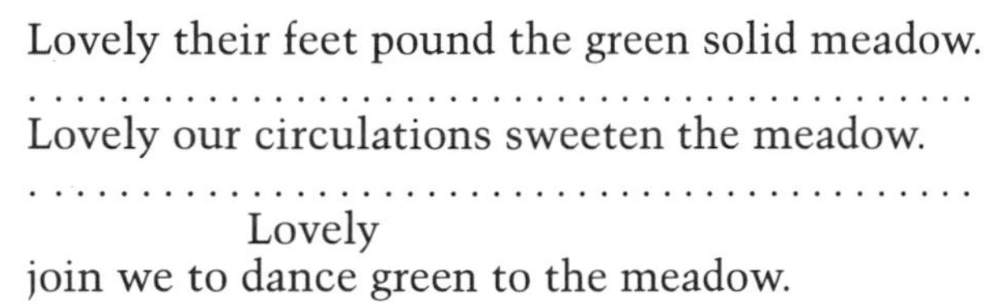

> Lovely their feet pound the green solid meadow.
> . . . .
> Lovely our circulations sweeten the meadow.
> . . . .
> Lovely
> join we to dance green to the meadow.

The advance in pronouns is also an advance to green.

"How near . . . the most sophisticated poetic comes in its hidden yearning to the first force of the round dancers."

The dance is efficacious, as in "Evocation," where, as he says, he renders "lovely the fall of Her feet" and evokes Kore. The *fall* being autumn also, as in the next line *spring* is also springtime, "where Her feet spring," where finally all the seasons dance, "the slow rounds of winter, pounds summer's heat." The harvest festival of this consummate poem tallies the Eleusinian mysteries. The peasants' celebration at the dance of the Hallows overlays the earlier rites (figure as "The Ballad of Mrs Noah" does, folk culture keeping alive excluded traditions). And he—the occasion of the poem is his response to an earth-tremor in San Francisco—his response is still another overlay, these layers forgotten when

> The Earth shakes. Kore! Kore!

when She "shakes the stores of ancestral grain," when Her presence revives generative tradition, when She wakes us, shakes us awake, this

> Kore! O visage as of sun-glare, thunderous
> awakener, light treader!

Evocation prompts invocation: "Will you not wake us again? shake the earth under us?" And prompts the need to tell his love, to praise the "Queen of our dance-floor!" And to enter the dance:

> Therefore I join them, dancing, dancing . . .
> a thresher among Threshers. Kore! Kore!
> (for I was thinking of her when the quake came, of
> radiant desire underground)

Radiant desire underground. What remembering, re-embers. "This is the new grass that springs from the ground" ("Keeping the Rhyme"). "Who will remember thy green flame?" he asks in "Food for Fire, Food for Thought," the concluding poem, where the desire, spoken in "Yes, As a Look Springs to Its Face," is answered. This earlier poem permits Whitman, who recommended candor, to speak for him:

> as earth, light and grass illustrate the meadow,
> there's a natural grace I hope for

> that unknowing a poem may show
> having its life in a field of rapture . . .

As with Whitman his poems are "part-songs" of those known and unknown whom he has loved, "a special green and flowering" inviting their embrace.

> Yes, though I contrive the mind's measure
> and wrest doctrine from old lore,
> it's to win particular hearts,
> to stir an abiding affection for this music,
> as if a host of readers will join the Beloved
>
> ready to dance with me, it's for the
>   unthinking
> ready thing I'm writing these poems.

So, at the close, he is kindled anew by the love he seeks:

> flamey threads of firstness go out from your touch.
>
> Flickers of unlikely heat
> at the edge of our belief bud forth.

16 October 1979

Awakened desire is related to childhood. So is the dance and Kore, who for all the acknowledgment of her dread sovereignty in Hades is still the maiden. The book is rounded by childhood, by the initial poem on the meadow and by the concluding poem, where, he says, "We are close enough to childhood, so easily purged." Close enough to recall, as he does at the end of "Crosses of Harmony and Disharmony," the familiar melodies played by the then unrecognized goddess at a children's evening songfest, and to recognize in the bright air (also song) of spring "her call" and a sentiment, as he says, "not to be uprooted! a ground of delight!" We know the sentiment from the resonance in this poem of Crane's "Virginia," the third of a sequence of songs working backward to the still pristine moment of awakened eros, when, as Duncan has it in his poem, "Life trembles"—*trembles*, a heavily charged word, as in "the tremblings of love." As in Crane's "naked in the / trembling heart."

The essential movement of many poems and of the book is toward spring, day, light, life, love—not Kore in Hell, but Kore emergent in spring, the virginal Virginia of Crane's poem, the maiden. What moves me most and is the moving force of this book is the purity of desire, the overwhelming presence of yearning and longing. Duncan expresses this exquisitely in "The Maiden," where he would revive "Cora among the grasses" because "Hearts / revive with her." Here he does for Kore what he had done less fully for Venus in "The Venus of Lespuges"—clusters evidence of her manifold presence throughout history and spells out the nature of the emotion she arouses. The maiden, whose "modesty / imparts to her nakedness willowy / grace," is "Bright with spring." To see her makes the heart tremble and (in the play on *spring*) awakens thirst, an "unquenchable longing." ("It is well / of water we return to," he says later, thereby associating the maiden with mother, and purifying the relation of mother and son in the image of the Virgin Mary.) She is an imperishable youth and purity, and a forever mysterious *anima* figure, "the girl the man knows nothing of" and loves in fear and pain, thereby, as he says of Dante, gaining "New Life" (*Vita Nuova*) and apprehending "Love." She kindles love: "Fear is a flame in your propriety."

Longing and be-longing. "It is from longing my making proceeds," he explains in "The Propositions."

> Thy hand,
> Beloved, restores
> the chords [cords] of this longing.
> Here, in this thirst that defines Beauty,
> I have found kin.

And with Olson in mind—he is mentioned earlier in the poem—he tells how intellect serves the melody of longing (the ear / intellect / syllable of "Projective Verse") and the heart "has pulse in this longing," so that "What I call magic proceeds from the heart." And lest Olson fail to understand that the beat of the heart has its be-longing in the cosmos, in the "great Longing" of all that moves the "Dance" (of life), he evokes Olson's fine poem on spring, "Variations Done for Gerald Van De Wiele":

> What opulence of my temper does not advance its
> charges?
> What intricate shifting of mood in the world's
> weather . . .

In "Spring," the final section of his poem, Olson tells how the body and the soul answer the charge (change) of the seasons: "we move, / we break out, we love."

18 October 1979

Yearning is matched by suffering, the passion of a later phase of love, that is necessary for the purification of desire. And yearning, for one who has inevitably passed beyond it, requires the "inbinding," a return, as "Often I am Permitted to Return to a Meadow" tells us. In "*The inbinding mirrors a process returning to roots of first feeling*" much of what the book has unfolded and done finds its consummate statement.

In the first stanza of this poem *noise* = *chaos* and *music* = *order / form*.

> In noise the yearning goes toward tones
> because a world in melody appears
> increasing longing towards stations of fullness
> to release from memory a passionate order . . .

Yearning and *longing* are *towards* a condition already known in memory: fullness, passionate order, world—*cosmicity*, to cite Bachelard. But what is significant here, already hinted at by "stations of fullness," where *fullness* and *increase* suggest erotic ripening and *stations* calls up the cross, is that the *first feeling*, the well-being, he wishes to return to by means of art includes all later knowledge and is returned to for the sake of all mankind.

> the inbinding, the return,
> where certain vital spirits of an eternal act
> are bound to be present, [yes, bound in the present]
> echoes there in octaves of suffering and joy.
>
> The inhabitants of Love, the inhabitants of Light,
> that were Eros and Psyche,
> that was Christ at the intersection of two lines,
> is each melos of the melody, the limbs of the tree
> are . . .

The *passionate order* is the melody so prominent in the poem, music here equivalent to the dance in coordinating passion (see "The Dance"). But it is also what Crane, evoked elsewhere in the poem, called "the visionary company of love." *The inhabitants of Love, the inhabitants of Light*: those who live together in love and light (in the true household). The eternal act he summons / makes present in the inbinding of memory / art involves suffering and joy, love and light; and the *vital spirits* he recalls here are those who have been most important in this book in filling out the mysteries of Kore: Psyche and Eros, Christ. He makes them present now; his music revives them. You might say they enter the dance. He says, playing on *melos* (limb) and *melody*, that they compose the passionate living order of the Tree of Life (another mythic reference in the book that proposes *Roots and Branches*).

The Tree of Life supports the wholly natural grounding of the poem, its reliance on the seasonal round and the forces of nature. Accordingly, hell is winter, "the naked trunk [of the tree] / seen as frozen back from its springtide of touching" and can be accepted / included as "perhaps no more" than that, an inevitable phase passing "in turn" to the happier touching, the at-one-ment told in "God is a Oneness": "a Being in touch." Touch, as in Crane's "Voyages," is the manifestation of love and has the erotic import of Duncan's lines on spring's emergence:

> . . . once blushd first budding, they put forth
> hints out of natural force
> to keep the tips green, fingers at the fresh edge of
> touching.

In its own defense against "the noysome poets" who raise up "one tower of poetry," the poem incorporates the natural doctrine (of "The Natural Doctrine," where the wonder Duncan needs "as the new shoots need water" is awakened by the "actual language" of natural things). The poem he answers to—

> . . . the poem
> beyond all poetry I have actually heard
> has words as natural and expendable
> as a cold stream of the first water. . . .

And it is also the poem in which the gods still have "faces of being" and have not been dispersed/abstracted by thought ("fell apart into one thought").

To return to "first feeling" is a condition of the poetry he wishes to write. "First feeling" belongs to the meadow, the place, he says in "Often I am Permitted to Return to a Meadow," of "first permission, / everlasting omen of what is." He reaches it now, not so much in the ways wonderful and mysterious of that initial poem, as by way of the process noted in the title, as a result of all his studies, labors, practice. Not only is the return necessarily psychological (of the psyche) to the mother-ground, it is a return to organic roots (respect for natural things) and etymological roots (human history manifest in the word, comprising the WORD).

The concluding section begins with Old English words: *Feld, græs* or *gærs, hus, dæg, dung* (prefiguring the spelling lesson of "Passages 13"). These words enable us to enter "the dream," the realm of Poetry inclusive of all poetry, and hence the realm of Man (all mankind). They do it because "we share," are not exempt from the trajectory of life told in "field, grass, house, day and dung." So we join in the dance with "those that in the forests went," are permitted to return to the earliest historical time, to a world of wonder, of fairy, as the words of Piers Plowman summon it, and also the "*faire felde*" of mankind itself, the field which is indeed "*betwene*" heaven and hell. To include Piers is to include the folk, to adduce a spokesman of Man and an example of a "simple" poetry—*simple*, of course, in the sense of *humble* as against *vain*, but also in the sense of *simples*, a mixture of herbs, tonic, perhaps even magical. And necessary now if Duncan, in his yearning for our renewal, is

> to awaken the old keeper of the living
> and restore lasting melodies of his desire.

19 October 1979

Is the old keeper of the living the child in us? I think immediately of "*Finders Keepers* we sang / when we were children" and of the images of the dancing children that are so important in the conclusion of "A Poem Beginning with a Line by Pindar." Aren't these images, taken directly from "Often I am Permitted to Return to a Meadow," there because this long poem, like "The Inbinding," earns an assurance that "Often I am Permitted to Return to a Meadow" never really does?

The *meadow* is indeed, as Duncan says, a "property [pun] of the mind," a "made place." A primary image, in Bachelard's terms, valorized by all that is beneficent in childhood. How Bachelard would have delighted in this image naming the goal of return, of the most significant of reveries, that toward childhood, toward the mother, the place of well-being! The title, itself the first line of the poem, declares a marvelous opening of the field, a repossession of all that is of inestimable value to him, love (and devotion), security, creative power. And the music of the poem, of a sweetness such as Duncan attributes to Dante, is consonant, in itself enough to convey his wonder and gratitude.

This poem opens the field because it provides an instance of what is needed to enable poetry and of what poetry enables—it tells what the poet is "given," as Creeley readily appreciated. But it also opens the field because it brings forward the images and ideas subsequent poems will unfold (the meadow is "an eternal pasture folded in all thought" and words themselves are a fabric, a "field folded"); because it involves an essential mode of poetic activity, reverie; and because it merely opens a realm of experience, does not yet fathom it, is incomplete, inconclusive.

The tone tells this to a greater extent than the allusions to chaos, the sun's setting, the underworld, the round of the dance. After all, he is returning to a "place of first permission," recovering something lost. But the present condition is wonderfully nullified (dismissed, not included) in the act of return. None of the images of beneficence is to the slightest degree valorized downward, as say in "A Poem of Despondencies," where the meadow is a sexual bog and the "green is obscene." And we know from "Nor Is the Past Pure" that neither the pasture nor the past is pure.

Perhaps *fold*, so conspicuous in the poem, provides a clue? Not the etymological one (*feld, fold, flor*—field, earth, floor), however much the vowel-leading of "field folded." Rather another poet's conspicuous use of it, Hart Crane's, in "Voyages

I," where the poet, intimating the losses of childhood, says, "The waves fold thunder on the sand." Crane's setting, the sea, is also Duncan's, unmentioned here, and Crane's conclusion is also his, "The bottom of the sea is cruel."

In "Four Pictures of the Real Universe" note the "white flowers / lost in waves of morning green." And the concluding couplet, calling up the metaphor of music in "The Inbinding":

> Were it not for the orders of music hidden
> we should be claimed by the preponderant void.

Yes, where music provides the chords (cords) that "hold the stars in their courses," what matters are "outfoldings of sound from the seed of first light."

"The waves throwing themselves down in ranks upon the shore are what I hear." Because, like Crane, he, too, was to embark on voyages. In "Occult Matters" (*The H.D. Book*), he recalls his identification with Wynken, Blyken, and Nod, and how, employing the childhood rhyme in the context of his fearful Atlantean dream, he would set out alone on the dark sea to save himself, yet never to reach land. The Atlantean dream is an anxiety dream of disaster, even though the grassy hill—the world of the meadow—is the risen Atlantis. In "Atlantis," the entire poem is heavy with presentiment of a Dickinsonian beginning, "the long shadow."

> Presentiment—is that long Shadow—on the lawn—
> Indicative that Suns go down—
> The Notice to the startled Grass
> That Darkness—is about to pass—

But the field, so important in his dream, does not enter the Atlantis poem. He thinks instead of "the old scars of the sea," of the "longings" that hover over the "deep water," of the seas "overshadow[ing]" the shores (the deluge survived in "The Ballad of Mrs Noah"), and of "the theme of revival the heart asks for."

Duncan associates his Atlantean dream with the birth-memory of his mother's death in delivering him. And the dream enacts his birth and the consequence/burden of his mother's dying. The hill is the mound of her belly (as in the Harry Callahan photograph), the cave is the womb and its waters; and his loss of his mother is equivalent to Kore's loss of Demeter. The risen Atlantis of the hill has none of the salutary meanings we find in the poem. There is no wind. The grass of its own accord "bows" west, to the left, the sinister direction of death. There is no sun, and he is uncertain of the time of day. Even the round dance is fearful since he finds himself at its center, feels "caught in the wrong" and responds most to "Ashes, ashes. All fall down!" Finally, there is the cave-womb, unmentioned in the poem. Duncan also considers this a throne room. And again, as in the dance, his presumptive kingship is denied, now by the waters that break in and overwhelm him.

This dream-content energizes *The Opening of the Field*. What "Often I am Permitted to Return to a Meadow" doesn't tell us, the subsequent poems do. But only within the limits defined by *field*. This is not the book of the cave.

23 October 1979

Now isn't "A Poem Beginning with a Line by Pindar," in which he most fully addresses the present forces opposing the meadow, already in his thought? Doesn't "property of the mind" in

> . . . a meadow
> as if it were a given property of the mind
> that certain bounds hold against chaos . . .

both recall and have the same weighted position in the poem as that single isolated line in the concluding verses on liquid light in the first *Pisan Canto* (#74)? Reveries toward childhood do not belong to childhood, but to the aggrieved man who in the Pindar poem identifies, by virtue of their courage and persistence, with his aging masters, among them Pound. Hasn't he, like them, turned to poetry to secure his survival? Isn't the deepest work of this poem told in the fact that "A line by Pindar / moves . . . / toward morning"; that at the end, he is permitted to return to a meadow—the poetic work has been efficacious—and that he *sees*, as in "The Dance" ("What I see is a meadow . . . / the dew shining")?

Not quite, or not in that way. He says,

> In the dawn that is nowhere
> I have seen the willful children
>
> clockwise and counter-clockwise turning.

It is still dark, and the dawn that he sees belongs only to the poem, whose work alone in our dark time has permitted him to see the children dancing.

What is vouchsafed in personal terms in "Often I am Permitted to Return to a Meadow" and "The Dance" is not (yet) vouchsafed by history. This admission is a measure of Duncan's witness and truth.

24 October 1979

"A Poem Beginning with a Line by Pindar": one of the longest poems in *The Opening of the Field*, and a most brilliant one. A touchstone of Duncan's art, poetics, and vision. Its importance to him is evident in the fact that he uses it to explain his art and what, from childhood on, moved him to it. Its importance? It joins childhood-desire-return (that vision of redemptive love) to the lost America of love he would have us—the nation: "I too / that am a nation"—recover. It is "epic," as no other poem in the book is: the poet's task is cultural (political?); his poem, as well as it might considering its debt to Pound, has history in it. And where that history of love and lovelessness is marked by discontinuity, "continual ravage" itself a primary manifestation, he speaks of (and for) a continuity of poets, of those since Whitman who have stood and have urged us to stand with Eros in the conflict with Thanatos.

25 October 1979

When he recalls the occasion of the poem in *The Truth & Life of Myth*, he speaks of cooperating with the "aroused process." Yes, poetry and eros are one, and the process of poetry here is one of arousal (eros-al?). Pindar, named in the title and evoked in the first line—"*The light foot hears you and the brightness begins*"—rhymes in significant ways with Duncan: a poet of disorderly forms, who lived in a time of war, and celebrated poetry, its power of harmonizing, of ordering, of moderating the thundermakers, Zeus and Ares, and quelling the rebellious, like Typhon. But this, though taken up in the poem, is not what he immediately hears, what arouses him. He is awakened by the beat of the line, by the dance, the words of the line having become "powers in a theogony, having resonances in Hesiodic and Orphic cosmogonies where the foot that moves in the dance of the poem appears as the pulse of measures in first things." The poem has this cosmogonical depth, so that the strife at its core is of first things, and the *willful* children dancing their round dance at the close—"clockwise and counter-clockwise turning"—figure it, and figure the turns of history and myth, as Dennis Cooley observes. The very condition of experience treated in the poem. Inconclusive, never to be concluded. Like the "Whispers antiphonal" with which Crane "ends" *The Bridge*?

And isn't the dance of the children, and hence the meadow to which he wishes to return, prefigured by the recollection of the brightness of Kore, the "awakener, light treader"—where *treader*, in its sexual sense, is already pressing the poem forward to

> god-step at the margins of thought,
> quick adulterous tread at the heart?

God-step. What he hears is the dithyramb, "the song that makes Zeus leap or beget." Note: "My thought as a poet has grown in the ground of twentieth-century mythologists like Cassirer and Freud, found a key in Jane Harrison's definition of the dithyramb . . . and followed the mythopoeic weavings of Pound's *Cantos* in which 'all ages are contemporaneous.'"

In "The Adventure of Whitman's Line," he speaks of sexuality and sound as formal imperatives.

And note the emphatic *begins*. Isn't Williams already in his thought, "The Desert Music," with its opening, "—the dance begins"? And doesn't Pindar, the mere fact of reading a Greek poet, recall H.D.? So he has in mind his beloved predecessors, who, he says in *The H.D. Book*, "saw literature as a text for the soul in its search for fulfillment in life and took the imagination as a primary instinctual authority." *Generative imagination*, Pound called it, and this reminds Duncan of Carlyle's poet-as-hero and Carlyle's notion, so important to him, of "musical thought" that recovers the deep hidden melody of things.

The awakening (out of darkness?) is overwhelming. ("With poetry, the imagination takes its place on the margin, exactly where the function of unreality comes to charm or to disturb—always to awaken—the sleeping being lost in its automatisms"—Bachelard, *The Poetics of Space.*) The serial words are inadequate to the immediate fullness. Read them simultaneously, the first verse as an instant. He is awakened, surprised by, overtaken by a power—the instinctual authority of the generative imagination—and a presence greater than himself. The *god-step* belongs not to the head but to the heart, is at the *margins of thought,* not within its circle. Can you read that phrase and not think of Whitman's "In paths untrodden, / in the growth by margins of pond-waters," the decisive opening of *Calamus*? How is it the tread is *adulterous*? And that he asks, "Who is it that goes there?" calling up, as it does, Whitman's "Who goes there? hankering, gross, mystical, nude?" Hasn't he been struck by the eros (arrows) of Cupid (Eros)? Awakened by light, as Eros was? Awakened to love, as Psyche was?

Whose *quick* (quickening) *face* does he see, a noumenal presence? In "A Poem Slow Beginning" (it begins: "remembering powers of love / and of poetry") he names

> . . .—Dionysus in wrath, Apollo in rapture,
> Orpheus in song, and Eros secretly

Doesn't this recognition account for the suddenly composed and measured dance of the old order?

> notes of an old music pace the air,
> torso-reverberations of a Grecian lyre.

Pythian ode. Delphi. Apollo.

Duncan's perturbation is relieved by finding its ratio in this music. (See "The Dance.") And the *torso-reverberations* it evokes not only prompt the immediate description of Cupid (Eros) but call up Rilke, his great poem on the torso of Apollo and its injunction to change our lives. As the lives of both

Psyche and Eros were changed by the ensouling of love. As Duncan's life was changed. ("My Other is not a woman but a man," he says in the superb poem on homoeros entitled "The Torso.")

26 October 1979

Duncan says that the line of Pindar immediately evoked for him Goya's painting of Cupid and Psyche and—what goes unmentioned in the poem—the recollection of Apuleius' story. In the stanzas that follow in §I, he describes the canvas depicting Psyche's discovery of Eros and reads the meaning of the initial episodes of their story. He uses the painting as he uses painting elsewhere in his work ("At Christmas," "Fire") with remarkable skill, in this instance as the image of his own (re)awakened desire and knowledge of its consequences. He describes only Eros, "the bronze boy's slight body," attends the physical ("His thighs are flesh"). But the burden of his appreciation of the sensual is his awareness of the fact that the painting depicts the birth of yearning ("yearning, a rose [eros] that burns"), inevitable sorrow, a "carnal fate," he says, "that sends the soul wailing / up from blind innocence." In his telling phrase, Psyche and Eros have been "bruised by redemption." So everything, evil, darkness, ignorance, *serves* them: "Fate, spinning, / knots the threads for Love."

27 October 1979

Psyche and Eros. The myth belongs to his childhood, is essential autobiography. And essential myth, weaving itself into the history of the nation, into the lives of the poets, a history of love and loss already announced by "the soul's wailing."

Duncan's account of the myth in *The H.D. Book* is notable for two things: the omission of any reference to Erich Neumann's *Amor and Psyche: The Psychic Development of the Feminine* and his reading it as a fable of the poet. "The would-be poet," he says, "stands like Psyche *in the dark* [in the *selva oscura* of the self], taken up in a marriage with a genius, possessed by a spirit outside the ken of those about him." So it tells of the misgivings of his parents over his choice of vocation as well as his sense, against the fact that it troubled Williams, that the poet is a woman. It is significant, too, that he considers the Palace of Eros that Psyche initially enters the world of Culture, and puts what matters to him in a brief paragraph recalling the confession of sin in *The Truth & Life of Myth*:

> Psyche before her sin is a dilettante. To read, to listen, to study, to gaze was all part of being loved without loving, a pleasure previous to any trial or pain of seeking the beloved. The light must be tried; Psyche must doubt and seek to know; reading must become life and writing; and all go wrong. There is no way then but Psyche's search, the creative work of a union in knowledge and experience. At the end, there is a new Eros, a new Master over Love.

The resonances of Hesiodic and Orphic cosmogonies he hears in the first line of the poem evoke the story of Psyche and Eros as assuredly as they evoked Goya's painting. Everything concerning Eros comes to focus for him in this fable: love as "a primal authority, a cosmic need," the moving force of creation, cosmologically, historically, individually. Love is formative, and transformative. The tradition that has served this primordial force is also present ("Mount Segur, Mount Victoire, Mount Tamalpais"—it has migrated west! How true it is that "the information flows / that is yearning"!). Present in the very poets who figure in the poem. And that tradition reminds us of the fertile darkness our civilization denies—the chthonic darkness of the old matriarchal order, of hidden vitalities. Reminds us that exclusion is divisive, giving birth to the demonic and satanic, as in the political portion of the poem, and that our task is twofold, to recover the unity of darkness-and-light, body-and-soul, and to gather the dispersed Eros, yes, gather him to us.

Paradise is here / now. *Le Paradis n'est pas artificiel*. Present. My only world, as Paul Goodman said, given to him when people come across. "Paradise," Duncan says, "is Itself the inexorable power of Eros."

28 October 1979

Why the reluctance to mention Neumann? Is it simply that the Jungians, as he believes, avoid "the lowness of the story" and read "in high-minded symbols"? Or is it that he recognizes, as Rachel DuPlessis does in "Psyche, or Wholeness," the patronizing, patriarchal bias of Neumann's interpretation?

29 October 1979

The *magic* to which he refers in §II points back to the mystery of suffering, the transformation of good out of evil, and forward to the consideration of the plenitude of old age. It also speaks for the way in which the story works, the magic of its *passionate dispersion*, the fertile power of its seeds. For hasn't the story aroused him to his tasks? Isn't he now aware of where he stands, "In time . . . / from this threshold"? Isn't he, his thought moving toward the "old poets," already thinking of Williams, of *Paterson*, where Williams says that knowledge undispersed is its own undoing, the tight-packed seed now lost in the flux, the scum of contemporary America?

Isn't the reason Psyche and Eros never grow old and "Psyche is preserved" given in the very arousal enacted in §I? There Duncan recovers the phase of youth. But in §II he speaks from his awareness of aging, and so age is beautiful, especially that of the old poets, with whom he identifies. Beautiful because by way of *their faltering* and *their unaltering* he arrives at what is most important to him:

> words shed like tears from
> a plentitude of powers time stores.

In the increase of time, the old poets have great powers, as he acknowledges in *The H.D. Book*. He is stirred by "their passion . . . their ripeness, the fullness in process of what they are." But their writing, like his, has its source in the fact, fully confessed in *The Truth & Life of Myth*, that love moves us to tears.

Even more overwhelmingly confessed in one of his greatest poems, the recent tribute to Whitman in "The Adventure of Whitman's Line," where he remembers

> my own being at thirty-seven
> in the opening of the field of grass you made for me
> facing the nation we
> inhabit together aged in the wood Dante in the
> darkly bewildered *selva oscura*
> set out from and returns to—the human
> condition—almost with despair but
> persisting,
> gathering up from your spirit what almost faltering
> flame I could but resolute,
> reciting the lists of the Presidents, each man
> to the heart more appalling—

where (the insistence is almost unbearable) he remembers / knows now, "the rehearsals of unrelieved suffering of the human condition comes to."

Of course the powers that time stores may be the inflictions of illness and history, the strokes Williams suffered—the damage to his speech enacted in the verse—and the lightning of the gods / presidents, emphasized by the isolated italicized line, "*The Thundermakers descend*." "These little strokes" are also those of the pen, the writer's recourse. And Williams, who is too old to *recoil* (in two senses), can still *recall*, memory itself evoked by *descend.*

> The descent
>   made up of despairs
>   and without accomplishment
> realizes a new awakening   :
>   which is a reversal
> of despair.

Memory is an accomplishment, and with evening, love awakens.

But this is not yet the line of associations Duncan follows. The pun-garbled speech that introduces the presidents raises the specter of the atom bomb:

>   The present dented of the U
> nighted stayd. States. The heavy clod?
>   Cloud. Invades the brain. What
>   if lilacs last in *this* dooryard bloomd?

Like Crane before him, Duncan questions Whitman's "syllables of faith." Like Bill [Rueckert], in "Letter to Walt Whitman":

> Even your poems are failing us, Walt.
> Nobody can remember when lilacs last in the
>   dooryard bloomed.

Duncan's denunciation of the presidents has its precedent in Whitman's *The Eighteenth Presidency.* The roll call of names, working back from Eisenhower to Lincoln, is sufficient answer to the interlinear accusatory questions, all of them addressing of the lack of love. Lords of industry and war, the presidents are spoliators, Plutonic/Satanic powers breaking the "bride-sweet" of the nation, desecrating the "tender landscape," creating human misery.

> Where among these did the spirit reside
> that restores the land to productive order?

That's Eliot's question in *The Waste Land,* Pound's in *The Cantos.* Crane's, too, in *The Bridge,* summoned here by these splendid lines on its Columbian vision:

> For whom are the holy matins of the heart ringing?
> Noble men in the quiet of morning hear
> Indians singing the continent's violent requiem.

And now it is Wendell Berry's, who sees in love the common discipline of marriage / farming / poetry, the ground of genuine culture. The unsettling of America: the lost America of love. Ecos and eros. Earth / hearth / heart / household. Yes, "the heart is wrung," as Crane says in "Quaker Hill."

Not until *Bending the Bow* will he be so political, and poems like "Up Rising" are prefigured here. He envisions the "under side turning," the "up break" of

> lilac blossoms of courage in daily act
> striving to meet a natural measure.

Is he thinking of Williams' "Horned Purple" in *Spring and All*? Certainly, of Kore.

30 October 1979

§II enacts what it declares:

> It is across great scars of wrong
> I reach toward the song of kindred men
> and strike again the naked string
> old Whitman sang from . . .

Yes, it is a cross. Scars: "always the iron dealt cleavage" (Crane). *Kindred* = kind red, and Crane's "Where are my kinsmen . . . ?" The naked string strikes up for a new world, its song the "vernal strophe" Crane struck in "Atlantis" from the "deathless strings" of the bridge. And Emerson's iron string. The bow and the lyre of *Bending the Bow.*

Finding his tradition, he assumes responsibility for its vision. *Song* must make *wrong* good, restore the *natural measure* his very book is doing so much to restore. Nothing will do but the restoration of eros.

Nothing will do but the restoration of Eros! The logic of meditation brings me to "Psyche's tasks"!

31 October 1979

§III is dedicated to Olson because Olson is a kindred man, concerned with the initiation of another kind of nation. *Under side* in the previous section has already evoked him. In his essay on *The Maximus Poems*, Duncan's cites Maximus' respect for the *underpart* in support of Olson's Jungian psychic task: "Olson insists upon the active. Homo maximus wrests his life from the underworld as the Gloucester fisherman wrests his from the sea." But of course Whitman, already linked with Olson in "The Dance," proposes him. In the biographical notes of *The New American Poetry* (1960), he uses the very words of §II in explaining his debt: he had learned from Olson that "the task in poetry could be promethean. In Whitman's words: 'The theme is creative and has vista.'" And then he does what this poem is doing: "Here biography passes into the living present and has no summary." To name Olson is once more to assume responsibility, to be active.

To put Olson and Pound together is just, a *recognition*. He generously puts Olson in the poem, even for several lines follows the wider spacing of his practice. But Pound, the old poet of the *Pisan Cantos*, is (rightly) focal for him.

Pysche's tasks and the making of poetry are so closely related that to speak of one is to speak of the other. Sorting the seeds, as Duncan himself does at the start, is one of the requisite lessons of learning to love. It is also a lesson in poetics respecting the potency of words/images and natural measure ("in its right place"). See "Fire," where blocks of seed-words frame the poem and call up an Edenic childhood world.

All of the tasks are covered by "for the soul must weep / and come near upon death." *We*—the poem speaks for all of us—must harrow hell and resist (note the amendment of the story) melancholy/sleep, the not infrequent condition of some of the poems in this volume. And we must learn obedience (as he maintains in the *Dante* [*Etudes*]), learn the lesson of the *Pisan Cantos*:

> The ant's a centaur in his dragon world.
> Pull down thy vanity, it is not man
> Made courage, or made order, or made grace,
>   Pull down thy vanity, I say pull down.
> Learn of the green world what can be thy place
> In scaled invention or true artistry . . .

The transition to Pound, the "old man at Pisa," may refer to this passage as well as Psyche's story: "In the story the ants help." For what Pound had to learn was to sort the seeds mixed in his mind, the "six seeds of an error" that he confessed (the context: the Eleusinian mysteries so important to him). Duncan notes this in *The Truth & Life of Myth* and extols Pound's heroism ("he had taken upon himself a commitment to order, as the tragic hero Oedipus took a commitment to a law that condemned him"). To include one's errors, one's mistakes, also belongs to the inclusivity of open form.

The Cantos themselves furnish lines for the poem: one, Pound's characterization as a lone ant; another, on the wind (which if traced to Pound's "grass under Zephyrus" calls up the meadow); still another, "*man upon whom the sun has gone down*," evoking Odysseus and the westering adventure of humanism ("humanism is [Homer] coming in, and [Melville] going out": Olson). Pound was, as Duncan has it, "father of many notions," *notions* playing off *nations*, telling the inconsequence of his politics. Yet he is the one, in answer to Duncan's questions, who "let light into the dark" and "began / the many movements of the passion." Movements, as the placing of "West" suggests, now terminated, if not the movement of poetry certainly that of civilization. The evocation here of Tennyson's Ulysses (also in *The Cantos*) addresses the decline of the West. West ("cursed") is darkness and death. It is too late to seek a newer world.

1 November 1979

West is where he is. The West pioneered by his ancestors. It was once "legend": "It was the West. Its vistas. . . ." But the Whitmanian vista never obtained. Melancholy rather, and coiled like a serpent. To survive in the West was a harrowing of hell.

Light and love; and love, darkness, and death. Love, the tertium quid. Now the poem intensifies as Duncan himself struggles East, toward light and love. This, in fact, is the overall movement of the poem.

With Pound, Williams, Crane, and Olson, he is a "hero who struggles east / widdershins to free the dawn." The hero figured by Jason, mentioned in *The Truth & Life of Myth*, where Max Müller is cited as having seen "ritual mysteries of freeing the dawn's light in the tale of Jason and Medea and the Golden Fleece." Isn't this the ritual Crane undergoes in the night-journey of "The Tunnel," which brings him to the "River that is East," and to the dawn of "Atlantis," where he salutes Jason? Olson, the archeologist of morning, the Zaddik of the springs. East is always source, origin.

And how could one not think of Williams, as Duncan does in an appropriate context in "Ideas of the Meaning of Form"? He declares his preference for the very mixed condition he struggles with in this poem and quotes from Williams' "Asphodel," though not those lines, relevant to the poem, where Williams affirms his faith in light and imagination and love, and concludes

> So let us love
>   confident as in the light
>   in its struggle with darkness.

The quest for light and love brings darkness and death, death itself, in the awe-ful pun, "cupidinous," of a greedily erotic nature.

>   The light that is Love
> rushes on toward passion. It verges upon dark.

At this point Duncan tells of Psyche's discovery of Eros and her consequent loss of paradise. She may be said to enter history, to take up the burdens of time that "conquers legend," to come into the life we know ("my life," Duncan says), when wounded by Eros we endure the "pain / beyond cure" and travel "station after station."

Her story ends here. He has nothing more to tell of her. Are death and darkness, then, "delicious," to borrow Whitman's word of praise? Isn't "Out of the Cradle Endlessly Rocking" an analogue of Psyche's story to this point? Will nothing but death, the word whispered by the sea, assuage desire? Aren't we to read

> Rilke torn by a rose thorn [a rose: eros]
> blackened toward Eros. Cupidinous Death!
>   that will not take no for an answer

knowing that Rilke accepted death as continuous with, as an opening of life? Aren't we, as the next section affirms, to say "yes" to death?

2 November 1979

Yes. It is already fated in "yearning, a rose that burns" and "Bruised by redemption." And by the consonance of *eros* and *yes*, and the rhyme of *bless*. The affirmation rings as clearly as that of Molly Bloom! And since he accepts the "pain / beyond cure"—sees Eros "fair," as Psyche does—he can welcome arousal, can return to the poem's opening in the recollection of another footfall, another dance of being, in his youth. Again, the brightness begins. And with the advent of imagination those transformations whose ultimate signature is the restoration permitted by his reverie toward childhood, his return to the meadow.

Duncan says "yes" to eros because it is also the empowering agency of imagination, of images that are eidolons, of those bright presences. Imagination is not merely the catalyst Eliot speaks of. The "catalyst force" here awakens imagination, as the poem itself demonstrates; it is the "tread," "that foot informed / by the weight of all things." Art has deeper roots than the mind alone, as Olson said in regard to Eliot in "Projective Verse."

Eros / dance / imagination / transformation. Duncan's verses here inevitably remind me of Crane's "The Dance," the Passion by which he would "dance us back the tribal morn." The transformation of lust, the positive-negative *unprepares*, the image of the lamp—and finally the hesitancy of "toward morning"—particularly remind me of him.

The poem insists on transformation in the reiterated "gives way." In answer to "Who is there?" (recall "Who is it goes there?"), he exclaims "O, light the light"—to be read in two ways, in fear (as the "cry for a comforter," as answered, for example, at the end of "Adam's Way") and in wonder. The verse supports both, for with the light all hostile forces give way and he comes again to the "place of first permission." There is no better commentary on what is happening here and in the remainder of the poem than

> Often I am permitted to return to a meadow
> as if it were a given property of the mind
> that certain bounds hold against chaos,
>
> that is a place of first permission,
> everlasting omen of what is.

And no better commentary on *given, chaos,* and *omen* than the Pindar poem.

Now more of the Atlantean dream is admitted. Now the dream is prefaced by the knowledge of loss, the inevitable dismemberment of Eros/Osiris that occurs in "Our [life] histories." So that childhood has a claim on it—to be *Finders* and *Keepers.* The reverie toward childhood involves re-member-ment.

And, as he says in "Nor Is the Past Pure," it is "not permitted without corruption," without the knowledge of the necessary and fertile dark also told in that poem.

> And we came up out of the dark hole
> into All Night of the World. Do we
>   not remember centuries of cold?
>
> . . . .
>
> O seed occult we planted in the dark furrow!
> O potency we rested and covered over!
> O life thriving lightwards, gathering strength!
> The image of our longing is the full head of seed,
>   the wheat-gold ready
>
> . . . .
>
> Again and again return underground
> to the dark fires, the Satanic thriving.
> The First Prince is of Light ignorant.
>   Toward *scientia* he strives.

> The Seed evil, the sprouting by desire, the
> shoots of beauty, the flowering art,
> the seed good, good, good, the good ear
> full and ripe, trembling with sound
> that joyfull we return to the underground!

Light and dark are equivocal terms, necessarily both/and, interlocked in transformation. The seeds of the poem are now the germs of self and art, their transformation imaged in "flowering." In saying that "Death is prerequisite to the growth of grass," Duncan again says "yes" to death, and in speaking of the "adultery" of the middenheap from which Kore springs, he comments on the quickening "adulterous tread" that stirred the growth of this poem.

Still more of his Atlantean dream is permitted to return: "the lonely psyche goes up thru the boy to the king / that in the caves of history dreams."

Does he enter the dance in the Pindar poem, or merely watch? And the secret of the round dance? The eternal round, the movement of restored innocence that destroys London Bridge, the kingdom, the power structures of loveless men—in the Unreal City of Eliot's poem where death has undone so many, where the planting seems to be fruitless.

Duncan answers Eliot, as all the courageous old men had had to. His answer? *The Spirit of Romance.* "We have come so far that all the old stories / whisper once more." *Whisper* the delicious word *love.*

> Mount Segur, Mount Victoire, Mount Tamalpais . . .
> *rise to adore the mystery of Love*!

The pinnacle of the poem! Truly.

And isn't he thinking of Williams' *Paterson* (the note at the end of Book I) in the prose passage in which he comments on the making of his poem? And continues it, taking up Pindar's and Psyche's recklessness as his own, as that which permits the information to flow, the poem beginning with a line by Pindar to move toward morning and the vision of the willful children (does recklessness gloss *willful*?) turning in the counter-motions of the dance. *Turning.*

The introduction of the prose paragraph is daring. It closes (off) the poem even as within it it begins again, resumes it. It raises the pitch of the poem at the same time as it subdues it. At the end, the vision of the children is only recollected, is historically only promissory, to be made good as it already has been by the *work* of the poem, by the yearning it sets flowing, the fountain it releases. *Yearning, morning, turning.* A tropic flowering or falling or both of "the virgin flower of the dark"? Kore. Queen of the dance-floor, the earth itself. Isn't Duncan's conclusion Williams' in *Paterson V*?

> We know nothing and can know nothing
> but
> the dance, to dance to a measure
> contrapuntally,
> Satyrically, the tragic foot.

4 November 1979

He has knotted threads for Love. "What I can catch and what catches me at work." *Knots the threads for love,* he says again in a letter to Olson (February 6, 1960), following it with, "I know it *is* for something missing that the line of the poem goes out." Isn't that the adventure here, taking *adventure* from his appreciation of Whitman's line? From the noiseless, patient spider?

Poem as event. "The form of the poem is the immediate condition of its content. The intent of the poem is the meaning of the way it is composed as part of what is happening in the poem."

Collage: inclusivity. His reading, memories, visions, personal and family history, dreams, kinships; history and myth; painting; Olsonian and Poundian form (as visual touchstones), Whitmanian catalog; politics; etc. "And we've, both of us," he wrote Olson (August 28, 1955), "got Grandpa [Pound] to thank for the way station of the ideogram (which allows for movement . . . for individual discovery)."

Movement. The dance of thought itself. What, hearing the "god-step at the margins of thought," is enacted. He thinks with—by means of—the poem, as Williams said in defense of his own profundity.

And, as here, the poem pictures his listening. How *melos* begets *melody*; how "the melody of events" enters the "generative memory" and awakens the soul, awakens the sense of relation and ratio so that a poem conforming to no previous form has form, is informed by its own patterns of relationship, its equilibrations.

The poem unfolds through you, through/in your reading. "Everything," he says on the Berkeley tape, "must tune up."

And the information flows. This poem demonstrates the uses of the collective consciousness, the endless generativity of texts (literary, scholarly, visual). It transfers energy.

It belongs in the Book of the Earth because it teaches us that love participates in the inseparable phases of life and death. Transformation is its essence. Labor—there is no way but Psyche's search, the "old labors," he says in "A Storm of White," that death proposes. Labor is necessary:

Thus the Evil is seed, terror
    held by courage (our labors) nourished
by devotion (our labors)
    anticipates Beauty.

Yes, beauty, as the old man at Pisa reiterates, is difficult.

7 November 1979

Each volume has its own formal rhythm, emotional trajectory. After the Pindar poem, the poems of *The Opening of the Field* work through despair and despondency (blackness) to a flicker of recovered belief in renewing love. (The image of wood and budding prefigures the "tree" of *Roots and Branches*.)

The tree, already present in "The Structure of Rime V," belongs to the pervasive vegetative metaphor. First the meadow of childhood, then the tree of life, the cross, whose "bleeding branches" speak the worst doubts, declare against Duncan's hope, so prominent in *Roots and Branches,* in the awakening of Adam Kadmon, the re-membered Man. The World Tree and the World Man. ("The Kabbalah does not praise artichokes," he says in *Roots and Branches,* thinking perhaps of Whitman tasting the artichokes in Ginsberg's poem?)

The well-being (precarious) of the concluding poem of the first volume is picked up in the initial, title poem of the second. (A life work is more than a book.) A spring poem, a morning poem of awakened psyche (butterfly), all the more restorative because the Monarchs also sail the seas, their airy sailing transforming the usually fearsome image of sea/ship/lover. This exquisite poem "echoing" the desire to perfect the spirit plays on the idea of correspondence, on the relation of self and world, spirit and sense; and the very desire to be transported to "an inner view of things" is burdened by the need for connection between spirit and sense, imaginary and real, figured in the Whitmanian "filaments woven and broken." The butterflies' flight in the sensuous March air trace for him "unseen roots and branches of sense." They "almost restore / an imaginary tree of the living in all its doctrine." Lacking are the hidden, sensual roots, fully acknowledged elsewhere, especially in the mandrill, another Bearskin; emphasized in Wynn Bullock's cover photograph.

In "The Structure of Rime XVI"—this series threads both volumes—a "voice dreaming within the bear skull" laments the loss of love: "*The winged denizens* [*bees*] *of light are gone.*" (Bees are more important and frequent in Duncan's work than butterflies, and the butterflies in the initial poem do the work of bees Duncan endorses in Rilke. They transform the visible into the invisible, their work connects one world with another. Duncan himself remarks in "The Matter of the Bees" in *Caesar's Gate* (1972) that "Psyches are butterflies, but souls are also bees." This commentary on his childhood memories of bees, on their mythic-matriarchal lore, on his confusion of *insect* and *incest* is rich in connections. Even *apis* calls up *ape.*) At the end the outcry is Whitman's, the concluding phrase of his poem of connecting, "A Noiseless Patient Spider," a poem Duncan explicitly refers to in *The Opening of the Field*, and the direction is rootward:

> O my soul,
> now man's desolation
>   into his beginnings return!

In "The Structure of Rime VI," the soul floats like a butterfly, but childhood freedom is jeopardized by the old women who come from caves and close the doors to the meadow.

The tree is an image of connection.

The airy opening of *Roots and Branches* is soon foreclosed. This is not a book of springtime nor a happy book because it returns to childhood and especially to adolescence, to the "despised and outcast modes of adolescence, that so troubled me." It does not have the equilibrum of *The Opening of the Field* because it moves into previously unsearched depths. It opens more, is more open in its disclosures and its forms. More inclusive. Risks more. Has more at stake. A book of survival.

Yet it ends with a poem of spring and resurrection, with the turning earth itself, "an actual earth of value" (Olson), mother earth beneficent.

His element, he says in "Returning to the Rhetoric of an Early Mode," is earth. He is the "servant of the green," of the tree, the "verdant rhetorical," "rich as a tree / in full foliage of metaphor, flower, fruit." (The one living tree of Poetry, where *melos* makes *melody*, mentioned by Eve in "Adam's Way.") Yet in this poem it's the psychic ground and seed of grief, self, and yearning that claims his imagination, not so much the literal earth of what Bachelard calls a material imagination. "Hidden wherein / the workings of ecstatic form."

"*Lie down, Man, under Love*," the counsel of "The Structure of Rime VII": "*The streams of the Earth seek passage thru you, tree that you are, toward a foliage that breaks at the boundaries of known things.*"

8 November 1979

Kabbalists' Tree of Life. Yggdrasil, the World Tree. Vertical topology—and *tropology* (from tropism). See John Scoggan, *MAPS* #4.

> The universe of the Tree's activity, when mapped, vertically, gives formal recognitions to the processes of creation: life-and-death as the dried-up ends that are renewed from beneath. . . . TURNING (i.e. vertical topology) as all post-modern *Pictures of the World*. . . . a topology that is *vertere*, of turning interactions, like roots and branches moving around the actual twists that occur between things in any organism's experience of its immediate universe.

So "It is the earth turning / that lifts our shores from the dark" ("Apprehensions") and dawn is the wave the earth makes in turning ("The Continent").

We grow and wave from the spine like flowers and like branches on a tree, Olson says in "A Syllabary for a Dancer." Noting, in *The Special View of History*, that "only love is order in the vertical of the self," he offers the tree as an image of cosmology: "ground . . . roots, stem, and photosynthetic growth out in the air among leaves." Duncan says the dancers mimic flowers, and in "Now the Record Now Record," he enjoins the tree (as Williams did the chicory) to strain upward, to

> Push forth green points of working desire, tree!
> I likewise!
>   *Verde, verde, que te quiero verde,*
> whose leaves are loves and who breathes
> close upon the breath of his lover
>   photosyntheses of his most being . . .

(Note the exquisite prosody. *Whose / who*; *are / and*; *leaves / loves / breathes*; *breathes / breath*; *whose / close*; *loves / lover*. And *photosyntheses*, where light is the miraculous agent of the fact that *leaves breathe*, have being; that the tree, like the verse, is active, in motion. ". . . by their syllables . . . words juxtapose in beauty"—Olson, "Projective Verse.")

Only roots and branches. No flowers as in Williams' *Root, Branch, and Flower,* the title he suggested for his autobiography? Yeats's *great-rooted* blossomer. As Duncan said of the noble old poets in *The H.D. Book,* "They move in their work through phases of growth toward a poetry that spreads in scope as an aged tree spreads its roots and branches, as a man's experience spreads; their art in language conveying scars and informations of age . . . accumulations of what he is in his life, in his cooperation with the world about him." Trees: serial poems.

Persistence, as H.D. has it in *The Guest,* where she writes (and he cites): "But the roots of that flower [the tradition of Romance] still flourished and sent out thorny branches." So here, in his return to the verdant rhetorical, his inclusion of poems like "Sonneries of the Rose Cross," "Two Entertainments," the adaptations of "Arethusa" and "Cyparissus," and "Adam's Way," with its theosophical themes. Disturbing to Olson? He brings Olson and Spicer together in "Forced Lines"!

Do not forget that for this student of Harvey the heart-arteries-veins comprise a tree.

And Bachelard: "Imagination is a tree," its integrative work the work of art. That "a root is always a discovery," a fundamental or primary image because only an image that involves ambivalence—the root works among the dead yet feeds vertical aspiration—serves the imagination.

Renewal from beneath.

9 November 1979

The field is deeper, and the distress. The ground of the tree is family history and immediate history (his-story = his tree). Now there is explicit autobiographical probing and homoerotic acknowledgment. The daring, the defiance of his forms, the challenge to fathers (to his and to Olson in the poem to Rodilla, where he proposes the poetics of his work)—this is part of the crisis told by the title, "Nel Mezzo Del Cammin Di Nostra Vita."

The book is nearly twice the size of *The Opening of the Field*. In two parts, chronologically disposed in keeping with the serial nature of his enterprise: "The whole / planned to occupy life and allow / for death." There are experiments in seriality and more ambitious collages, though nothing as ambitious as "Passages." And more diversity, like Rodilla's tower (tree?) an "accretion of disregarded / splendors / resurrected against the rules," a "fairy citadel," yet to this end: " 'to do something big for America,' " his work, like Gaudi's mentioned here, the imagination's holy work, to gather us as Gaudi's Church of the Holy Family names it, into that polis, that America of love. Yes, to gather the "children / under one roof of the imagination."

A book of architecture, not a broken tower but a tower of broken bits ("an ecstasy / of broken bottles," recalling the transformed broken glass in *Paterson*, in *Tribute to the Angels*, and raising up the hidden jewel of "Apprehensions"?). Built by the son of an architect, who was not, finally, cowed by the Carpenter-God, and in the poem built after his own fashion and to his own ends. A "fairy citadel," indeed; the protective house, hearth, heart, where outlawed love and work (poetry, itself a work of love) have their being.

Troubled still by the question of "manhood" and vocation (see the counter-gesture of Chapter 1 of *The H.D. Book* begun about this time). By his mother's disapproval, the overbearing of his father's wishes. Seeking/defining true mothering, true fathering. Did H.D., herself so autobiographical in her work, prompt his autobiographical search? this descent to the cave, the hidden matrix, mother-ground? This is chiefly the book of the mother, like *Maximus II*. The mother lost in birth, the mother he knew, his spiritual mother H.D., and the all-subsuming Great Mother who ameliorates his ambivalence and sustains his faith. Mother Nature, who, at the end of "Adam's Way," is the Nurse of all nurses saving the children from the sea and the dark, coming with her light. Who, at the end of "Osiris and Set," "revives ever": "She remembers. She puts it all together." She gathers her children.

Autobiography is descent. *Re-membering*, in order to ascend, to day and love. The prominent myths, other than his own composite creation in "Adam's Way," are those of Osiris and Orpheus, myths of great suffering and erotic despair. ("Cyparissus" offers a version of the later in keeping with the image of the tree.)

Survival now means transforming the roots (hidden) into branches (revealed). Poetry itself is the act of faith that quells dread and helps him light(en) the dark. The fundamental movement of Duncan's work involves recoveries, sallies, risings, dawnings, rebirths. Is it in the nature of poetry to end in despair? to not rush in to fill the void? Isn't *The H.D. Book* a concurrent assertion of this, necessary enabling work? His concern with H.D. threads both parts of *Roots and Branches*. Both parts end on a rise, the second greater than the first.

11 November 1979

Return to innocence, and confusion. The initial poems are alive with desire, point back to the green world of *The Opening of the Field*, yet bear the uncomfortable burden of homoeros. Day, in "Roots and Branches," has its sensual counterpart in "Night Scenes." Here, as in other poems of the city, the streets are "sexual avenues" ("arteries," as in Crane's "Faustus and Helen"?) where, in cruising, he seeks "to release Eros from our mistrust," to "release the first music," find again the "wholeness green lovers know," *green* having a double meaning. A similar pristine quality informs the dream of homoeros in "A Sequence of Poems for H.D.'s Birthday": "To be in love! . . . // And youth in love with youth!" But in that dream, itself finally one of decadence, the mother counsels aloofness. In fact, all the introductory poems are mixed and marked by the acknowledgment in the poem on the Kabbalah that he knows nothing of the left or the right.

In what ways is the long, major "A Sequence of Poems for H.D.'s Birthday" for H.D.? Not, certainly, in the direct way of "Doves." Perhaps because it does large work, enters on such troubled psychological ground, makes conspicuous the matter of "*Dream Data*," and would have her understanding. Only she answers, helps?

Sequence here is characterized by diversity of forms, as also in the even longer, more complex "Apprehensions" (it includes "The Structure of Rime XIV"). In this instance most of the verse is "regular," some in rhyme and off-rhyme. The exceptions are "*Dream Data*," in restrained open form, and the explicit autobiographical section in prose. Were it not for its anticlimactic nature I would include the subsequent prose letter to the carpenter-father relating another dream; but as it is it prefaces the poem to Rodilla. *All these poems make a tight sequence.*

How focal "*Dream Data*" is may be gauged by this—as well as the preface to *Caesar's Gate*. And by how deep the issues it opens are—birth, parentage, identity, loyalties, vocation—and by the trust and redemption sought in the other sections. Four sections, in appropriately conventional (recognized) verse forms, are prayers to father and mother. Section 2: "Give me a hand, / out of the hell that is still underground // into the sunrise share, the new man." Section 3: a litany in praise that defines acceptable godhead and hence permits the declaration, "I am your son" (how grievous this need, as in Olson's imploring epigraphic verses to *Call Me Ishmael*, a book in which he, like Melville, agonizes over paternity). Section 5, to his mother to "be a nurse to me," to assure him that in going forth "into myself to be a man," the very work recalled and still enacted in this book, his errant ways will not deny him home (the crux of filial love). Section 6, concluding the sequence, an address to the Lady that acknowledges the terrible mother and the transformation he seeks and hopes to find in Sophia, the radiant spiritual mother.

> . . . I acknowledge you are most there
> when, tossing at night, head down, I watch
> (a witch's figure kept by old hatreds)
> the dark emerging from its stinking hole,
> you will lead me from despair.

The dark and the light lady and his confusion over mothers in the séance reported in section four. His version of Creeley's perplexity over real and ideal wives and his subscription to the tradition of Romance he finds in Creeley (see his review of *For Love*). Is this a cohort against Olson? Conspicuous here,

"A Dance Concerning A Form of Women" juxtaposed to the poem on Rodilla that cites "Against Wisdom as Such." Another poem, "Thank You For Love," the title naming book and act, paying tribute to Creeley's prosody by adopting it as his own—the poem itself ending in an echo of Creeley's concluding lines ("Into the company of love / it all returns"), the lines with which Duncan concluded his laudatory review. And then "Sonnet 3" in which he follows the vernacular of Creeley's practice in "Guido, vorrei che tu e Lapo ed io." Creeley:

> Guido
> I would that you, me & Lapo
> (So a song sung:
> *sempre d'amore* . . .)

Duncan: "Robin [Blaser], it would be a great thing if you, me, and Jack Spicer." What would be great? ". . . to weave themes ever of Love." To remember the verses in which "Our lusts and loves [were] confused in one" *and* for each to be "glad / To be so far abroad from what he was."

These poems are not tangential. What he says of Creeley applies to himself. The "Lady is both archetypical and specific" and her function, in Creeley's words, is to "give a man his / manliness." But manhood for Duncan means MANhood. He beseeches the Lady to re-member him in the image of MAN. No more than the ground are the roots and branches his own.

14 November 1979

There are no political poems in this book, though their source is here, as also in the previous book, in his concern with law-Law, with the necessary disobedience (see Psyche's); in his defiance of domineering authority; in his wish, in the letter to his father, to be allowed his "helpless little happiness of the human world," his "pathetic homestead" in the face of "the marches of relentless power." Homestead/Father here is the paradigm of beleaguered democracy; of poet/poetry versus institutional/political power. In the Pindar poem there are presidents, poets, and children, the later—and the meadow they desire and inhabit—defenseless, threatened by the former. There are no political poems here of the kind in *Bending the Bow*, and the interesting thing is that there they figure mostly in "Passages," that that sequence of essentially autobiographical poems gives them the requisite personal and mythic context. Duncan's politics moves us because it is not merely a matter of current issues but is as deep and as necessary to him as poetry, something demanded by ensouling, by his understanding of the Heraclitean (cosmological) and Freudian (psychic) notions of strife.

15 November 1979

"Our consciousness, and the poem as a supreme effort of consciousness, comes in a dancing organization between personal and cosmic identity." The previous entry brings that to mind, as does my apprehension over "Apprehensions," a "difficult" poem, the longest here and clearly one of the most important. "Apprehensions": intellectual understanding, the grasping of the mind, played off against fear, the apprehensiveness of something unpleasant—and *prehension*? a Whiteheadean term signaling event, the poem as event, in the happening/writing of which the fear is apprehended (thief of uncertainty that it is) and overcome (not dismissed but verified and included)?

The quotation on personal and cosmic identity comes from "Towards an Open Universe" where he cites a section of this poem as evidence of his imagination of the cosmos, of having his being and poetry in-and-of-it. An essential essay, with *essential* having the emphasis of essential autobiography; a necessary gloss, the poem itself also exemplifying what he says of musical thought and aperiodic structure.

Musical thought: addressing *deep things*, the *primal element of us . . . and of all things*, Carlyle says; "Poetry . . . we will call *musical* thought. The Poet is he who *thinks* [apprehends?] in that manner. See deep enough, and you see musically." Duncan concludes the poem with this declarative statement of all it includes / does:

> There is no life that does not rise
> melodic from scales of the marvelous.

(Do not overlook the serpent / jewel evoked by *scales* nor the appended phrase that does not let *us* forget the ground from which we attempt by "living apprehension" to rise: "To which our grief refers." Nor for that matter the conclusion of "The Law," immediately preceding "Apprehensions," where the muses command "strains of wild melody against the grain," and "*What is* / hisses like a serpent / and writhes // to shed its skin.")

Aperiodic structure. First, periodic structure, which originates in the balanced rhythms of day and night, the tides, the pulse beat; which has formal correlatives in "rhyming lines and repeating meter"; which Duncan says, following Schrödinger, expresses our desire to return to "the inertia of uncomplicated matter." Periodic forms are entropic, are associated with the "chemistry of death." Duncan cites Schrödinger's biological adaptation of thermodynamics: "*Living matter evades the decay to equilibrium*." That is, matter is alive when it is in a state of disequilibrium, "'When it goes on 'doing something,' moving, exchanging material with its environment.'" Like a tree, like an aperiodic poem; both complicated forms in which the elements, like atoms, play "individual role[s]." Aperiodic forms, then, are tropic; they resist entropy with eros, with desire. Note Duncan's comment: "What interests me here is that this picture of an intricately articulated structure, a form that maintains a disequilibrium or lifetime . . . means that life is by its nature orderly and that the poem might follow the primary processes of thought and feeling, the immediate impulse of psychic life."

Poems like "Apprehensions" are intricately articulated structures. So are serial books like *The Opening of the Field, Roots and Branches, Bending the Bow.* Open: in disequilibrium, to keep alive the activity of/for a lifetime. And this disequilibrium is not disorderly, without order, *melos* making *melody* ("the given and giving *melos* / melodies thereof"). Aperiodic forms answer "to impulse not plan," and this not only permits the poem to follow but to have the fullness of immediate psychic life. Yes, the life of the psyche, which is why the poem is necessary and Duncan goes on to define *apprehension* in the following: "Each poet seeks to commune with creation, with the divine world; that is to say, he seeks the most *real* form in language. But this most real is something we apprehend; the poem, the creation of the poem, is itself our primary experience of it."

16 November 1979

Is "The Venice Poem" periodic, "Apprehensions" aperiodic? That's the direction, in any case. And "The Venice Poem" comes to mind because it too turns on an ambivalent jewel—"This jewel / from which proceeds / as if rays / a melody."

"Apprehensions" is the poem of the cave, and the first poem of the book to put explicitly its central issue: the ascent of MAN. "Adam's Way," in the second part, is a companion work. The centrality of "Apprehensions" is evident in its filiations, for example, with "Osiris and Set" and "The Continent."

And isn't *the* "theme"—it has been nagging me, and I find it now in leafing through the text—the lines of "The Continent" that resume these lines of "Apprehensions" ("To survive we conquer life or must find / dream or vision"):

> the thought returns
> that we conquer life itself to live,
> survive what we are.

The opening section of the poem is a notable instance of the ideogrammic mode of the entire poem. The complexity is of many interconnected strands. As H.D. explains in defense of her "personal approach / to the eternal realities,"

> each has its peculiar intricate map,
> threads weave over and under

These are sorted out at the end in a Whitman-like catalog that insists on the order inherent in all things (*i.e.* "the orders of stars and of words"), on the very marvelousness of this. Which is what the poetic work discovers: "All things are powers within all things. // There is only one event." (Is there an echo here of Pound's touchstone from Erigena: *omnia quae sunt, lumina sunt*"—all things which are, are lights?) The work of the poem—and Duncan's belief in its reality—is verified at the end when the dream of the cave/cave-in is found to have anticipated the discovery of an actual abandoned cesspool. The first line of the poem, repeated later, proposes this work: "To open Night's eye that sleeps in what we know by Day." The work of the poem, brought forward in the activity of meditation, is to recover MAN, who, having been taken out of time (in the thought of theosophists) has left an empty space, a grave/cave in the earth: "and the hero bloom as he will toward that end / the poem imitates by admitting a form." The activity of meditation, involving the imagination of cosmologies, theosophies, fairy tales (earth as toad-mother), is re-memberment, and restores his sense of the universe as a whole. And as having a hole, a "grievous excavation," the emptiness, the incompleteness, "to which our grief refers"; the cave-grave-womb where he sees (as *Eidos*) the gleaming, jewel-like snake of MAN's possibility. The poem works not to the denial but to the appreciation of this necessary hidden condition. It would make us "Dragon-wise," as in Duncan's comment on Freud's saying that myths lie "in our blood, Dragon-wise / to darken our intelligence." Yes, to *deepen* with the necessary shadows.

17 November 1979

A lovely acknowledgment of Olson in the sixth section of "Variations on Two Dicta of William Blake." The context is the context of many of these poems, the part and the whole, divisiveness, yearning. The heart (responsive to breath, projecting the line in "Projective Verse") figures here in just those terms Olson used in speaking of the mind in relation to the syllable ("the mind is the brother to this sister . . . is the drying force, the incest"). The heart, the "dark organ," is "a part / of the whole yearning." It yearns for wholeness, and the whole itself seems to be characterized by yearning. And in lines that themselves prosodically confess it the heart of one poet is moved by the other.

> —the poet's voice, a whole beauty of the man Olson,
> lifting us up into

Answered. Joined by words. Transference of energy (love).

> where the disturbance is, where the words
> awaken
> sensory chains between being and being,
> inner acknowledgements
> of the fiery masters—there
> like stellar bees my senses swarmd.

Much more than Emily Dickinson's test, the tingling of the spine, is involved. He is moved, *charmd*, by both the poem and the man, a danger that he recognizes: "Here, again, I have come close upon what harm? / where the honey is. . . " Isn't he telling us why he considers Olson Promethean, "a Big Fire Source"? The assonance of *charm, swarm, harm*—the hum of the very bees, so brilliantly evocative, *stellar* indeed! carrying so many associations to language and sexuality, the visible and the invisible, enacting here what the butterflies do in "Roots and Branches." Calling up the meadow poem.

The despair of this part of the book is resumed and overcome in "Osiris and Set." A myth as important to this stage of ensouling as Psyche and Eros was to the earlier one. And as important to him as it was to Olson, who used it to tell his anxiety over paternity. Only for Duncan the myth tells of his own dismemberment, the contest or *agon* of his *members* ("Osiris and Set / members of one Life Boat are"). Drama, as he says, "is the shape of us"; the whole being that we are is broken from within ("Osiris-Kadmon into many men shattered, / torn by passion").

The poem summons many anxieties: the Atlantean dream; the knowledge of the "dark mind," the evil within himself (the psyche is a cosmos) that "scattered the first light"; homosexual seduction; loss of innocence, attributed here to Set as "Father." The image of the "radiant jewel" recalls "Apprehensions," and the desire for ascent from the cave. This rebirth-rememberment is the work of Isis, who for Duncan is not sister-wife but mother, "our Mother" who "revives ever," who "remembers . . . puts it all together." So in this realization "the sistrum / sounds through us" (as in Williams' "The Desert Music," "the music volleys through"). So Nut, as Olson wished, again arches the earth and we "nurse at the teats of Heaven"—

Dark sucks at the white milk.
Stars flow out into the deserted souls.

In our dreams we are drawn towards day once more.

"Osiris equates O-sir-is or O-Sire-is," and following this verbal play, H.D.-Isis asks (in *Trilogy*), "O, Sire, / is this union at last?" Isis, the Mother who re-members by remembering—isn't Duncan already paying tribute, as he will in what follows, to H.D., the Mother-Muse who inspires his art, his own remembering? Aren't these the most telling lines?

. . . We are
ourselves tears and gestures of Isis
as she searches for what we are ourselves . . .

Our selves.

18 November 1979

Windings (1961–63). Two books in one. Why does this title recall Yeats? Wind ("the wind is my god"); windings (coils/recoil, curved passages, twinings/weaving, wounds, cerements, spiral stairs ascending, swirling waters, vertical topology). The whole process of descent/ascent, unity/separation told in the adaptation of Shelley's "Arethusa": "into the full of life winding again. . . ."

"Adam's Way," like Psyche and Eros, fables the evolution of the soul, the coming into the divided life, the yearning. Samael, the Satanic presence who awakens in Eve "the grievous knowledge of the denial of love" (the burden of Duncan's essential autobiography), tells her that yearning will come of eating of the tree of knowledge: "*There* will be news of Love." The play ends there, with the discovery of death and darkness, the only solace the coming of the Mother with "a little light."

By its objectivity and distance, the play modulates the personal extremity of this half of the book. Its keynote, struck at the end, bears repeating: "we conquer life itself to live, / survive what we are." And struck at the beginning, in a dream following on the death of his second mother in 1960, a dream in which he finds himself in a death-like, birth-like state resisting the summons of life because "I have lost heart, / my mind is divided." Heart here, as he explains in prose "Afterthoughts," is also the heart of his first mother, lost in giving him birth, and, by extension, H.D.'s heart, since he fears that her death will be exacted as the price of *The H.D. Book*. And since the Great Mother is evoked by mothers, her heart too. What is most distressing in this resumption of self-soul history—and now it concerns only mothers—is the uncertainty that puts in question his faith in the Great Mother. More than that? his inability in his own case to accept the Eleusinian mystery of life out of death?

In the second of "Two Presentations," a poem remarkable for the patency with which he works with its occasion, he considers the death of the second mother in terms of the death-abandonment-motherlessness of his own birth. She, too, is in the swirling waters—

> Are you out there alone then like that?
> Or did your own mother come, close in,
> to meet you.

His aunt believes that on death our mothers await us, but he is not sure, not even of the Great Mother:

> But, of that other Great Mother
> or metre, of the matter . . .

Mētēr, Mater, Materia, Matrix, Matter. Yes, the Great Mother is the mother of all things, of poetry (meter), too. And his fear of forfeiting love—his greatest fear—touches that. He writes, remember, "to win particular hearts." The dread he feels comes from the fact that

> My letter always went alone
> to where
> I never knew you reading.

The windings are tortuous / torturous. When he reaches "A Part-Sequence for Change," he is, as he reiterates, "Deeply estranged." Deep fears invade him—

> The boy I was watches
> not without fear
> black places in the darkening room

—and he is overcome by what he feels to be the desertion of the powers upon which he relies. Yet there is a stubborn physical counterforce in him that rises up like spring, "changes and turnings of the heart" that blossom like a tree—

> . . . break from the tree
> . . . .
> the swarm of too many buds
> for melody
>
> and the ascendancy of the shadow
> in the blossoming mass.

So in the instinctual round of things fears give way to pristine possibility, to the restoration of the green world. The buds are too many, but their swarming—hear the bees in a*sc*endan*cy* and blo*ss*oming ma*ss*—sounds the advent of love and poetry. Such is the case in respect to hearing Olson in "Variations on Two Dicta of William Blake" and in respect to recalling H.D. in "After Reading H.D.'s *Hermetic Definitions*." In the latter, another poem remarkable for the way in which he uses the occasion (now to show his reliance [trust] on subconscious processes), the bees remind him of his service to the Queen and that he, like H.D., writes by instinct, and under the injunction, "*Write, write or die.*"

This puts the extremity. Even with the change of "A Part-Sequence for Change," the necessary work of ensouling remains. Now, in "The Structure of Rime XIX," he stands "Under the branches of tears," unable to find the art with which to survive, dismayed, it seems, by the lack of correspondence between self and world. The subsequent poems of this series (XX, XXI) offer counsel: to lose (and loosen—as in "Come, Let Me Free Myself") heart, to yield the ego and give over grasping, to both free from confinement the thrush held in his hands and attend the world outside himself; to follow the less willful way of the women who serve the natural order and thereby release the sound of the wood, the bird-notes at the edge of silence.

The concluding poem, "The Continent," fulfills much of this counsel. Now he attends the turning world, has all the world before him, Gaia, who, as the title indicates, is Pangaia, Gondwanaland, as Eduard Suess named the ancient continental mass, the "one continent," Duncan now affirms, "moving in rifts, churning, enjambing, / drifting feature from feature" (like an open poem?). And the turning Earth, whose Eleusinian mysteries are worldwide, from time zone to time zone, and everpresent.

19 November 1979

"The Continent" closes the book with this evocation of the still active primordial Mother. But some of the counsel of the Master of Rime involves the primordial and calls up "Doves," Duncan's finest (deepest) tribute to his Mother-Muse.

"After Reading H.D.'s *Hermetic Definition*," separated from "Doves" by the interval of one poem, is prefatory, the doves already present in the overcast sky—"doves / (that may be her *nun*'s) grey." Now in response to news that H.D. has had a stroke impairing her speech, he writes to tell his love, his speech, he claims (though the poem proves otherwise), inadequate, like hers. Doves, in fact, names a language prior to words, "the actual language," of Duncan's "The Natural Doctrine," that "is written in rainbows." In losing the power of speech, H.D. gains another, gains the privileged condition of the first / primordial world, where *things are*, un-named. The process of naming is reversed, from thing to word to word to thing: Soul is to tongue, as thing is to word, as secret is to its name. H.D. is admitted—at the window opening into the dove-grey air and light of morning—to the "first world" where "initial things" (like Kabbalistic letters, themselves divine agencies of creation) go.

So the doves, immemorially associated with the spirit (and with priestesses of the Earth-Mother), replace words, and in H.D.'s paralysis, are her *mouthings*—this "Mother of mouthings," the evocation at once of the Mother-Muse of all *muthos*, the Tree of Life itself with doves murmuring in the branches, and of H.D. Dove-sounds *recur* (as here) in the "hurrrrrr / hurrrrrr / hurrr" (and again in "The Continent" where Gaia is "murtherer, murmurer, demurrer"). I hear it too in "love's watery tones," which combines the lovely and the fearful and recalls the musical shuttle of Whitman's great reminiscence song.

She is admitted to creation, restored, I think, to *her* Mother-Muse, in her extremity met by the Mother. In images as applicable to Duncan as to H.D., she has released the dove from her cupped hands and thereby broken the "nets of words." The loss, told by "The Lady holds nothing in her two hands / cupt. The catches of the years are torn," is immediately, consequently, compensated by "And the wood-light floods and overflows / the bowl [now the golden bowl of consciousness?] she holds like a question." Even more:

> Voices of children from playgrounds come
> sounding on the wind without names.

So *windings* are sounds without names, and bring her (and us) to the place of first permission. To the serenity of the time before words, which is equivalent to the time after words. To an emptiness (humility) readily filled/answered by "love's watery tones," by the dove's call, the "*whirr* of wings in the boughs [of the Tree of Life]," which is also the leaf sound and the voices of children, all of them gathered in *verging*: "the voices in the wind verging into leaf sound," where *into* tells of leafing, of springtime, and the returning green world.

The meadow is an image of the primordial, of that new occasion of self and world. The leafing recalls the swarming buds of "A Part-Sequence for Change" and the "disturbance of words" of "Often I am Permitted to Return to a Meadow":

> She it is Queen Under The Hill
> whose hosts are a disturbance of words within words
> that is a field folded.

The Primordial.

22 November 1979

> There was never any more inception than there is now.
> . . . .
> Urge and urge and urge,
> Always the procreant urge of the world.

More than ever Duncan answers to the primordial in *Bending the Bow* (1968). He engages with creation, with the cosmos as "a field of fields," a realm of life (all life: "human" and other).

He takes the turning—and evolving—world into his keeping. Taking up a (the) public task, he becomes the poet as hero.

The Opening of the Field is (primarily, not exclusively) the book of the meadow and the dance, *Roots and Branches* of the cave and the tree. *Bending the Bow* is the book of daylight duties. Here, as in the title poem, he becomes the bowman of morning. Olson had been—still was—its archeologist, but not its bowman. Duncan's book is actively political, his poetry is political act. Now he makes literal what he said in speaking of the poetics of act in respect to *The Maximus Poems*: "Beauty is related to the beauty of an archer hitting the mark." He bends the bow with a warrior's intensity (just as in the cover photograph he stares grimly at us, *confronts* us, who may after all belong to the enemy) to send the arrow, the arrow of Eros, at Thanatos. Poetry—Orphic song: for the bow is also the lyre—is at war for life. *BIOS*, Greek, stands for both bow and life. Life is strife. Poetry has become public, which is not to say that it is any the less personal, but that like the individual it finds its fulfillment in community, has accepted responsibility for survival.

In becoming public, it has taken possession of the house. The poet now speaks in and for "the company of the living," and his voice no longer issues from the cave but from the earth (*hearth* contains *earth*)

> . . . from the hearth stone, the lamp light,
> the heart of the matter where the
> house is held
> ("Tribal Memories")

Olson recognized the change, though, curiously, without acknowledging the political aspect, just as in speaking of

Mailer's achievement in *The Armies of the Night* he found it sufficient to praise the prose, the writing. Having received one of the "Passages" that extend beyond *Bending the Bow*, he remarked: "He's become a BIG poet, like Yeats. I mean that quality, suddenly. At 49 he put on the robe. And he writes in that marvelous—but its big, its ode-*ique*—paeon would be useful. And not Blake, but I mean beautifully American."

BIG. What he speaks of in "Projective Verse" as "projective size" and, taking bearings from *The Cantos*, as pointing to the solution of the problem (his, in *Maximus*) of "larger content and of larger forms."

Beautifully American. Yes, but not for any reason he offers us.

The mandate, from Dante and Whitman, companions in Duncan's thought about whom he wrote companion essays, on Dante in 1965, on Whitman in 1969, both "perennial source[s]" and presences during the composition of *Bending the Bow*. And would anyone but Duncan (and Pound) put them together? these poets, on whom, as the contention between Eliot and Crane reminds us, the issue of the American long poem centered? Duncan has many distinctions, but one of the greatest may be that he fulfills the tradition of Romance of the one and the tradition of "Democracy" of the other *and* joins them in an ecological vision neither had. In the essay on Whitman, which of all his writings tells us most precisely what his "project" is—what is at the generative center of his work, what he serves—he speaks of allegiance to an all-inclusive ecological order, knowing, as he says, that "the well-being of Nature becomes the condition of our humanity."

Thinking of this and his insistence on the primordial—creation is always before us here/now, not behind us—I hear *him* in "Solitary, singing in the West, I strike up for a New World."

23 November 1979

Poet as hero, but not as he once defined him, a Canute playing sovereign to the sea. The hero now takes "orders" and is concerned with the "orders" of art, orders coming to him from Dante and Whitman. In "Passages 35" (in *Tribunals*, 1970), Duncan tells us that he is citing from the Temple Classics edition of *The Divine Comedy* translated by John Aitken Carlyle, "the text . . . belonging to the mystery of these Passages." John calls up Thomas Carlyle, and the brotherly tie deeply links Dante's work to "The Hero as Poet" (the poets: Dante, Shakespeare), which, in turn, leads Duncan to Pound's *The Spirit of Romance* (originally published by the publishers of Temple Classics) and Pound's prefatorial declaration, "The study of literature is hero-worship." So poetry, as he says, has a liturgy, his, here, involving those who serve "the Goods of the Intellect," what in "Orders" ("Passages 24") he spells out

For the Good
il ben dello intelletto, the good of the people,
the soul's good.

Duncan declares almost all of his "goods" when he writes of the many connections between Dante and Whitman. Enough to cite now, "Whitman's politics, like Dante's, is the politics of a polis that is a poem." (Doesn't the polis become cosmopolis in the poem, and the psyche cosmopolitan? Isn't that, finally, his heavenly city? And isn't polis, as in *Maximus*, a *nest*, a rounded household befitting cosmicity, wellbeing?) And this, to fill out the liturgy: Whitman . . . comes to fulfill and sees himself as fulfilling . . . the vision of the poet that begins, for [him], in Carlyle's *Heroes and Hero-Worship* and passes on through Emerson's writings."

"Yes, truly, it is a great thing for a Nation that it get an articulate voice; that it produce a man who will speak-forth melodiously what the heart of it means!"—Carlyle, "The Hero as Poet."

"The theme is creative and has vista." / "He is the president of regulation." Duncan cites these lines from the 1855 Preface to *Leaves of Grass* in "A Poem Beginning with a Line by Pindar." There, initially, Whitman commanded his political voice, gave him the "orders" he then considered a "Glorious mistake." Now he endorses them, and in "Fire" ("Passages 13"), where his political outrage first finds expression, he cites an entire paragraph of Whitman's speech, "The Eighteenth Presidency," according to Gay Wilson Allen, Whitman's last attempt at "practical" political action.

May we not say of Duncan what he says of Whitman, that he writes the definitive politics of his time, "'his time,'" he explains, "being the time created in his poetic vision?"

24 November 1979

Our time of strife:

1964 Free Speech Movement at Berkeley
1965 Systematic bombing of North Vietnam begins
Selma-Montgomery march
Invasion of the Dominican Republic
First anti-war march on Washington
Malcolm X assassinated
Watts
1966 Sit-ins against the war and the draft
1967 Exposure of CIA infiltration of NSA

The Resistance formed in California
March on the Pentagon

According to the Notes—with the Introduction an unusual feature of this volume—the title comes from Heraclitus, Fragment 51: "People do not understand how that which is at variance with itself agrees with itself. There is a harmony in the bending back, as in the case of the bow and the lyre." A tension (harmony) of opposites, "a contrapuntal communion of all things." Yes, the All, as Herigel says of the Zen of archery: "When drawn to its fullest extent, the bow encloses the 'All' in itself."

Duncan's cosmology is Heraclitean-Whiteheadean; like Olson's and some other postmodern poets'. But more than any other poet, he turns to Heraclitus to evoke the political burden of the book. The title of his most important political essay (written at about the time of the essay on Whitman; Whitman is Heraclitean) is "Man's Fulfillment in Order and Strife." Its opening sentence is "War is both King of all and Father of all"—Heraclitus, Fragment 25, which Fragment 26 unfolds: "War is the common condition . . . strife is justice . . . all things come to pass through the compulsion of strife."

These fragments—did he hear Eliot, as in Heraclitus, too?—are a mandate. He goes to war, bends the bow, because it is necessary to *harmony* and *fulfillment*. "A new order," he says in the essay, "is a contention in the heart of existing orders"—whether the orders of polity, psyche, or poem. "The very life of our art is our keeping at work contending forces and convictions." So the book includes his strife with Blaser over translating Nerval. But more important it is itself both the means of his engagement and the model of the order he summons, just as much as Dante and Whitman, in the forms of their poems, proposed orders, one retrospective, the other prospective (not "at the end of a civilization but at the beginning").

Whitman opened the field to the political voice that now speaks out in these poems *and*, as we can better see now, elicited their form. Whitman and Dante are sources of Duncan's work because each "projected a poem central to his civilization and his vision of ultimate reality—*Leaves of Grass*, like the *Divina Commedia*, being not an epic narrative but the spiritual testament of a self-realization." But *Leaves of Grass* serves him where the *Divina Commedia* does not because its form is not the "paradigm of an existing eternal form" but an organic, evolving form of "the ever flowing, ever Self-creative ground of a process." *Leaves of Grass*, like his own work, is moved "by generative urgencies toward the fulfillment of a multitude of latent possibilities"; it *grows*, "as a man grows, composed and recomposed, in each phase immediate and complete, but unsatisfied." *Unsatisfied*: picking up both Whitehead's and Whitman's *satisfaction*.

So, as he explains in the Introduction, the sonnets with which he begins conclude a series begun in *Roots and Branches* and initiate "a theme of love that moves in other poems" (enclosing and interpenetrating the public with the private, with the necessary condition of love: he bends the bow, as he says of Freud, between Eros and Thanatos, and like Odysseus, to secure the household, the heart). And "The Structure of Rime" continues, even as "Passages" with which it merges in "Passages 20" extends beyond the book, into *Tribunals* and now to periodicals. "Passages" constitute a new, another departure, wholly representative: "I enter the poem as I entered my own life, moving between an initiation and a terminus I cannot name." Then, "The Narration for

Adam's Way" brings the play forward, or sends us back to it, that *way* also a passage; and the translations of Nerval take us to the Duncan issue of *Audit/Poetry* (1967), itself a rich miscellany. The Introduction, evoking an end of things, "the last days of our own history," demands a hearing, brings to the reader's attention explanations of a lifework without which he might not fully understand how poetry can give us a place to survive, be a lifeline. And the Notes give him some sources unnamed in the text, resources should he follow them up.

All for the sake of these interrelated *orders*.

Cosmos	evolutionary process Whitehead Heraclitus (strife)	God the great household
Polity	"a nation of nations" ("Trans-National America")	Democracy the commune of communes
Psyche	ensouling* Freud (strife) re-memberment	MAN heart-hearth- household
Poem	open, aperiodic, serial, inclusive	Poetry a commune, a "grand collage" serving the above**

* "For the ego is not the whole psyche, only one member of a commune."—James Hillman, *Re-Visioning Psychology*.

** And fertile in resonances, ratios, correspondences.

All, as he says in "Orders," where, like Pound and Olson, he feels the force of the story of the Wagadu in "Gassire's Lute"—"The city that is within us," he remarks in *The Truth & Life of Myth*, "haunts all of Poetry," the city held in the heart—all because

> There is no
> good a man has in his own things except
> it be in the community of everything;
> no nature he has
> but in his nature hidden in the heart of the living,
> in the great household.
> The cosmos will not
> dissolve its orders at man's evil.

25 November 1979

With politics, the voice of outrage enters the book. Always concerned with boundaries, he now draws the line, as Paul Goodman did in *The May Pamphlet* (1945) and Gary Snyder does in *Turtle Island* (1974), all of them in the realization, in Goodman's words, that "a man is dependent on his mother Earth." (Do not forget the political activity of his early manhood, his connection with the anarchist writers at Woodstock—he remembers Vanzetti in discussing the good of the commune in the essay on Whitman and acknowledges Kropotkin elsewhere—and his writing for Dwight Macdonald's *Politics*. Nor the fact that he draws the line by going out of bounds, by introducing discord into the established—closed—order; the discord, for example, of the homosexuality of many of these poems, homosexuality having been the subject of his essay in *Politics*; and by confronting the established poetic line and closed forms with a phrasal prosody, a "restless" ordering. This is how *poetry* goes to war, this is to make a *political* book.) So now, as he explained in the case of *Trilogy*, one must expect, must include, the anger, outrage, despair, fear, and judgment that accompany apocalyptic statements, that rise up from the "besieged spirit." For, as in H.D.'s time (World War I and II), life itself is under attack, the heart is under attack. The war, in its social and psychological aspects, is the "old war against Tiamat." And since the psyche exists within the social psyche (a psychic society) the artist must fight the psychic contents by admitting them in himself and in his art, *by including what we know but refuse to acknowledge* (refuse on penalty of social disintegration, as he recalls E. R. Dodds saying of the Greeks). In psyche, society, and poem he must permit the return of the repressed—include even madness. And for psyche, society, and poem, he must recover the power of Eros, go back to the heart of things.

When the heart is under attack the imagination must provide "a new heart and a new reality in which there is a germ of survival." This has always been Duncan's work, and now we can readily read it as he reads H.D.'s, Pound's, Williams'—and Whitman's—as an "evolution of forms in which life survives."

Do not all the great long (cultural) poems respond to war-in-our-time? And isn't *Bending the Bow* notable for this reason? for making a place in poetry, as no other contemporary poet has, for this war, our recent war and the continuing war within the cosmos and the human spirit? Who besides Duncan (maybe Ginsberg?) has seen the issue so fully, as eternally present, history itself enacting myth; seen the necessity of strife to fulfillment, and, in taking on himself the necessity of waging war (within and with the poem), given us so many germs of survival?

There is another way of assessing his politics and coming to an understanding of what it means to be a political poet.

There's Bill Reuckert's schema:

WORD

CULTURE

NATURE

WORD, what Duncan would call the collective consciousness or Poetry, the achievements of all mind and imagination; CULTURE, something less than that, the present social use we make of these riches of mind and heart and of the resources of NATURE. Now Duncan brings the good(s) of the WORD and of NATURE, *allied by him*, to a faltering CULTURE that pollutes, corrupts, and destroys both of these essential generative sources.

27 November 1979

Cosmos includes *polity, psyche, poem*; and cosmogony (myth) accounts for what is generative—and regenerative—in politics, psychology, and art. As much as before, Duncan is concerned with reviving the old orders, but now, polarizing in response to political urgencies, he treats them in the context of good and evil (evil defined politically, as authority, power *over* us, as Satan and Ahriman). In *The Truth & Life of Myth*, itself a work of this time arguing for the recovery of the sense of myth (for what is at war are also mythic and rational modes of understanding), he says of "Chords" ("Passages 14"—*Chord* is one of the god-words in the subsequent spelling lesson): "I . . . evoke[d] cosmic powers from the oldest myths as they appear in the Orphic theogonies, to bring into the immediate reality, where the political powers at war seem all powerful, awareness of or the presence of the very numen of the Universe."

The universe itself is at war with war: "The cosmos will not / dissolve its orders at man's evil."

Not only is myth presently enacted in historical and psychic events but it is presented for use by way of our restored sense of its presence. It is present for us because—in these poems more than ever before—it is present to him. He *experiences* myth, the presences in them, not only the cosmogonal, but the seasonal / vegetative / diurnal, the redemptive myths. And since all are myths involving strife, he accepts the necessity of the present war, and sees in it the "forbidden hallucínogen / that stirs sight of the hidden / order of orders!"

The Orphic theogonies are prominent now because Orphism revives the old orders, the Eleusinian mysteries, at the same time as it introduces elements familiar to us in Christianity—sin, purification, atonement, the "passion," immortality. Orphism joins Demeter and Dionysus, Mother and Son. In the cosmogony of the World-Egg it restores the primacy of Eros. And, in Orpheus, it gives the poet a cultural role, his music being of the kind Carlyle commended in "The Hero as Poet" ("See deep enough, and you see musically; the heart of Nature *being* everywhere music, if you can only reach it"). The hero as poet, but also the poet as homosexual. All of these elements are here.

"Orpheus out of a professor's studies"—he cites W. K. C. Guthrie in the Notes. A learned poet, as much as Pound and Olson to be gauged by his reading, some of it entered in "The Architecture" ("Passages 9"), where it is appropriately part of his inner space, of his "recesses," heart, hearth: Hesiod, Heraclitus, *The Secret Books of the Egyptian Gnostics, La Révélation d'Hermès Trismégiste, Plutarch's Morals: Theosophical Essays*, Avicenna, *The Zohar, The Aurora*, the works of George MacDonald (spiritual allegories and fairy tales), Amerindian lore.

"And, before he composed the theogony [in "Chords"] . . . hadn't he," he asks in prose "Reflections," "heard the great passages of Charles Olson's *Maximus* resounding theogony?" Inevitably, he recalls "Against Wisdom as Such," but now "wisdom" is read favorably in the light of "wisdom texts" that for him, as for Olson, awakened these salutary resonances.

He refers to *Maximus II*. Incorporates it, for example, "Maximus, at the Harbor" in the "Okeanos roars" of "Passages 30," the *katavóthra* of "Gravelly Hill" in "Passages 6." Adopts a similar playfulness with titles: "In the Place of a Passage 22." Rivals it with his own brilliant theogony, Orphic, moreover, not Hesiodic (his Hesiod, the poet of *Works and Days*, from whom, in support of the goods of the intellect, he takes the account of the golden ones, alluded to in "Passages 19," celebrated as the hero-ancestors of the poet as hero in "Passages 35"). Generously. He is not at war with this kindred poet, and where acknowledgment is most important acknowledges him, twice, for example, in the Introduction, so much of which involves Duncan's poetics, is, in fact, a revision (*re*: vision) of "Projective Verse," moving from its concern for the syllable to the musical phrase.

Duncan and Olson share the same cosmological faith. Olson: "The spiritual is all in Whitehead's simplest of all statements: Measurement is most possible throughout the system." Duncan: "This is not a field of the irrational; but a field of ratios in which events appear in language. Our science presumes that the universe is faithful to itself: this is its ultimate rationality." And then, in what may be considered as updating Fenollosa, "And we had begun to see that language is faithful to itself."

Is mathematics for them—an imagination of the stars—before not after myth, as Giorgio de Santillana believes? "It was *measures* and *counting* that provided the armature, the frame on which the rich texture of real myth was to grow." (*Hamlet's Mill*)

Ratios, Correspondences, Articulations, Equilibrations. Key words, addressing the formal matter of coherence, of order—the problem of long and serial poems—where the most radical innovation for Duncan is phrasal composition. Here, he is Hermes, the lock-picker, who "invented the bow and the lyre to confound Apollo, god of poetry." Confound/confront. So now the phrase fits not by locking, but by unlocking ("I hate locks"—"A Poem of Despondencies"), and "what was closed is opened." Why? "The line of the poem is articulated into phrases so that phases of its happening resonate where they will"—here *and* there. Everywhere. In the entire "commune of Poetry."

This is one sense in which "Passages of a poem larger than the book in which they appear follow a sentence read out of Julian." Another: a life is more than a book. In reading Guthrie, he "heard the great passages of Charles Olson's *Maximus*," which tells us that the theogonic is only part of the association established here. Who are the poets mentioned in the Introduction and taken up in the work? Chiefly Pound, Zukofsky, and Olson. "Passages" is Duncan's *Maximus*, if not the one poem a poet writes all of his life, a poem that resumes all of his life and proposes thenceforth to be such a poem. It is the newest issue of his growth, of a generative urgency greater than that in subsequent serial poems, *A Seventeenth Century Suite . . .* (1973), which includes "Passages 36," and *Dante [Etudes]* (1974), though these poems, too, are resumptive. And like *The Cantos* and *"A"* and *Leaves of Grass*, it is "the spiritual testament of a self-realization."

2 December 1979

Passages. Does he take the title from the fact that the inspiration for the poem came from *passages* he copied out, those on the bounded and unbounded that preface the poem? And that the poem incorporates other such passages of his reading, passages in his chrestomathy? As he says in "Passages 6," these are "passages of a poetry, passages made conglomerate" (*conglomerate* replaces *condensare*, probably from Pound, in the reading at Berkeley). In prefatory remarks made on reading some of the sequence, he is exclusively concerned with its formal nature, with a sequence which has no "consequence," that is, has "no beginning and no end as its condition of form." "At the Loom" speaks for this weaving of "one fabric," a memory-field (hence the importance of the musical phrase) in which all the strands or parts "co-operate, co-exist" and memory itself (invoked in "Tribal Memories") is essential to the apprehension of form. Meant to be performed, read aloud, *Passages* makes a more than usual demand on our memory. And a wonderful performance it is! The ritual he says it is, the chant, requiring the use of the "high voice." Heretical, he says, in modernist literature, calling up (as with Ginsberg) "the Upanishads and Sutras . . . the Songs of Solomon and the Psalms of David." So the poet is once again priest, but, as "Passages 6 and 15" demonstrate, also a pedagogue, his drawing and writing on the blackboard (conspicuous also with Olson) summoning the cave-drawings of Pleistocene man. Tribal memories. By sight and sound.

Rites of passage? Those of love and poetry are remembered ("The Torso," "Shadows"). Passages out of the cave? Passages of music to "illustrate concords of order in order" ("Orders"). The dark, cunning corridors of history, from Eliot's "Gerontion," Eliot now acknowledged. The passages between the body and the universe, from Boehme; the passage(ways) fearful and joyful between rooms and stories; and passage from not-being to being, death to life, the supplication of the sequence, always in search of an opening, being, "Grant me passages from winter's way," which echoes, fittingly, Crane's "Permit me voyage, love, into your hands." These poems permit the passage of love.

Movement itself from phase to phase, event to event, this itself of the nature of cosmos and self. *Passages* is concerned throughout with creation, and is itself an enactment of "creational passion." Its ground in the WORD and NATURE.

> The principle of form for this poem, for all my poetry and works in the light of this poem, its originality, was posited . . . in the great ground of forms created in Man's Poetry . . . and, beyond, in the ground of all forms as apprehensions of the Real, in the physical and spiritual reality of the Universe as a present creation, a Self-making in process.

This poem resumes his life in the light of all human history: his-story is that story, and its myth(s) are those of the cosmos. So it may be said to be a theogony of creation, of the ever-renewable creation and love that countervails the evil of war (*unnatural violence* because, as Goodman says, it "reinforces the coercive and authoritarian establishment").

3 December 1979

The sequence, one fabric in itself, is woven into the book, its text of that texture. It is the prominent feature of *Bending the Bow*, served by everything else, often as reflexive commentary, as in the installments of "The Structure of Rime," which may dissolve into it because the "high voice" takes over its shamanism and "Passages" themselves are concerned with "rime, measure, correspondences, as kosmos." And also because they are the same poem, in different phases, both evoking Mnemosyne in their initial poems ("Mnemosyne is still the Great Mother, the Matrix, of the World we artists seek the Art of"); connected, as we see in the best commentary on them, the 1973 addition to the notes on *The Structure of Rime* that also prefaces the subsequent remarks on *Passages* (in *MAPS #6*). Other poems serve by modulating, for example, "Earth's Winter Song," which not only answers "In the Place of a Passage 22" but brings the most resonant imagery of the previous books again into play, and "An Interlude," where the dance is the "grand mimesis" of a Heraclitean cosmos. Or, as with *The Chimeras of Gérard de Nerval*, which follows "Up Rising" and permits another kindred poet to speak in behalf of what he values, indeed to speak most eloquently the "Golden Lines" that declare the ecological manifesto of the book—ancestral wisdom out of Pythagoras, one of the golden ones, guardians of the good. (And aren't these sonnets "rimes" of his own sonnets, love the essential element of any *ecos*, household and earth household? Didn't Olson say that the inclusive factors were *Eros, Economos, Ethos*?)

And then, a poem like "God-Spell," which in its position in the book, its phrasal scoring, its insistences and recapitulations is as much a "Passages" as any (here a way is found), yet not designated as one, perhaps because in moving to close the book it might bring the sequence to a close. Certainly it answers with some hope the rumors of the enemy first heard in "Tribal Memories," answers much that the sequence addresses—

> seeds of a rumor   from hearts long ago
> defeated faiths   blown out
> the ayre of the music   carries.

But the good news, gospel, *kerygma*, is followed by an afterword, by an "Epilogos," where the pun on *logos* is undoubtedly significant, a poem about love, about the heart of the matter, that ties back to the "Sonnets," and to "Doves" (in *Roots and Branches*), and by way of Keats's "Ode to Psyche" to "A Poem Beginning with a Line by Pindar" (in *The Opening of the Field*); a poem that in its *moan* tells us that, at heart, muthos has for its burden the story of the difficult journey to love; that as Ginsberg says in his lovely "Song" (out of Williams), "for the burden of life / is love."

4 December 1979

How intricately woven! *Passages* belongs to the entire corpus, and the entire corpus comments on it. It is not only the intricate art, the remarkable loomcraft (of lines thrown, vanishing, as he says, on the air—but caught by ear), that marks this work as masterful—I am tempted to single it out as his greatest work, but then what would I say of the still greater sequence of *The Opening of the Field, Roots and Branches, Bending the Bow*, which, as ground, contributes so much to the resonance—the intensity—of *Passages*?

If you think of *Passages* as comparable to "Song of Myself" (Robert Duncan, a Cosmos) in relation to *Leaves of Grass*, note its chronological place in the work: it does not initiate but re-visions an already considerable life-work.

What is it *now* you think to say of it? What resonances does it have for you?

The deep interiority of it, and the need to see / make the cosmos a household ruled by love. (There are poems in *Bending the Bow* that seek to ameliorate the relationships with mother and father.) The sequence is moved by reverie toward childhood, by the desire for cosmicity, that well-being, first known in the womb-room of the World-Egg (the "rimed round / sound-chamberd child"), then known in other rooms, for example, the room he has been the architect of in "The Architecture," where all his precious goods sustain him and which leads back (out) to the garden—*out* because he is also, significantly, moved by "the lure of the world / I love," where *lure*, as in "lure of feeling," has a Whiteheadean meaning.

Reverie toward childhood: reverie toward love, to the values of warmth and light, milk and love (the "milk and light" of the Orphic theogony in "Chords," the "warm" of "The Architecture"). To the values—Edenic, he rightly says—that are evoked by the seed-words framing "Fire," words that in their counter-clockwise turning recall the children in their dance in the Pindar poem, and whose terminal "jump" recalls the plash of the frog in the poem first heard in childhood and remembered in *The Truth & Life of Myth*.

And doesn't this reverie account for the quantum leap of "Fire" ("Passages 13"), the sudden flare-up of rage? This remarkable poem, reminiscent of "A Poem Beginning with a Line by Pindar," puts the political issue in the inclusive terms of the meadow:

> They are burning the woods, the brushlands, the
>   grassy fields razed;   their
>   profitable suburbs spread.
> Pan's land, the pagan countryside, they'd
>   lay waste.

Again in "The Soldiers," where he (we) fight(s) from "the heart's [deep] volition": "The Industrial wiping out the Neolithic!" And in "Passages 33," these unbearable lines:

> A million reapers come to cut down
> the leaves of grass we hoped to live by . . .

Though the meadow is evoked, it is now the heart/hearth/house that carries its values. Just as commune now speaks for the dance. We may measure Duncan's course by the fact that this book of the bow is the book of the household and the commune, written under threat of burning and laying waste and darkness and death, existence itself more precarious than ever. It is so in the contrapuntal lines of "Passages 36," where his only refuge is

> this room where we are,   this house,
> this garden,   this home
>   our art would make

His goods are his weapons: love and poetry, and in them is "the passage from sleep to day again." "Passages 30," the concluding installment of *Bending the Bow*, ends with the release of Chrysoar and Pegasus from the body of the slain Medusa ("from the dying body of America"), Pegasus again striking the earth and raising "new springs" of poetry. Are we to recall in "Steed of Bellerophon" that Duncan himself had "conquered" the *Chimeras* of Nerval? And "Epilogos," in its summoning (I wrote *summing*) of love, reminding us of the coda to *A Seventeenth Century Suite*, a sequence which may be thought of as Duncan's equivalent to H.D.'s *By Avon River* (which also considers poetry a house: "O, what a house he [Shakespeare] built / To shelter all of us"). Here, at the end, "our little household" stands to the cosmos as Duncan, in the assurance of love (the night nurse now replaced by the lover), stands to the enveloping darkness.

> You clothe me round
> And to the shores
> sleep knows upon a further deep
>   solemnity
> into the infancy of a darkening bliss
>
> Love sets me free.

6 December 1979

The act of poetry also renews his faith. That is as true of *Bending the Bow* as of the other books, where the movement at the end is upward. But darkness now is not only private and public war. It is oncoming, always ever-present death, which is why I feel the strong insistence on eros—generative energy—and on responsibility: on conscience and obedience in the *Dante [Etudes]*, on playing out the full significance of Whitman's line in "The Adventure of Whitman's Line." Could anything more conclusively confirm his lineage with this poet of love and death (the "unrelieved suffering of the human condition") than his own striding, in the appended poem, with Whitman's line? This consummate poem *justifies* and *answers* the poet whose birth in 1819 rhymes with Duncan's in 1919, a poet he now acknowledges to have had his place (with H.D.) in the formative years of his adolescence. Whitman, he says, addressed "the central pathos" of his life and spoke to him of a tender and boundless love that is justified even now, a century later, only "in the mutualities of personal courages and personal recognitions" ("dear father, greybeard, lonely old courage-teacher," Ginsberg says)—a love, he adds, "in which and from which I too must adventure to create whatever common ground of humanity and my alliance with the intent of life itself."

Adventure: advance. "It is only in a new poetry [not his alone: he speaks representatively for a generation of poets] that the transmission of poetry is ever justified, is ever carried forward."

Eros and responsibility. And persistence. ". . . courage now in this persisting, the painstelling a new phase of the life-story. . . ." ("The point is not to be happy but to persist"—Rilke, cited by Goodman.) Courage now when "Urge and urge and urge / Always the procreant urge of the world" rhymes, he says, with his findings, but he nevertheless feels that "we have lost inceptions, it must seem ever there was once more inception." And more love? The "lost America of love" of

Ginsberg's poem? That poem sounding again in Duncan's soundings, the burden of that loss suggesting a meaning of *line* not explicitly noted here, the spider's filament "seeking the spheres to connect them," that reaching out for relation, to establish the self's *place* (not dominion) in the great household.

In bringing forward as no one else has the burden and work of love in Whitman's poetry, doesn't he also bring forward Whitman's insistence on nurture? Doesn't he set a table for all? Hasn't he in "The Feast" (*Tribunals*) become father-mother, gathering us to the "pleasures of the household," to a "fortunate feast," where, as in the first days before the threat of ecological disaster, we may once again, in our need, regenerate ourselves, "feeding on milk as though we were born again"? Milk and light and warmth and love. A culinary poem that beggars Snyder's "How To Make Stew in the Pinacate Desert."

And doesn't what he tells us of Whitman's—and his—poetry, of that line of poets, answer affirmatively Ellison's query, "Could politics ever be an expression of love?" Hasn't Ellison himself answered it in a single sentence that better than he knew reads back to Whitman and Duncan? "The way home we seek is that condition of man's being at home in the world, which is called love, and which we term democracy."

"Poetics, like politics, is an art of the intensification of what we take to be the principle of individuality in the realization of its identity and unity (or fulfillment) as essential part of a society. It is not in whatever social attitudes we protest that the *politics* of our poetry is to be read, but in the actual society of events that that given poetry presents and in the character of the life of the members of that society." (*MAPS* #6).

> I will not make poems with reference to parts,
> But I will make poems, songs, thoughts, with reference
> to ensemble,
> And I will not sing with reference to a day, but with
> reference to all days,
> And I will not make a poem nor the least part of a
> poem
> but has reference to the
> soul,
> Because having look'd at the objects of the universe,
> I find there is no one
> nor any particle of one
> but has reference to the
> soul.
> —Whitman, "Starting from Paumanok"

Lineage? How is it Pound figures in the succession? By what he said at the beginning of his career in "Psychology and Troubadours" of the "germinal consciousness" that is "close on . . . [and] ever at the interpretation of [the] vital universe."

"The grand formal courage of Whitman's Personalism in *Leaves of Grass* was to present not argument or rationalization, but, as Pound declares his own purpose in writing, 'one facet and then another'—an ideogram of Self, a conglomerate Image. Once I returned to Whitman, in the course of writing *The Opening of the Field* when *Leaves of Grass* was kept as a bedside book, Williams' language of objects and Pound's ideogrammatic method were transformed in the light of Whitman's hieroglyphic of the ensemble."

"In Whitman there is no ambiguity about the source of *meaning*. It flows from a 'Me myself' that exists in the authenticity of the universe. The poet who exists close on the vital universe then exists close on his Self." *Then.*

Creeley, in speaking of Whitman, appreciates most his substantiation of the authenticity of the personal. But Whitman, as he now tells us in "Desultory Days" (*Later*, 1979), means less to him than Dickinson, lacks her "existential / terror," is only a "Mr. Goodheart," whose vision, though loved, he could never believe. Doesn't Duncan believe because he is (more than any poet in our time) a poet of cosmos, always admitting his derivativeness, his ground(s), his sources, the self's reliance on the authenticity of the universe? Isn't this poet, so long disturbed by his Atlantean dream, now, of all our poets, most at home in the world?

7 December 1979

Forward and *back*.

The dancers come forward to represent unclaimed
things.

* * *

We must go back to sets of simple things,
hill and stream, woods and the sea beyond,
the time of day—dawn, noon, bright or clouded,
five o'clock in November five o'clock of the year—
changing definitions of the light.